**Energy Policy and
Forecasting**

Arthur D. Little Books

A series of books on management and other scientific and technical subjects by senior professional staff members of Arthur D. Little, Inc., the international consulting and research organization. The series also includes selected nonproprietary case studies.

Acquisition and Corporate Development
    James W. Bradley and Donald H. Korn

Bankruptcy Risk in Financial Depository Intermediaries: Assessing Regulatory Effects
    Michael F. Koehn

Board Compass: What It Means to Be a Director in a Changing World
    Robert Kirk Mueller

Career Conflict: Management's Inelegant Dysfunction
    Robert Kirk Mueller

Communications Network Analysis
    Howard Cravis

Corporate Development Process
    Anthony J. Marolda

Corporate Responsibilities and Opportunities to 1990
    Ellen T. Curtiss and Philip A. Untersee

The Dynamics of Industrial Location: Microeconometric Modeling for Policy Analysis
    Kirkor Bozdogan and David Wheeler

Energy Policy and Forecasting
    Glenn R. DeSouza

The Incompleat Board: The Unfolding of Corporate Governance
    Robert Kirk Mueller

System Methods for Socioeconomic and Environmental Impact Analysis
    Glenn R. DeSouza

Energy Policy and Forecasting

Economic, Financial, and
Technological Dimensions

Glenn R. DeSouza
Arthur D. Little, Inc.

An Arthur D. Little Book

Lexington Books
D.C. Heath and Company
Lexington, Massachusetts
Toronto

Library of Congress Cataloging in Publication Data

DeSouza, Glenn R.
  Energy policy and forecasting.

  Bibliography: p.
  Includes index.
  1. Energy policy—United States—Mathematical
models. 2. Economic forecasting—United States—
Mathematical models. 3. United States—Economic
conditions—1971–   I. Title.
HD9502.U52D47   333.79'0973   79-9671
ISBN 0-669-03614-5   AACR2

Copyright © 1981 by D.C. Heath and Company

Published simultaneously in Canada

Printed in the United States of America

International Standard Book Number: 0-669-03614-5

Library of Congress Catalog Card Number: 79-9671

To my parents,
Francis and Teresa DeSouza

Contents

List of Figures   ix

List of Tables   xi

Preface   xv

Chapter 1   **Introduction**   1

Background   1
Summary of Contents   4

Chapter 2   **Public-Sector International Energy Modeling**   7

Background   7
Oil Market Simulation (OMS) Model   8
International Energy Evaluation System (IEES)   11
World Integrated Model   15
Conclusions   17

Chapter 3   **Electricity-Demand Models**   19

Energy-Demand Accounting and Trends   20
Electricity-Sales Modeling Overview   22
Residential Sales Model   30
Commercial Sales Model   49
Industrial Sales Model   52
Electric Peak-Demand Modeling Overview   60
Residential Peak-Demand Model   63
Industrial Peak-Demand Model   69
Other Contributions to Peak Demand   71

Chapter 4   **Coal-Demand Analysis**   73

Major Recent Published Studies of Coal Demand   73
Broad Context for Coal Demand   75
Electric-Utility Sector   78
Metallurgical-Coal Demand   89
Industrial-Fuel-Coal Demand   96
Synthetic-Coal Market   102
Coal Exports   106
U.S. Coal Production   109

Chapter 5   **Energy-Supply Models**   117

Oil- and Gas-Supply Models   117
Electric-Utility-Supply Models   123
Evaluating New and Existing Technologies   130

Chapter 6   **Regulated Energy Pricing**   137

Financial Theory and Utility Regulation   137
Rate-Level Issues   141
Conventional Rate Structures   143
Innovative Rate Structures   146
Electricity-Price Forecasting   154
Representative Power Costs for New Base-Load Units   158

Chapter 7   **Public-Sector U.S. Energy Modeling**   165

Background   165
Structure of the System   166
Governmental Forecasts   173
Critique of Forecasts   175

Chapter 8   **U.S. Energy Policies**   179

National Energy Conservation Policy Act   179
Energy Tax Act   182
Powerplant and Industrial Fuel Use Act   183
Public Utility Regulatory Policies Act   185
Natural Gas Policy Act   186

Notes   189

Bibliography   197

Index   211

About the Author   219

List of Figures

3-1   Electricity Sales and Generation, 1950–1978   24

3-2   Overview of Sales and Peak-Load Model   29

3-3   Daily Load Curve for Peak Day   61

7-1   MEFS Model Overview   167

List of Tables

3-1	Energy Conversion Factors	21
3-2	Relationship between Energy and GNP	21
3-3	U.S. Consumption, by Fuel and Sector, in 1978	22
3-4	National Electricity-Use Patterns	23
3-5	Annual Electricity Use in Kilowatt-Hours per Unit for 1979	35
3-6	Illustrative Profile of Single-Family Electric Space-Heat Customer	35
3-7	Illustrative Profile of Single-Family Nonelectric Space-Heat Customer	36
3-8	Illustrative Profile of Multifamily Electric Space-Heat Customer	36
3-9	Illustrative Profile of Multifamily Nonelectric Space-Heat Customer	37
3-10	Proposed Mandatory Appliance-Efficiency Improvements	47
3-11	Historical Pattern of Commercial Electricity Use	50
3-12	Commercial Unit-Electricity Coefficient	50
3-13	Fuel Shares of Commercial Building Inventory in 1975	51
3-14	Unit-Electricity Intensity Index, by Building Type, in 1975	51
3-15	Basic Comparison of Electric Motors and Pumps, 1977	53
3-16	Historical Patterns in Industrial Electricity Sales	56
3-17	Residential Summer Model	68
3-18	Definition of Variables in Residential Summer Model	69
4-1	U.S. Primary Energy Demand in 1979 and Forecasts for 2000	76
4-2	Historical Patterns in Electric-Utility and Total Coal Consumption	78
4-3	Comparison of Recent Forecasts of Electricity Generation	81

4-4   Historical Shares of Electricity Generation, by Primary
        Resource   81

4-5   Current Status of Nuclear Power and Capacity Plans, as of
        31 March 1980   82

4-6   Forecasts of Nuclear Capacity   83

4-7   Current Status of Coal-Fired Capacity along with Expan-
        sion Plans, as of December 1979   85

4-8   Forecasted Shares of Electricity Generation, by Primary
        Energy Resource, in 1990   85

4-9   Forecasted Shares of Electricity Generation, by Primary
        Energy Resource, in 2000   86

4-10   Forecasted Electric-Utility Coal Consumption   88

4-11   Patterns in U.S. Raw-Steel Production   91

4-12   Patterns in Pig-Iron Production   92

4-13   Patterns in Coke Requirements for Blast Furnaces   93

4-14   Patterns in Coke Production   93

4-15   Patterns in Metallurgical-Coal Demand   94

4-16   Comparison of Forecasts of Metallurgical-Coal Demand   96

4-17   Estimated Boiler-Fuel Use in 1978   99

4-18   Estimated Non-Boiler-Fuel Use in 1978   101

4-19   Comparison of Forecasts of Industrial-Fuel Coal Demand   102

4-20   Projections of U.S. Coal Exports   108

4-21   WOCOL Disaggregation of U.S. Coal Exports, by Type,
        in 2000   109

4-22   WOCOL Disaggregations of U.S. Coal Exports, by Im-
        porting Region   109

4-23   Historical Market Patterns in U.S. Coal Consumption and
        Production   110

4-24   Comparison of WOCOL, EIA, and NEP III Consumption
        and Production Forecasts for 1990   111

4-25   Comparison of Coal Consumption and Production Fore-
        casts for 2000   111

4-26   Demonstrated Regional Coal Reserves and Reserve-
        Production Ratios   112

4-27   OTA Regionalized Coal-Production-Share Forecasts   113

4-28   EIA Regionalized Coal-Production-Share Forecasts   114

4-29   WOCOL Regionalized Production-Share Forecasts for
        2000   114

6-1   1990 Incremental Power Costs Based on New Western-Coal
        Unit in 1990   163

7-1   MEFS Scenario Assumptions   174

7-2   MEFS 1985 Price Forecasts   174

Preface

In recent years a number of books on energy have been published. These books either contain detailed treatises on specific energy technologies or present somewhat simplified discussions of the energy-policy alternatives available to the United States. As such, they are not especially helpful to economists and business analysts who are engaged in or would like to be engaged in energy-policy analysis and forecasting.

This book is addressed specifically to economists and business analysts and should be useful to them in a number of respects. First, it provides an introduction to the technological characteristics of energy demand and supply. Second, it contains a synopsis of the key elements of U.S. energy legislation. Third, it describes econometric, deterministic, and financial methods that can be used to identify trends in energy demand, supply, and price and to predict the probable impact of energy legislation on such trends.

This book, although introductory in nature, reviews complex contemporary energy issues and problems. For example, the chapter on regulated rate making describes the Public Utilities Regulatory Policy Act of 1978 and explains such electric-rate design initiatives as time-of-day rates, marginal-cost pricing, interruptible industrial rates, and lifeline rates.

The methods and models discussed in this book include approaches developed by me and models formulated at the Energy Information Administration, the National Energy Laboratories, the MIT Energy Laboratory, and various academic institutions. In this context, a number of highly publicized state-of-the-art models (for example, the Mid-Range Energy Forecasting System) are described and critiqued.

This book reflects my casework experience at Arthur D. Little, Inc., and I acknowledge my debt to various individuals at the company. I am particularly indebted to Neil Talbot, who impressed on me the necessity for using interdisciplinary and practical methods in energy forecasting. I am grateful for the guidance provided to me on various occasions by Ted Heuchling, Kirk Bozdogan, and Demos Menegakis. I thank Betty Mystakides for her meticulous checking of the tables and Joanne Gioiosa for her skillful typing of the manuscript.

1 Introduction

Background

Among the nations of the world, the United States is exceptionally well positioned in terms of energy resources. It produces about as much oil as Saudi Arabia, and it is the free world's largest producer of coal, natural gas, and nuclear energy. In contrast, many of the other industrialized nations, especially Japan, are overwhelmingly dependent on imported energy. However, the United States does depend on oil for 47 percent of its energy usage, and almost half this oil is imported.

In 1979, the United States imported 3.1 billion barrels (BB) of oil at a cost of about $21 a barrel, with the chief suppliers including Saudi Arabia (0.49 BB), Nigeria (0.39 BB), Libya (0.24 BB), Algeria (0.23 BB), Venezuela (0.25 BB), Canada (0.19 BB), and Mexico (0.16 BB).[1] The payment for imported oil represents a serious drain on the balance of payments and contributes to domestic inflation and recession. Even more alarming is the prospect of another oil cutoff, which would have disastrous economic and social effects.

Recognizing the hazards attendant with oil dependence, the U.S. government has instituted a comprehensive program designed to reduce oil imports by promoting or mandating (1) general energy conservation, (2) the substitution of oil by nonscarce domestic energy forms such as coal, and (3) the increased domestic production of oil and gas.

It is generally felt that the United States has a significant potential for conservation, in that other nations with equivalent standards of living consume much less energy per capita than does the United States. Conservation can involve an adjustment in lifestyle or an enhancement in the efficiency with which energy is used. Lowering thermostats in the winter would be an example of a lifestyle conserving adjustment, while adding attic insulation would be an example of an efficiency-increasing (or waste-reducing) measure. Governmental conservation policy has been primarily directed at efficiency improvements. Representative elements of the government's conservation strategy are summarized as follows:

1. Tax credits, subsidies, grants, and other measures are provided to encourage the consumer to conserve energy (for example, a tax credit is available for residential investments in insulation, caulking, weather stripping, storm windows, and other items).

1

2. Mandatory standards are promulgated to ensure that manufacturers will make available to consumers devices that are energy-conserving (for example, proposed rules have been published requiring that by 1986, appliance manufacturers produce clothes dryers, water heaters, and so forth that meet minimum efficiency standards).

3. Various measures are employed to foster energy-conserving techniques among industry (for example, all companies that consume at least one trillion Btu's per year in each of the ten most energy-consuming industries must report their energy consumption to the Department of Energy and show that actions are being taken to conserve).

4. Corporate automotive fuel-efficiency standards to conserve energy use in the transportation sector are promulgated.

Oil is used for industrial steam raising, electricity generation, space heating, and other "low-priority" applications, where more abundant energy forms could be used. Coal is the most important of these abundant energy forms, but solar energy, biomass, and other renewable energy sources also can make limited contributions. Electricity, despite its high cost, also can be regarded as an abundant energy form, since it can be produced from coal and uranium, both of which are available in this country. Some of the measures introduced by the government to replace oil by other energy forms are as follows:

1. Financial incentives are provided to encourage users to substitute coal for oil and gas (for example, new industrial oil and gas boilers are generally denied the usual investment tax credit).

2. The use of oil and gas is prohibited in low-priority uses where coal can be used (for example, the use of oil and gas is generally prohibited in new base-load electric plants).

3. Financial incentives are provided to accelerate the use of solar power and other renewable resources (for example, reduced-interest loans and tax credits are provided to individuals who install solar heating and cooling equipment).

4. A program is set up to foster the commercialization of the electric car.

In the transportation and petrochemical-feedstock areas, the potential for replacing oil and gas is very limited. This makes the continued availability of oil and gas imperative. However, conventional U.S. sources of oil and gas are being rapidly depleted. To offset this decline, the government has initiated the following policies:

1. A price-decontrol program is instituted whereby the price of oil and natural gas will be allowed to rise, thereby encouraging greater exploration and making secondary and tertiary recovery techniques more economic.

2. A Synthetic Fuels Corporation, a special-purpose federal entity, is set up to stimulate private-sector production of synthetic oil or gas (from coal, shale, and so forth) through the provision of price guarantees, purchase guarantees, loan guarantees, joint-venture arrangements, and other financial and institutional inducements.

The formulation of national energy policies has been accompanied by considerable debate. The divergence of opinion concerning the appropriate strategy is evidenced by a comparison of the recent Harvard and MIT energy studies. The Harvard Energy Futures Report cites conservation and renewable energy forms as offering the cleanest and most practicable route to evergy independence.[2] However, the MIT World Coal Study sees coal as the panacea.[3]

Such differences of opinion probably result from alternative perceptions of the negative economic and environmental effects associated with most energy policies. The nature of these effects will depend on the policy option. For example, the policy to replace oil boilers with coal boilers is likely to increase the emissions of air pollutants, while the policy to accelerate residential conservation by governmental financial incentives will mean higher taxes to provide the requisite funds.

There are typically diminishing returns associated with a specific energy policy. In the case of conservation, for example, initial expenditures directed at quick-fix problems will result in greater energy savings per dollar than subsequent outlays. In addition, in some cases, the potential for a specific policy may be limited by technical constraints. For example, it is very feasible to use coal rather than oil in large industrial boilers, but it is not feasible to directly use coal in industrial applications requiring clean direct heat.

The presence of diminishing returns and technical constraints makes it advantageous to use energy models to identify that mix of policies that will achieve a given reduction in oil imports with the minimum impact on living standards and environmental quality.

To quantify the costs and benefits associated with alternative energy policies, the government has, in fact, often applied sophisticated energy models in a policy-evaluation framework. The energy-policy models have been used to prepare forecasts of energy consumption, production, imports, prices, GNP, industrial production, air pollutants, water effluents, and other key variables for different scenarios. Each scenario embodies a set of assumptions relating to future events and policies. By comparing the forecast results of two scenarios, each with different policy assumptions, it is possible to gauge the probable impact of those policies on the different variables.

Energy modeling has not been confined to the national level. In fact, much of the innovative modeling has been conducted at the sectoral level. An excellent example of sophisticated sectoral modeling is provided by the demand and supply models used in the electric-utility sector. The demand models are used to prepare long-term forecasts of electric generation and peak demand that take into account the effect of population, income, industrial output, appliance wattages, building thermal integrity, electricity price, load management, and other technical, economic, and policy variables. The supply models are used to identify the mix of base, intermediate, and peaking units that can meet the forecasted demand at minimum cost while satisfying system-reliability criteria.

A wide range of analytical methods have been used in national and sectoral energy models, including econometrics, input-output tables, and linear programming. These methods have been fitted to technical and economic data to provide a basis for forecasting in a manner that incorporates economic and technical factors. The technoeconomic orientation of energy models differentiates them from traditional macroeconomic and microeconomic models, which rely solely on economic constructs.

Summary of Contents

The purpose of this book is to provide a reasonable indepth description of the characteristics of the energy sector, along with the methods used to model these characteristics. To this purpose, a number of tables containing historical data are presented, and many operational models are described.

The material in the book has been organized into eight chapters. Each chapter is relatively self-contained, so that it is possible to use this book selectively.

Chapter 2 describes some of the major models used by the federal government in evaluating international energy events. The models described include the International Energy Evaluation System and the World Integrated Model.

Chapter 3 introduces the reader to the characteristics of electricity use and provides technical and economic data relating to such usage. This chapter also specifies the models used by electric utilities to forecast residential, commercial, and industrial electricity sales and contribution to peak demand.

Chapter 4 explains the major factors determining the demand for coal and the manner in which the effect of these factors can be quantified. Particular attention is devoted to coal demand for electricity generation, industrial boiler fuel, and metallurgical coking. The role of competitive energy forms is also described in the chapter.

Chapter 5 discusses energy-supply characteristics and the use of technical and econometric methods in projecting supply. A brief survey of important contributions to the literature is included.

Chapter 6 is devoted to the rate-setting process, with particular attention paid to the formulation of electric rates. Time-of-day pricing, marginal-cost pricing, and interruptible rates are among the issues covered in this chapter.

Chapter 7 describes and evaluates models used in the public sector. In particular, the comprehensive Mid-Range Energy Forecasting System used by the Department of Energy is discussed and critiqued.

Chapter 8 describes some of the major policies instituted by the government that relate to the energy sector.

2

Public-Sector International Energy Modeling

This book is basically about the modeling of energy demand and supply in the United States. Nevertheless, it is essential to devote some attention to the international energy sector, in that it was the escalation in international energy prices that precipitated the domestic crisis. The purpose of this chapter is to describe models used by the U.S. government in forecasting international energy prices and balances.

Background

While the sporadic disruptions in the supply of oil have received the greatest public attention, the energy crisis is also one of price. The June 1979 meeting of OPEC set oil prices between $18 and $23.50 a barrel, a far cry from the $3 a barrel that prevailed 6 years ago, although "only double" the 1974 level. As we enter the 1980s, the question is how much higher can oil prices go? A related issue is the impact these new prices will have on the already debilitated economics of the consuming nations.

To answer these and other questions, analysts have increasingly turned to computer models. Among the earliest efforts in this direction was the project carried out by the Workshop on Alternative Energy Strategies (WAES).[1] This was an ad hoc international project involving participants from fifteen countries and carried out under the direction of Carroll Wilson at MIT. The Workshop estimated energy demand and supply by region to the year 2000. These projections were made separately, and a comparison of supply and demand, therefore, identified deficits (or surpluses), which in the real world would be eliminated by the price mechanism. The conclusion of the study was that without serious action on the part of consuming nations, the demand for oil would outstrip supply by about 1990, and possibly even as early as 1983.

The first session of WAES was held in October of 1974, and the results of the project were published in 1977, after about two and one-half years of work. While the study involved analytical methods at various points, it did not result in a formal model. As such, WAES provided useful insights but has not served as an ongoing tool for policy analysis and forecasting.

This chapter is based on my article, "International Energy Models in the Public Sector: A Critical Guide," *Journal of Energy and Development* 1(1979): 95–106. I thank the editors of the journal for their gracious permission to reprint the material.

Another project at MIT—and one that is still current—is the World Oil project, run by Professors Morris Adelman, Robert Pindyck, and Henry Jacoby, with funding from the National Science Foundation.[2] Associated with this project are separate demand and supply models. These models can be integrated to analyze, among other issues, OPEC behavior. While the models as such are neutral, the reader should note that Professors Adelman and Pindyck have at various time come out with the opinion that oil prices will not rise significantly.[3]

While the MIT Energy Laboratory and other organizations remain actively engaged in energy modeling, the quantitative analysis of energy issues has come to be dominated by the Energy Information Administration (EIA) of the U.S. Department of Energy. This predominance has been achieved as a result of the vastly superior resources available to the government. The EIA was established by the Department of Energy Organization Act of 1977 (Pub. L. 95-91), taking over the functions of such groups as the Federal Energy Administration. EIA's charter included the collection of energy data and their analysis, and to this purpose, EIA has developed a sophisticated modeling capability.

The objective of this chapter is to provide a nontechnical yet indepth description of two EIA models—the International Energy Evaluation System and the Oil Market Simulation Model.[4] Also described, by way of comparison, is the energy component of the World Integrated Model, a private-sector model now in use in some government agencies.[5] This model provides an interesting contrast to those of EIA, in that energy is analyzed along with economic, trade, and agricultural variables, thereby taking into account feedbacks of different sorts.

Oil Market Simulation (OMS) Model

Description

As is well known, the period up to 1973 was characterized by a remarkable stability of oil prices. The sustained increase since that date is largely attributable to production restraints on the part of OPEC in the face of growing demand from the importing nations. During the 1973 embargo, OPEC reduced production by about 5 million barrels a day (MMBD), an amount approaching 10 percent of world production. Since then, it has continued to restrain output levels. The 1978 OPEC output averaged 29.9 MMBD versus 31.0 MMBD in 1973.[6] At the same time, the United States has been unable to reduce its imports. In the wake of the embargo, President Nixon announced the launching of Project Independence to make the United States free of foreign energy sources by 1980. Yet, in the first quarter of 1979, the United States imported oil at the rate of 8.5 MMBD versus 6.1 MMBD during 1974.

The Oil Market Simulation (OMS) Model of the EIA is centered around the precept just defined, namely, that the price of oil will rise as long as nations wish to import more and OPEC refuses to acquiesce. Basically, the model operates by identifying the oil price that will drive desired imports down to the point at which it equals what OPEC is willing to produce (export). OPEC production is an exogenous input to the model, and so it is possible to use the model to examine the effect of various OPEC strategies on oil price.

The OMS Model is small, long-run, and multiregional. It contains about thirty equations and is designed to predict oil price through 1995, taking into account conditions in the United States, Canada, Japan, Europe, the less-developed countries (LDCs), the Communist Bloc, and OPEC.

The model predicts oil demands for each of the seven regions. The demand equations relate oil demand to oil price and GNP. The price-demand relationship is quantified by a price-elasticity parameter. This parameter varies by region, with a typical short-run (that is, 1-year) value around -0.1, indicating that a 100 percent increase in oil price will cause a 10 percent decrease in demand in that year. Similarly, the effect of the GNP increase on oil demand is quantified through an income-elasticity parameter. The value of this parameter ranges around +0.7, indicating that a 100 percent increase in GNP will cause a 70 percent increase in oil demand.

The OMS Model predicts oil supply for the six non-OPEC regions. The supply equations relate oil supply to oil price, with the response of supply to price quantified by a price-elasticity parameter. A typical short-run value for this parameter is +0.1, indicating that a 100 percent increase in oil will increase supply by 10 percent.

In addition to its demand and supply equations, the OMS Model contains equations to predict the change in GNP resulting from a change in oil price. The effect of oil price on GNP is modeled through a feedback elasticity. A typical short-run value for the U.S. region in -0.05, implying that a 100 percent increase in oil price will depress GNP by 5 percent. The feedback elasticities for other regions are set at twice the U.S. value to reflect their relatively greater dependence on imported oil.

As is well known, the short-run effect of an oil-price increase on oil demand, oil supply, and GNP is quite a bit lower than its long-run impact. This is particularly true in the case of oil supply. A rise in oil price can have a short-run impact on oil supply by making secondary or tertiary recovery techniques economic. Its long-run impact is to encourage more drilling, the effect of which will be felt only years later. Although they are not discussed here, the reader should note that long-run dynamics are incorporated into the OMS Model.

The demand, supply, and GNP equations constitute the OMS Model. The model is solved by locating the market equilibrium. This is said to occur when net demand—the excess of demand over supply—equals the user-entered value for OPEC production. Equilibration is performed by varying price. If, for example, net demand is greater than OPEC production, the price is raised, depressing net demand to equal OPEC production. As price is raised, the following adjustments, all of which depress net demand, occur: (1) oil demand decreases as consumers switch to substitutes; (2) GNP decreases, which further reduces demand; and (3) oil supply increases.

Evaluation

A model can be evaluated on three basic criteria: (1) structure, (2) parameters, and (3) forecasts. Is the structure logically complete? Are the parameters statistically unbiased and intuitively plausible? Do the forecasts seem to agree with informed opinion? These are the sorts of questions an evaluation must answer.

Taking structure first, the OMS Model scores high. It takes into account, in a reasonable and systematic manner, the key force affecting world crude price. A particularly attractive attribute of the model is that it has but one goal, and a very important one at that, namely, the prediction of oil price. Because of this specialization, the model has a clarity of structure not evident in models attempting to fulfill more than one purpose.

On the negative side, it must be said that the model does not go far enough structurally. It fails to define or use the elasticity associated with net demand, a concept that has important implications in that it defines the market facing OPEC and so influences OPEC's production strategy. The net demand elasticity defines the percentage decrease in oil imports caused by a 1 percent increase in oil price. Its value is determined by the oil demand and oil supply elasticities of the importing nations, and if they are inelastic, then net demand also will be inelastic. It can be shown that if the net demand elasticity is between 0 and -1.0, an OPEC cutback will raise price by an amount sufficient to raise total revenues. This implies that (in the short-run, at least) OPEC can produce less but earn more.

The OMS Model is bereft of such microeconomic theoretical foundations. It should be possible to restructure the model so that it endogenously pinpoints the OPEC production (and so the price) that will result if OPEC behaves as a pure monopoly. Of course, to a large extent, OPEC's output is determined by considerations that are not identical with those of a pure profit-maximizing textbook monopoly. Thus it makes sense to also allow the user to exogenously input an OPEC production that will override the monopoly one.

The parameters of the OMS Model, some of which have been presented in the description of the model, are not conventional econometric estimates. Rather, these elasticities are, for the most part, values implied by prior runs of EIA's multifuel U.S. and international models. The U.S. model is known as the Mid-Range Energy Forecasting System (MEFS), and the international model is called the International Energy Evaluation System (IEES).[7] This means a conventional parameter evaluation, based on data, estimation technique, and so on, cannot be applied. Instead, all that can be assessed is whether the parameters realistically depict probable response patterns.

In general, the short-run parameters appear to reasonably approximate oil-market behavior—although there are exceptions. For example, the foreign feedback elasticities are set at 2 times the U.S. value, implying that a rise in oil price will impact other countries twice as hard as the United States. As it turns out, experience does not confirm this rather arbitrary assumption. Japan and Western Europe—two of the OMS regions—have shown far more resilience to oil-price hikes than has the United States.

The OMS equations contain lagged dependent variables. This means that if the short-run elasticity is s, then the long-run elasticity is $s/(1 - d)$, where d is the coefficient attached to the lagged dependent variable. This means, for example, that if d is 0.90, then the long-run elasticity is 10 times the short-run value.

The inclusion of a lagged dependent variable means that the short-run elasticity approaches its long-run value in an exponentially decaying manner. The smooth pattern implied by this structure is clearly incongruent with the tumultuous oil market. A more appropriate choice would have been the flexible Almon approach, which can allow for a variety of lagged responses.

In the final analysis, a model must be judged on how well it forecasts. The EIA released forecasts in May of 1979 corresponding to five scenarios—A, B, C, D, and E.[8] The forecasts are reported in both real (1978) and nominal dollars. According to EIA, the nominal dollars are based on projected inflation rates of between 5.2 and 5.6 percent a year.

The EIA predictions seem most optimistic. Nominal oil prices in 1985 vary between $22.50 and $33 a barrel. Furthermore, for three of the five scenarios (including scenario C, which is regarded by EIA as most likely), the price is $22.50 a barrel. This is patently absurd if one considers that this implies hardly any increase in nominal oil price between late 1979 and 1985.

The EIA forecasts should not be cause for rejecting OMS as useless. To a large extent, these forecasts are the result of assumptions entered into the model. For example, in scenario C, 1985 OPEC production is 34.7 MMBD versus the approximately 30 MMBD of today. Such an increase, if it came about, would have a dampening effect on oil price. Similarly, EIA's inflation forecast is clearly optimistic in that it falls on the lower end of the probability spectrum.

EIA's optimism is all the more surprising in that the report discussed here is dated May 1979. Whatever the reason for such optimism, it is clear that if the EIA forecasts are to be taken seriously, more realistic scenarios must be used.

International Energy Evaluation System (IEES)

Description

The International Energy Evaluation System (IEES), another EIA model, is a valuable resource for those interested in energy balances by geographic region. This model forecast energy balances for thirty-three international regions, with additional country-specific information available on request. IEES also forecasts energy prices—the exception is the world oil price, which is exogenous to the model. IEES, like OMS, is an EIA model—although a much larger one. A rough guess would be that IEES contains several hundred times as many equations as OMS.

In IEES, major energy-consuming and energy-producing nations are classified as regions. Thus Japan, Germany, and France are each a region—as are Indonesia and Iran. However, India, Malaysia, Taiwan, and so forth are collapsed into an Asian region. If requested, however, the EIA can break out the forecasts corresponding to a country that, like India, is part of a multinational region.

The core methodology for IEES is based on the Mid-Range Energy Forecasting System (MEFS) Model, developed in 1974. The MEFS Model, earlier known as Project Independence Evaluation System (PIES), forecasts energy balances and prices for ten U.S. regions. IEES and MEFS are based on the premise that energy markets, with the exception of oil, are workably competitive. Given this premise, demand and supply curves are derived (circa 1985 and 1990) for each fuel. These curves are entered into a linear program that locates the intersection of demand with supply and thus identifies equilibrium prices and quantities. While the basic logic of IEES and MEFS is similar, there are differences between these models. The major difference is that in IEES, unlike MEFS, the approach used to derive demand and supply curves varies by region. For example, regions in the OECD block are analyzed with a sophistication approaching that of MEFS, while other regions are modeled in a much simple manner.

IEES, it should be emphasized, is not a single model—rather, it is a system of integrated models. There are models to generate energy demand and supply curves, and then there is the model that integrates these curves to find price. The entire analysis is performed twice, once for 1985 and once for 1990.

The purpose of the IEES Demand Model is to derive for each region and each fuel type a demand curve depicting the quantities that would be consumed at various hypothetical prices. IEES derives these curves from econometric fuel-demand equations. In these equations, fuel consumption is a function of price and other variables. To derive one point on the 1985 demand curve, 1985 values for the nonprice variables and a hypothetical price are entered into the equation to give one quantity estimate. This procedure is repeated continuously—each time with a different price to generate different quantities. The price-quantity relationship traced out by this procedure is the demand curve.

IEES contains a model for each of the three major fossil fuels: coal, oil, and gas. The objective of these models is to develop a supply curve (for 1985 and 1990) showing the quantities that would be extracted at various hypothetical prices. The models are highly disaggregated, and in the case of oil, for example, there is a curve for each major crude type.

The supply curves are a connection of points, with each point defining a specific quantity-price relationship. The derivation of a point is a complicated procedure that depends on the fuel, the policies of the country of analysis, and the data available. In general, however, it is correct to state that the supply points are not econometrically derived. Instead, they are the result of technical analysis, expert judgment, or governmental estimates.

The supply curves generated by the primary fossil-fuel models understate the cost that the consumer will pay. These curves do not include the cost of transporting the fuel, nor do they include the cost of converting the primary fuels into the secondary energy forms demanded by the consumer. To bridge this gap, IEES contains transportation and conversion models. The Transportation Model of IEES simulates the movement of primary and secondary energy between the thirty-three regions. Each fuel is treated independently and is allowed to move by a number of alternative transport modes—tanker, pipeline, barge, and rail. For each fuel-mode combination, the cost of transport between regions is calculated. Besides cost, the model takes into account capacity. Fuels move on the cheapest route, but when there is a capacity constraint, a costlier alternative is used.

The Refinery Model of IEES is concerned with estimating the cost of converting crude oil to the set of petroleum products demanded by electric utilities and consumers. The petroleum products modeled include gasoline, residual oil, distillate fuel, and jet fuel. In computing the cost of conversion, the model takes into account that yields and other operating factors depend on the output slate of the refinery and the chemical composition of the crude it receives. It should be noted that the Refinery Model is dynamic in that it allows for capacity expansion. These capital expenses are included in the costs of conversion.

The Electric Utilities Model of IEES is concerned with the cost of converting coal, residual, distillate, natural gas, and nuclear fuel into electricity. The model also covers electricity generated by geothermal power and hydropower. In its costing algorithm, the model includes the capital expended in installing new generating capacity. The model assumes that capacity increments will come about in the most efficient manner. Thus the model will select high-capital, low-operating cost units (such as coal-fired steam turbines) for intensively used base capacity. For infrequently used peak capacity, the model selects units (such as gas turbines) that have low capital costs but high operating costs.

In the final stage of IEES, the disparate demand and supply curves (note that supply includes transportation and conversion) are integrated to' find equilibrium consumption, domestic production, imports, and prices. The equilibration is performed through the price mechanism, and equilibrium occurs when consumption equals the sum of domestic production and imports.

The equilibration is performed in a so-called Integration Model. This model actually is a linear program that is executed a number of times until a solution is obtained. The linear program is a representation of the supply network. Its objective function is the minimization of supply cost. The first run-through of the Integration Model involves

1. Assuming initial demand prices and reading off the demand curves, the quantities demanded at those prices.
2. Using the linear program to compute the least-cost method of supplying the quantity demanded.
3. Reading off the supply prices associated with the least-cost method.
4. Adding markups and taxes to the supply prices to give demand prices.

The demand prices of step 4 will, in general, not be the same as those assumed in step 1. As a consequence, a second iteration will be required. The assumed price in step 1 of the second iteration will be the average of the price in steps 1 and 4 of the first iteration. The iterative process will be stopped and equilibrium will be declared when the difference between the prices in steps 1 and 4 is below a specified tolerance level.

It should be pointed out that the equilibration is, in fact, performed simultaneously for all fuels and regions. Thus the solutions of the Integration Model provide an energy balance for each region. These balances indicate the consumption, production, and imports of each fuel.

Evaluation

The size of IEES precludes the sort of appraisal of parameters and forecasts that was performed for OMS. Instead, the purpose of this evaluation will be to identify the structural problems with the IEES Model.

It is necessary to start out by stating that IEES is an extremely impressive product. Clearly, a great deal of work has gone into its development, and it is undoubtedly among the largest and most comprehensive of international energy models. Its linear-programming approach to integration can be challenged as simplistic in its assumption that the energy market can be competitively approximated, but it is hard to suggest a better way to integrate demand and supply.

From the user's point of view, the major structural problem with IEES is that there is absolutely no way to evaluate the potential accuracy of its forecasts. The model contains a vast number of parameters—most of them deterministic. In such a system, the possibilities for significant errors are impossible to isolate, and the mechanism by which errors are propagated is a complete unknown. Thus the user has no analytical means for bounding IEES forecasts. This, by itself, need not be a matter of concern. By using a deterministic model to backcast, historical mean forecast errors can be computed. Unfortunately, IEES has not been used to backcast, and as a consequence, one does not even have an empirical guide to the reliability of IEES forecasts.

A more theoretical structural problem with IEES is the manner in which it handles the interaction between the economy and energy prices. GNP is an exogenous input to IEES, where it is used to derive energy demand. Now, of course, GNP is sensitive to energy prices, and so the GNP entering IEES might well be inconsistent with the energy prices coming out of it.

Finally, the reader should note that while IEES individual components are reasonably sophisticated, they do not approach the state of the art. This is most apparent in the very rough analyses of the LDCs, but the same criticism can just as easily be made about the IEES treatment of the other regions. For example, in predicting electricity demand in the developed regions, IEES does not take into account the effect of appliance saturation, time-of-day pricing, load-shaving controls, and other developments that affect both the amount and periodicity of electricity usage.

World Integrated Model

Description

The models reviewed so far have been EIA products with a focus exclusive to energy. Agencies other than the Department of Energy (of which EIA is a part) are also coming to be directly involved with energy issues. One indication of this has been the acquisition by some of them of the World Integrated Model (WIM), an international multidisciplinary model. WIM is discussed here not because it offers anything startling in the way of energy modeling, but because it provides a contrast to the more specialized energy models.

WIM was developed by Professors Mesarovic of Case Western Reserve and Pestel of Technical University (Germany), under the sponsorship of the Club of Rome. It forecasts economic, demographic, energy, raw-material, agricultural, and trade variables for each of twelve international regions, taking into account both regional and topical interdependencies. This discussion will be restricted to the energy components of WIM, which cover the production, consumption, and pricing of the five primary energy sources: coal, oil, natural gas, hydropower, and nuclear power.

In WIM, energy production is determined by the stock of capital and a capital-output ratio. The product of these two terms gives maximum energy production, which may or may not be realizable depending on the level of energy reserves. The stock of capital changes from year to year. In each year it is adjusted to reflect the retirement of completely depreciated capital and the investment in new capital. A similar accounting procedure is used to keep track of reserves. The amount of reserves available is adjusted down to reflect production of energy and up to reflect new discoveries.

Aggregate energy consumption is predicted in WIM as a function of GNP and a total energy-price index. Next, the consumption of each of the five energy forms is calculated by multiplying aggregate energy consumption by a vector defining the market shares of each energy form.

The production and consumption predictions of WIM are brought together to compute energy deficits and surpluses. For those regions where production exceeds consumption, we have an energy surplus; while in those regions where production is less than consumption, there is an energy deficit. The surpluses are summed across regions to give worldwide export capacity, and a similar procedure is followed with deficits to give import requirements.

The relationship between import requirements and export capacity constitutes the basis for price determination in WIM. The model starts with an exogenously specified price, which is modified in subsequent periods to reflect market conditions. When import requirements exceed export capacity, price is raised; and the converse is true.

Evaluation

Computer Sciences Corporation (CSC) undertook a survey of international models.[9] Their survey included the UN–IO Model, the Bariloche Model, the SARU World Model, the MOIRA Model, and WIM. They concluded in favor of WIM on the basis of its "flexibility and adaptability to a wide variety of forecasting tasks."

Where the analyst is interested in a broad range of issues, of which energy is but one, WIM might offer a viable alternative to specialized models, such as OMS and IEES. However, the assertion that WIM is more accurate than the specialized models because it takes into account topic interactions is not tenable. Any gains in this regard are more than offset by the inaccuracies caused by the abstract and aggregative mode of analysis.

WIM's energy analysis is certainly abstract. It fails to explicitly deal with the individual characteristics of each energy form. Furthermore, its depiction of energy production as determined by capital (subject to resource constraints) does not deal with the reality of OPEC.

Equally bothersome is the highly aggregative manner in which WIM analyzes the energy market. It focuses on the demand and supply of the five primary energy resources (oil, coal, gas, hydropower, and nuclear power) and does not concern itself with the stages of production. Thus the role of the refinery and electric utilities in converting primary energy into secondary forms is ignored. This means, for example, that the effect on coal and oil demand of a legislative order to convert oil-fired electricity-generating capacity to coal cannot be represented in such a model.

Another manifestation of WIM's aggregativeness is its treatment of energy demand. It does not break out fuel demand by end use. For example, it would be appropriate to disaggregate oil demand by gasoline, space heating, electricity generation, industrial use, and so on. This sort of disaggregation could allow the model to incorporate such developments as mandatory automobile fuel-efficiency standards.

Conclusions

The predictions of international energy models have had a mixed reception to date. Some analysts have accepted them as scientific and objective; others have dismissed them as naive and uninformed. The proper attitude is one of cautious and selective acceptance. International energy models embody in one logically structured and easy-to-use package a vast amount of data, along with the combined wisdom of their creators. Consequently, the answers they provide can only enhance the analysts' work. All the same, these answers must be scrutinized carefully. To a larger extent than is commonly realized, the solutions of these models reflect the biases of their operators. As we have seen, the output of the models is often more sensitive to scenario assumptions than to anything else. Hence the user must select his or her own scenario, rather than accepting the one EIA regards as most likely.

In conclusion, it must be emphasized that despite all the problems that have been identified in this chapter, models are a reasonable approach to analyzing the complicated international energy market. Furthermore, many of these problems are not irreparable, and with the experience gained by continuing application, the utility of these models is bound to increase.

3 Electricity-Demand Models

Energy plays a vital but invisible role in American society. In the residential sector, energy is used for space heating, space cooling, water heating, lighting, cooking, refrigeration, freezing, clothes washing, clothes drying, television, and so on. The major commercial uses of energy are heating, cooling, lighting, water heating, and the operation of office machinery. In the industrial sector, the functional energy uses are direct heat, process steam, machine drive, coke production, electricty generation, electrolytic processes, space heating and cooling, and lighting. Significant amounts of energy also are used by industry as raw materials for the production of petrochemicals. The transportation sector requires energy to power automobiles, trucks, buses, aircraft, trains, and ships.

Many of the functions just listed can be satisfied by alternative forms of energy. In the residential and commercial sectors, for example, the heating options include natural gas, oil, and electricity. In the industrial sector, process steam can be raised by coal, oil, or natural gas. The chief exception is the transportation sector, where oil is often the only practical energy form.

Energy consumed in the residential, commercial, industrial, and transportation sectors represents end-use demand; that is, the energy is acquired to satisfy a specific need, not for conversion into a secondary energy form. However, the energy consumed in the refinery and electric-utility sectors represents intermediate demand. Refineries convert crude oil into gasoline, distillate heating oil, residual fuel oil, and other petroleum products. Electric utilities convert coal, oil, and natural gas into electricity. In addition, utilities generate electricity from hydropower and nuclear power. The products of refineries and utilities are delivered to meet end-use demands.

During the last few years, economists and engineers have become quite activity engaged in projecting energy demands. Not surprisingly, the methods used by these two groups have differed.

Economists have applied the technique of econometrics to energy demand, and this has long been their standard approach to forecasting macroeconomic and industrial activity. In the econometric method, equations describing behavioral responses are statistically estimated from data extending back about 20 years. For example, residential electricity consumption is modeled as a function of population, income, and electricity price.

Engineers have developed end-use (that is, technological) models, the equations of which describe the process utilizing the energy. For example, in an end-use model, residential electricity consumption is forecasted taking into account the number of appliances, their rated wattages, and their hours of use.

The purpose of this chapter is to explain and illustrate end-use and econometric models of projecting electricity demand. Electricity has been selected because it provides the best example of modeling techniques. It must be emphasized that these techniques, with minor modifications, can be used for forecasting oil and natural-gas demand.

Energy-Demand Accounting and Trends

Energy Units

Usually, energy usage is reported in physical units. For example, we read of barrels of oil, cubic feet of natural gas, and short tons of coal. When, however, comparisons between energy forms are to be made, it is necessary to convert energy from physical units to standard units. The standard energy unit measures the heat content of the fuel. In the British system, the standard unit is the *British thermal unit* (Btu), which is defined as the quantity of heat necessary to raise the temperature of one pound of water one degree Fahrenheit.

Physical energy units can be converted to standard energy units by applying conversion factors. The conversion factor defines the number of standard units contained in one physical unit. For example, the conversion factor for residual fuel oil is 6.29 million Btu per barrel. Conversion factors for ten of the most important energy forms are presented in table 3-1.

Energy-Demand Patterns

Energy is a necessary component in the production process, and over time, U.S. energy consumption has tended to rise in tandem with GNP. Table 3-2 shows the relationship between aggregate energy use and GNP for the years 1950, 1955, 1960, 1965, 1970, 1973, 1975, and 1978. If the relationship was perfectly stable, the Btu's per dollar of real GNP should have remained constant. As the table shows, this has not been the case. In the aftermath of the oil embargo, the ratio decreased from 60,000 Btu/dollar in 1973 to 50,000 Btu/dollar in 1978. This decrease implies that the same production is achieved with less energy.

Darmstadter, Dunkerley, and Alterman have prepared some interesting international comparisons of the energy-GNP ratio.[1] They show that per dollar of GNP, the United States uses more energy than all industrialized countries except Canada. The energy-output ratio of the two North American nations is about 50 percent higher than those prevailing in Western Europe and Japan. The

Table 3-1
Energy Conversion Factors

Energy Type	Conventional Unit	Conversion Factor
Residual fuel oil	Barrel	6.29 million Btu
Distillate fuel oil	Barrel	5.83 million Btu
Motor gasoline	Barrel	5.25 million Btu
Jet fuel	Barrel	5.57 million Btu
Natural gas	Cubic foot	1.03 thousand Btu
Electricity	Kilowatt hour	3.41 thousand Btu
Anthracite coal	Short ton	25.4 million Btu
Bituminous coal	Short ton	14.8 to 29.3 million Btu

Source: U.S. Department of Energy, Energy Information Administration, *Federal Energy Data System* (Springfield, Va.: National Technical Information Service, June 1978), pp. C–6 and C–7.

Table 3-2
Relationship between Energy and GNP

	Gross Energy Consumption (Quadrillion Btu)	GNP (Billions of 1972 Dollars)	Energy-GNP Ratio (Btu per 1972 Dollar)
1950	33.92	533.5	63,580
1955	39.66	654.8	60,568
1960	44.52	736.8	60,423
1965	53.31	925.9	57,576
1970	67.12	1075.3	62,419
1973	74.66	1235.0	60,413
1975	70.79	1202.3	58,812
1977	76.56	1332.7	57,447
1978	78.01	1385.1	56,321

Source: Gross Energy Consumption Data from 1950 to 1970 from U.S. Department of Energy, Energy Information Administration, *Annual Report to Congress*, Vol. III (Washington: U.S. Government Printing Office, May 1978), p. 7; values from 1970 to 1978 are from a publication from the same source entitled *Energy Data Report*, p. 2; GNP data are from *Economic Report of the President* (Washington: U.S. Government Printing Office, January 1979), p. 184.

greater energy intensity of the U.S. economy does not necessarily imply that industry is inefficient or consumers are profligate. Differences in climate, geography, and industry mix account in part for the international variations in the energy-output ratio.

Table 3-3 shows U.S. consumption of energy for the year 1978 disaggregated by fuel and sector. In that year, this country consumed 6.82 billion

Table 3-3
U.S. Consumption, by Fuel and Sector, in 1978

	Oil (Billion Barrels)	Gas (Trillion Cubic Feet)	Coal (Million Short Tons)	Electricity (Billion Kilowatt-hours)
Residential/commercial	1.10	7.28	10.4	1126
Industrial	1.39	8.40	131.9	799
Transportation	3.68	0.52	–	–
Electric utilities	0.65	3.22	481.1	–
Total domestic consumption	6.82	19.42	623.4	1925

Source: U.S. Department of Energy, Energy Information Administration, *Energy Data Report* (Washington: 1980), pp. 3-5.

barrels of oil. Of this amount, the transportation sector accounted for 54 percent; the industrial sector, 20 percent; the residential and commercial sectors, 16 percent; and the electric-utilities sector, 10 percent. Natural-gas consumption in 1978 equaled 19.42 trillion cubic feet. The industrial sector accounted for 43 percent of natural gas consumption; the residential and commercial sectors, 38 percent; the electric-utilities sector, 17 percent and the transportation sector, 2 percent. Coal consumption equaled 623.4 million short tons, with the electric-utilities sector accounting for 77 percent of the coal consumed and the industrial sector 21 percent. In 1978, 1925 billion kilowatt hours of electricity were consumed. The residential and commercial sectors accounted for 56 percent of electricity consumption and the industrial sector 40 percent.

Electricity-Sales Modeling Overview

Background

Electric utilities prepare two types of long-term (10 to 20 years) forecasts of electricity use. First, they forecast how much electricity they must produce, measured in kilowatt-hours (kWh) or megawatt-hours (MWh). This forecast is composed chiefly of sales to customers, but it also includes company use and transmission and distribution losses. Second, they forecast the maximum hourly demand (for example, peak demand) made on the system during a period (for example, a year).

Electricity-sales forecasts are a key input in the utility financial-planning process. The amount of revenue earned by a utility will depend on the total kilowatt-hours sold, as well as on the distribution of sales among the residential, commercial, and industrial customer classes. Typically, electricity-sales forecasts in kilowatt-hours, disaggregated by customer rate class, are entered into the corporate model to be used in projecting revenue.

Electricity-sales forecasts are also used in projecting fuel requirements and costs, both of which depend on the electricity sales and the customer class distribution. The class distribution is relevant in that because of distribution losses and other factors, the cost of selling a kilowatt-hour to a residential or commercial customer is more than for an industrial customer.

Despite the crucial nature of electricity-sales forecasts, the preparation of such forecasts was until 1973 accorded limited attention. Electricity use increased each year with a dependable regularity, and utility planners felt quite justified in extrapolating out past trends. The oil embargo and the pursuant increase in energy prices rudely disturbed the comfortable pattern in electricity growth. Total U.S. electricty sales in 1974 were below the 1973 level, and since that time, nationwide sales have grown at about one-half the historical levels. Table 3-4 presents historical U.S. electricity data, and these values are also pictorially depicted in figure 3-1.

Higher electricity prices were not the only new factor affecting electricity use. Slowdowns in economic and demographic activity and the increasing saturation of electric appliances also played a role. In addition, governmental intervention, as manifested in building insulation standards, appliance-labeling requirements, and other programs to conserve energy, had an effect on electricity use.

Counterbalancing these forces were developments that caused customers to view electricity with increasing favor vis-à-vis liquid and gaseous fuels. First,

Table 3-4
National Electricity-Use Patterns
(*in billion kWh.*)

	Residential	Commercial	Industrial	Other	Losses	Total Generation
1950	72.2	50.6	146.5	22.1	37.7	329.1
1955	128.4	79.4	260.0	29.0	50.2	547.0
1960	199.3	120.0	328.6	38.6	66.8	753.3
1965	291.0	200.5	428.7	33.6	101.5	1055.3
1970	466.3	306.7	570.9	48.5	98.6	1491.0
1973	579.2	388.3	686.1	59.3	147.8	1860.7
1975	584.7	401.7	675.3	68.2	187.8	1917.6
1978	670.4	459.5	800.5	73.2	202.7	2206.3
1979	679.2	471.7	833.7	73.1	189.9	2247.6

Source: Energy Information Administration, *Statistics and Trends of Energy Supply, Demand, and Prices* (Washington: U.S. Government Printing Office, May 1978), p. 103; Energy Information Administration, *Monthly Energy Review* (Washington: U.S. Government Printing Office, May 1980), p. 63.

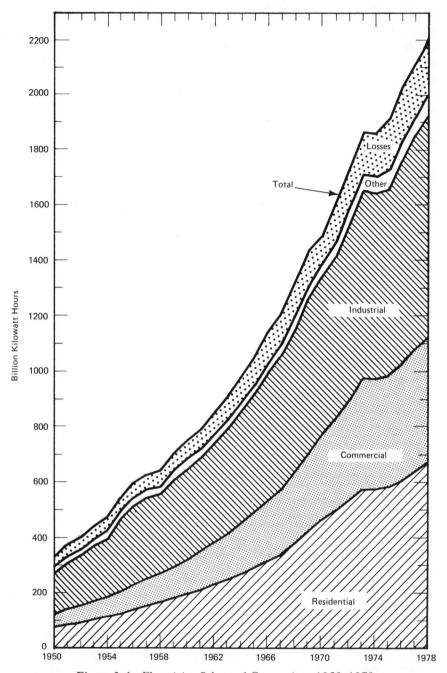

Figure 3-1. Electricity Sales and Generation, 1950-1978

electricity prices were rising at a slower rate than those of oil or natural gas. Second, the supply of electricity was reliable, which was not the situation for oil and gas. The result was that where the economics seemed reasonable, as for example with the heat pump, customers opted for electricity in increasing numbers.

Electric utilities reacted to the new forecast environment by adopting modeling methodologies that would more fully account for the forces influencing load growth.

Model Evaluation Criteria

The purpose of a model is to forecast the future, and the best model is one that forecasts accurately. Unfortunately, by the time we find out whether a long-term electricity-demand model is accurate, it is too late. Thus in evaluating such models it is necessary to use a priori criteria that can indicate the likelihood that a particular modeling methodology will produce accurate forecasts. These a priori evaluative criteria include simplicity, statistical validity, and level of detail.

Simple models are not necessarily accurate models, but models that are simple enough to be generally understood inspire confidence, while complicated "black box" models implicitly require that the uninformed reader trust the discretion of the modeling group. Thus, other things being equal, simplicity is a desirable feature in a model.

In the context of simplicity, it should be pointed out that mathematical complexity may, in fact, introduce inaccuracies. This is illustrated by the use of fuel-choice methods for forecasting electricity use, which is particularly common among government agencies entrusted with the task of forecasting the demand for all energy forms. In this approach, total energy use is forecasted as a function of economic and demographic variables and an overall energy-price index. Next, the shares of electricity, coal, oil, and gas are determined as a function of relative energy prices using very complex multinomial logit or probit methods.

This approach is both complex and unrealistic. Its assumption that the customer demands energy and then selects among fuels does not represent customer behavior. Electricity is a premium energy form, and its use is generally restricted to motors and other applications where fossil fuels cannot be used. Electricity does compete with natural gas and fuel oil in certain applications, but there is limited direct substitution between coal and electricity. Moreover, the substitution dynamics among eletricity, oil, and gas reflect, to a considerable extent, issues such as supply reliability, which the logit/probit models cannot handle.

The *statistical validity* of a model refers to the ability of a model to replicate the past accurately. Such validity can be quantified by using the model to backcast electricity sales and then comparing the backcasted values with the actual values. These comparisons can be summarized in the form of such statistics as the mean absolute error. The *mean absolute error* is the average difference between the actual and forecasted values, and the lower is its value, the more statistically valid is the model.

It should be noted that statistical-validity measures, based as they are on historical comparisons, tend to overstate the model's ability to forecast the future. This is true because when such statistics are computed, the actual values of the exogenous or independent variables are known. In actual forecasting, the values of these exogenous variables must themselves be forecast. However, if a model has been used in the past, its track record can be tested—this is a harder test, because the accuracy of the independent-variables forecasts is also being tested.

Even if the future values of the independent variables are known with certainty, the forecasts of a statistically valid model can be inaccurate. This inaccuracy can result as new factors that are not incorporated in the model develop in the future. This leads us to the next evaluation criterion—the level of detail.

The more detailed is a model, the greater is its ability to incorporate new developments or test the effect of possible new policies. For example, a residential-electricity model should be able to take into account changes in customers, weather, appliance saturations, appliance-efficiency standards, building insulation standards, and other determinants of use. Clearly, a residential model that forecasts electricity use on an appliance-by-appliance basis will be better able to take into account such factors than one that forecasts residential electricity demand only in the aggregate.

The three criteria of simplicity, statistical validity, and level of detail are not complementary. In general, there is a tradeoff involved, and this is especially true for the criteria of statistical validity and level of detail. Consistent detailed historical data on electricity use by appliance are not available, and so it is not possible to validate detailed electricity-sales models. Conversely, statistically valid models are too aggregative to incorporate many of the new developments affecting electricity peak demand. Next, the evolution of forecasting models in the electric-utility industry will be traced out.

Evolution of Forecasting Methodologies

The three types of forecasting models used by the electric-utility industry each have undeniable superiority with respect to one criterion. The time-series model is simple, the econometric model is statistically valid, and the end-use model is highly detailed. However, each has significant weaknesses on the other criteria, as the following discussion will demonstrate.

In the *time-series approach,* electricity sales are projected solely as a function of time. The degree of complexity can vary from simple trending to the use of autoregressive and moving-average terms, as in the Box-Jenkins approach.

In the *econometric approach,* historical data extending back about 15 years are used to fit equations relating electricity sales to such underlying economic and demographic determinants of usage as electricity price, natural-gas price, per-capita income, industrial value added, and number of customers. Future assumed values for the economic and demographic determinants are then inserted into the fitted equations to give forecasts of electricity sales.

In the *end-use approach,* electricity sales are forecasted separately for each major application or process utilizing electric energy. For example, residential electricity sales will be disaggregated by space heating, air conditioning, water heating, clothes drying, cooking, and so on.

While the three types of methodologies overlap and are not necessarily mutually exclusive, most forecasts have an orientation toward one type or another. During periods of stable growth, such as the 1950s and 1960s, time series is preferred, and this, in fact, was the approach generally used by the electric-utility industry through 1973. The preference for it was based on its simplicity and the absence of any clear indication that other methods would be more accurate. Whatever structural changes were occurring were themselves correlated with the passage of time (for example, appliance saturations were gradually increasing over time; electric rates, in real dollars, were gradually declining over time; population was gradually increasing over time). In addition, if there were changes in structure, they counterbalanced each other, to maintain the famous "double-10" growth rate of 7.2 percent annually, which led to an approximate doubling of sales each decade.

After 1973, forecasters became unsatisfied with time-series methodologies as a result of the negative deviation in electricity sales from the trend, a deviation, moreover, that seemed likely to persist.

The principal alternative approach, which had already worked well for some companies, such as the Southern California Edison Company and the Public Service Electric and Gas Company of New Jersey, was econometric models, and there was a spate of econometric studies in the 1974–1976 period. Because the econometric models were able to incorporate slowdowns in income and population growth and rises in electricity prices, they produced forecasts of electricity sales that were significantly lower than those produced by time-series methods. There is no doubt that econometric models are a valuable forecasting tool that in many cases provides the best method of forecasting.[2]

However, some serious problems have emerged, among them

1. The level of aggregation involved (for example, the use of total residential-sector electric-energy consumption without disaggregation of electric heating, air conditioning, and so forth)

2. The difficulty of including the impact of new policies, such as load-management programs and mandatory appliance-efficiency standards
3. The problems of relating the energy-sales forecasts with the peak-demand forecasts required for system-planning purposes
4. Generally, the uncertainty of how realistic econometric estimates derived from historical data are for forecasting future trends

These problems with econometric models have led some of the larger electric-utility systems and commissions to develop end-use models.[3] These models, because of the considerable detail they contain, are able to delineate the various factors—economic, technological, and legislative—that can cause the future trend in electricity sales to depart from the historical norm. In general, their application has produced forecasts that are usually even lower than those produced by econometric models.

A good illustration of the general technique of end-use modeling is provided by the manner in which the end-use model forecasts residential electricity used for space heating. To forecast the annual electricity use attributable to this application, the number of electric space-heating units is multiplied by the annual electricity use associated with a single unit. The number of space-heating units is forecasted, taking into account increases in the number of customers and the fraction of new customers likely to have electric space heating (that is, the penetration rate). The space-heating penetration rate is often forecasted econometrically, typically as a function of the relative life-cycle price of electricity and natural gas, with an adjustment made to reflect the availability of gas. The annual electricity per unit factor is reduced over time using informed judgment to reflect the introduction of heat pumps, the improved insulation of new buildings, and the lowering of thermostats.

End-use models are highly appealing conceptually, but their implementation creates a problem. Data on electric energy use by application are not readily available. In the residential sector, reasonable approximations can be made, and to a lesser extent, the same can be said about the more complex commercial sector. In the industrial sector, however, the diversity of electricity uses and the paucity of data make end-use modeling very difficult.

Modular Structure

The forecasts of electricity sales and peak demand involve the construction of a number of submodels or modules. These submodels are linked in the sense that the projections of one submodel become the input to another.

Figure 3-2 contains an overview of the modular structure. The regional submodel predicts electric customers (customers are synonymous with households), per-capita income, and industrial value added for the service territory

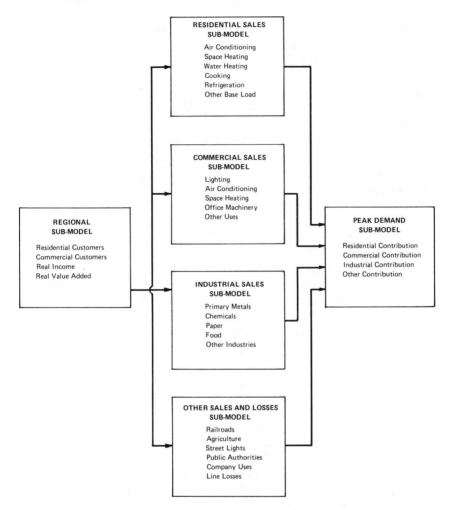

Figure 3-2. Overview of Sales and Peak-Load Model

served by the electric utility. The regional submodel typically utilizes econometric techniques. Economists have been developing regional econometric models for about 15 years, and the techniques for forecasting the variables that constitute the regional submodel are well documented.

An alternative is not to build a regional econometric model, but to rely instead on forecasts from state economic agencies. These agencies routinely disseminate projections of population, households, per-capita income, and value added. A problem with relying on these projections is that they are not always available on a service-territory basis. Another problem is that the agency forecasts tend to be overly optimistic. However, for the purpose of this chapter, it will be assumed that reliable economic and demographic projections are available, and there will be no discussion of regional modeling.

The three sales submodels forecast annual (or monthly) electricity use in the residential, commercial, and industrial sectors. The sales forecasts are based in part on the economic and demographic projections of the regional submodel. The logic of these submodels will be discussed in detail.

The purpose of the other sales and losses submodel is to predict the remaining constituents of the load. The other sales category includes railroads, streetlighting, agriculture, public authorities, cooperatives, and other utilities. Losses occur as the utility steps down the voltage so as to deliver electricity to the customers. Generally, simple procedures are used to forecast these categories. For example, losses are projected as a function of residential, commercial, and industrial sales. The logic of the other sales and losses submodel will not be discussed.

The peak submodel predicts the maximum hourly load imposed on the system. The peak can be calculated as a function of the annual sales forecasts. The sales forecasts are put on an average hourly basis by dividing them by 8760, the number of hours in the year. The average hourly loads are then multiplied by factors that define the ratio of peak to average load.

Residential Sales Model

Factors Affecting Residential Electricity Use

As mentioned earlier, the application of end-use models to forecast residential electricity sales was the result of dissatisfaction with the highly aggregative structure embodied in econometric models, a structure that makes it difficult to quantify the impact of specific mandatory and voluntary conservation actions on electricity-use patterns. Residential end-use models are able to deal with the conservation issue, as well as the plethora of factors that are likely to cause future electricity-sales growth to be significantly lower than that experienced historically. Some of the more important long-run determinants of residential electricity use are reviewed next.

Number of Appliance Units. By far the most important determinant of residential electricity use is the number of electricity-using appliances in the service territory. The number of units of a particular appliance type (for example, dishwashers) is determined by the number of electric customers and by the appliance saturation ratio.

The number of electric customers corresponds to the number of households. Because household size has been declining, households, and therefore customers, have been growing at a faster rate than population. In the future, population growth is expected to stabilize, but since the decline in household size is expected to persist, customers should continue to grow faster than population.

The electric-appliance saturation ratio defines the fraction of customers who own the appliance. For essential appliances, such as refrigerators, saturation is complete, while the saturation ratios for dishwashers and other "luxury" appliances are quite low, as are the saturation ratios for cooking, space heating, and other applications where fuels other than electricity can be used.[4]

For a variety of reasons, the saturation of electric appliances is expected to increase. The saturation of luxury appliances should increase as rising real incomes permit more customers to acquire such appliances. The saturation of electricity in space heating, water heating, and other applications traditionally dominated by natural gas should increase because of the perceived unavailability of gas and its escalating real cost.

The increasing saturation of electric space heating is deserving of special mention, because space heating is the major residential energy application and because electric-heated homes typically also use electricity in water heating and other functions. The choice between electricity and gas depends on the initial (installation) cost of the system, the efficiency of the system, and the cost per Btu of energy.

The initial cost of an electric-resistance system is lower than that of a gas heating system. This has made its use quite popular in the warmer regions (where operating costs are low) and in areas where the supply of natural gas is constrained or perceived to be unreliable.

The electric-resistance system has an efficiency of 1.0, that is, for every Btu of energy used, there is a Btu of heat delivered, while the gas heating system has an efficiency of 0.6. However, the higher efficiency of the resistance system is not sufficient to offset the much higher cost per Btu of electricity, and as a consequence, the annual operating cost of a resistance system is generally higher than that of a gas system. However, the differential should narrow, because gas prices are rising faster than electricity prices.

The electric heat pump is a technology that can offset the lower Btu costs of gas. The heat pump, which works on a principle similar to that of an air conditioner, can heat and cool a home. The heat pump has a winter seasonal performance factor of about 1.5, meaning that over a season, it is 1.5 times as efficient as a resistance system. It is expected that the seasonal performance factor of the heat pump will improve over time as better units are introduced. Counterbalancing the greater efficiency of the heat pump is its significantly higher installation cost.

It is possible to compute the life-cycle costs of heat pumps, resistance systems, and gas systems. The life-cycle costs would be computed from the initial cost and the expected operating cost. Furthermore, it also would be appropriate to include air conditioning costs in the calculus, since the heat pump also provides cooling. In theory, the option providing the lowest life-cycle cost will be adopted.

In practice, all three options will continue to be used. First, there are a number of noneconomic factors that influence the fuel-choice decision, including consumer perceptions about reliability, cleanliness, and convenience. Second, the fuel-choice decision in about three-quarters of the single-family units and practically all the multifamily units is made by the builder, who, unlike the homeowner, is more concerned with initial cost than with life-cycle cost.

Appliance-Efficiency Standards. Electricity consumption is expected to increase at a rate that is slower than that of the number of appliance units. One reason for this expectation is that new and more efficient appliance units will be introduced into the stock.

The manner of measuring appliance efficiency depends on the appliance. The efficiency of electricity use in lighting is calculated as lumens (a measure of light flux) per watt of electricity. The higher are the lumens per watt, the more efficient is the lamp. Fluorescent lighting is more efficient than incandescent lighting, and sodium vapor lighting is more efficient than fluorescent.

The efficiency of room air conditioners is measured by the energy-efficiency ratio (EER). The EER is the ratio of cooling capacity to wattage, and the higher is the EER, the more efficient is the unit. The cooling capacity of an air conditioner is measured in terms of Btu's of heat removed. A 1000-watt unit with the ability to remove 6000 Btu of heat in 1 hour would have an EER of 6.0. For a unit with similar capacity but only using 750 watts, the EER is 9.0. There is considerable potential for enhancing air-conditioner efficiency.

The efficiency of electric water heaters is expressed in a manner that identifies the heat loss. If the efficiency is 85 percent, this means that 85 percent of the energy is used to heat the water and 15 percent is lost. The losses occur as a result of conduction through the jacket walls and distribution pipe.

The efficiency of electric-resistance space-heating systems is effectively 1.0, in that for 1 Btu of electricity use, there is 1 Btu of heat. However, the electric load required to keep the thermostat at a certain level can be reduced by insulating the ceiling and walls, by adding storm windows, and by otherwise reducing the heat loss caused by air infiltrations or conduction through the building shell. It must be pointed out, however, that electric-heated homes are as a class much better insulated than oil- or gas-heated homes. In addition, as noted earlier, the electric heat pump has a winter seasonal performance factor of 1.5, which means it provides 1.5 Btu of heat for each Btu of energy consumed.

The Energy Policy and Conservation Act of 1975 (Pub. L. 94-163), as amended by the Energy Conservation and Production Act of 1976 (Pub. L. 94-385), required that voluntary energy-efficiency improvement targets be set for thirteen categories of appliances, including air conditioners, water heaters, clothes dryers, and kitchen ranges. The targets defined the percentage efficiency by which appliances manufactured in 1980 should exceed the efficiency of those manufactured in 1972.

The *Federal Register* of 15 July 1977 (pp. 36648–36670) contained proposed efficiency targets. The targets were 30 percent for room air conditioners, 18 percent for electric water heaters, 8 percent for electric clothes dryers, and 3 percent for electric ranges.

The voluntary target program was eliminated by the National Energy Conservation Policy Act of 1978 (Pub. L. 95-619), which made appliance-efficiency standards mandatory. The Department of Energy (DOE) is required to set standards for the thirteen categories of appliances, and it has contracted Arthur D. Little, Inc. to assist in this matter. Proposed rules were published in June of 1980 in the *Federal Register.*

Changes in Building Design. New homes will typically require less electricity for space heating and air conditioning than existing homes. First, a greater proportion of new homes are likely to be multifamily units (for example, apartments), which, because of their smaller size and shared walls and ceilings, use about one-third as much heating energy as single-family units.

Second, new homes are likely to be more energy-efficient because of the institution of building energy codes. The most widespread code at this time is Standard 90-75 of the American Society of Heating, Refrigerating, and Air Conditioning Engineers (ASHRAE: 90-75). The Energy Policy and Conservation Act made federal energy-conservation grants to the states conditional on, among other things, their adopting residential insulation standards consistent with ASHRAE or with the Housing and Urban Development Minimum Property Standards (HUD–MPS).

The Energy Conservation and Production Act required the publication of Building Energy Performance Standards (BEPS). While ASHRAE is prescriptive in nature (that is, it identifies those features a building must contain), BEPS is a performance standard (that is, it defines an allowable energy use per square foot and lets the building designer meet it any way he or she chooses).

The *Federal Register* of 28 November 1979 (pp. 68120–68181) contains proposed rules for BEPS. The DOE has estimated that if the proposed BEPS become effective, the energy savings will be greater than that associated with ASHRAE 90-75 or HUD–MPS. However, BEPS, will be binding on the states only if the Congress approves sanctions for noncompliance, which is questionable.

Conservation. In any one year, the proportion of new appliance units and new buildings to the total stock is quite low. Thus the effects of appliance-efficiency standards and building insulation standards are limited because they do not affect the existing stock of appliances and homes. However, this does not mean that the electricity use associated with existing appliance units and homes will remain constant. Such electricity use will decrease as real electricity prices encourage customers to conserve. It is possible to identify two generic types of conservation. The first type of conservation requires the customer to make an investment in a retrofit of his or her appliance so as to augment its efficiency. The second type of conservation requires the customer to alter his or her lifestyle to minimize energy use.

In the case of space heating, an example of the first type of conservation is the installation of storm windows, insulation, or other materials to reduce heat loss from the building. An example of the second type of conservation is the lowering of thermostats.

In the case of water heating, an example of the first type of conservation is the use of a fiberglass-jacket insulation kit to reduce heat losses. Lowering the thermostat on the water heater and reducing hot water consumption are examples of the second type of conservation.

The feasibility of the first type of conservation is usually evaluated by the customer using a payback ratio. The *payback ratio* is defined as the number of years needed for the savings in reduced electricity bills to equal the cost of the retrofit. Thus any rise in electricity prices or any reduction in the initial outlay will reduce the payback ratio and so encourage the investment.

Rises in real electricity price also will encourage the second type of conservation. The greater is the cost of energy, the more willing is the customer to alter his or her lifestyle.

Both types of conservation have been accelerated by programs to increase customer awareness of techniques to reduce energy use. For example, utilities are conducting energy audits for individual customers designed to identify various cost-effective conserving options. On a more general level, DOE is making available pamphlets on conservation.

Conservation also is being encouraged by legislative initiatives that reduce the cost of the initial investment in retrofits. For example, both the National Energy Conservation Policy Act of 1978 (Pub. L. 95-619) and the Energy Tax Act of 1978 (Pub. L. 95-618) contain provisions to stimulate residential conservation. Credit funds are to be made available for specified investments in residential conservation and a 15 percent tax credit also is provided for such investment.

Illustrative Profiles. The amount of electricity use consumed by a particular customer depends on the annual electricity use per unit and the number of units owned. Table 3-5 presents annual electricity use per unit for different appliances, disaggregated by single-family and multifamily customers. As the table shows for many appliances, the amount of electricity used per unit varies between single-family and multifamily customers. In the case of electric water heating, for example, a single-family customer uses about 5450 kWh a year, while a multifamily customer uses about 3650 kWh a year.

Tables 3-6 through 3-9 present detailed electricity-use profiles for various customers classes. It will be noted that single-family customers use more elec-

Table 3-5
Annual Electricity Use in Kilowatt-Hours per Unit for 1979

	Single-Family	Multifamily
Water heat	5,450	3,650
Cooking	870	670
Central air	2,600	1,800
Room air	900	800
Clothes drying	1,150	760
Refrigeration	1,230	1,125
Freezing	1,380	1,140
Color television	300	290
Dishwashing	300	200
Lighting	650	410

Source: Arthur D. Little, Inc., estimates.

Table 3-6
Illustrative Profile of Single-Family Electric Space-Heat Customer

	Saturation Ratio	Annual kWh/Unit	Contribution in Annual kWh
Space heat	1.00	10,600	10,600
Water heat	0.88	5,450	4,796
Cooking	0.90	870	783
Central air	0.22	2,600	572
Room air	0.40	900	360
Clothes drying	0.59	1,150	679
Refrigeration	1.06	1,230	1,304
Freezing	0.47	1,380	649
Color TV	0.88	300	264
Dishwashing	0.42	300	126
Lighting	1.00	650	650
Other	1.00	760	760
Total			21,543

Note: The contribution in annual kWh is calculated as the product of the saturation ratio and the annual kWh/unit.

tricity than multifamily customers, and electric-heat customers use more electricity than non-electric-heat customers.

Model Logic

The factors affecting electricity use fall into two classes: those affecting the number of appliance units and those affecting the annual kilowatt-hours per unit. The second class includes appliance-efficiency standards, changes in building design, and conservation.

Table 3–7
Illustrative Profile of Single-Family Nonelectric Space-Heat Customer

	Saturation Ratio	Annual kWh/Unit	Contribution in Annual kWh
Fossil-fuel auxiliaries	1.00	575	575
Water heat	0.25	5,450	1,362
Cooking	0.46	870	400
Central air	0.16	2,800	448
Room air	0.40	900	360
Clothes drying	0.53	1,150	609
Refrigeration	1.06	1,230	1,304
Freezing	0.47	1,380	649
Color TV	0.88	300	264
Dishwashing	0.42	300	126
Lighting	1.00	650	650
Other	1.00	715	715
Total			7,462

Table 3–8
Illustrative Profile of Multifamily Electric Space-Heat Customer

	Saturation Ratio	Annual kWh/Unit	Contribution in Annual kWh
Space heat	1.00	4,300	4,300
Water heat	0.89	3,650	3,248
Cooking	0.91	670	610
Central air	0.24	1,800	432
Room air	0.36	800	288
Clothes drying	0.24	760	182
Refrigeration	1.00	1,125	1,125
Freezing	0.10	1,140	114
Color TV	0.62	290	180
Dishwashing	0.30	200	60
Lighting	1.00	410	410
Other	1.00	380	380
Total			11,345

The residential end-use model reflects this classification of factors. In it, annual electricity use is calculated by multiplying the stock (number) appliance units by the annual kilowatt-hours per unit. Such an operation is carried out separately for each of i appliance categories (for example where $i = 1$ is space heating, $i = 2$ is air conditioning, $i = 3$ is water heating, $i = 4$ is clothes drying, $i = 5$ is cooking, and $i = 6$ is residual) and p housing types ($p = 1$ is single-family and $p = 2$ is multifamily).

Table 3-9
Illustrative Profile of Multifamily Nonelectric Space-Heat Customer

	Saturation Ratio	Annual kWh/Unit	Contribution in Annual kWh
Fossil-fuel auxiliaries	1.00	290	290
Water heat	0.11	3,650	402
Cooking	0.40	670	268
Central air	0.21	1,800	378
Room air	0.36	800	288
Clothes drying	0.21	760	160
Refrigeration	1.00	1,125	1,125
Freezing	0.10	1,140	114
Color TV	0.62	290	180
Dishwashing	0.28	200	56
Lighting	1.00	410	410
Other	1.00	380	380
Total			4,231

The appliance groups in the model are selected because they represent significant percentages of residential electricity use and/or because they represent applications that can be satisfied by an energy form other than electricity. The housing disaggregation is necessary because, for any given appliance, a multifamily home uses considerably less electricity than a single-family home.

For the base year (for example, 1979), the user inputs starting values defining the stock of appliance units for each of the i categories and p housing types. For subsequent years, the model calculates the stock of appliance units by adding to the base-year value the number of appliance units associated with new customers and the number of units purchased by existing customers who did not own the appliance in the base year.

The user also must input base-year annual kilowatt-hours per unit values (henceforth referred to as unit-electricity coefficients) for the i appliance categories and p housing types. In subsequent years, the model calculates the unit-electricity coefficients, taking into account the greater efficiency of new units and the possibility of voluntary conservation.

Apart from the base-year values, the user also has to input values that are required by the model to perform the subsequent-year computations. These values are for such variables as appliance penetration rates for new customers and unit-electricity coefficients for new appliances.

Presented next is a symbolic list of the equations in the residential model. For ease of exposition, no reference will be made in the listing to the housing and appliance disaggregation, because the presence of such disaggregation does not complicate the structure of the model but merely creates a requirement for more data. The listing also will focus on the year immediately after the base year. The subscript b will denote the base year and the subscript t the year after the base year.

In the listing, the labels used to identify the variables will reflect their status. The initialization or base variables are identified by the symbol BVR, the other input variables by the symbol IVR, and the output variables by the symbol OVR. The variables are numbered by their order of appearance: the first output variable is $OVR1$, the second is $OVR2$, and so on.

Equation 3.1 forecasts total residential electric customers by multiplying population by a customer-to-population ratio. The ratio is actually the reciprocal of the number of people per customer, with a ratio of 0.25, for example, indicating four people per customer.

$$OVR1_t = IVR1_t \times IVR2_t \tag{3.1}$$

where $OVR1_t$ = total customers in year t
$\quad IVR1_t$ = population in year t
$\quad IVR2_t$ = customer-to-population ratio in year t

Equation 3.2 forecasts new electric customers by subtracting from the total customers in year t the total customers in the preceding year b:

$$OVR2_t = OVR1_t - BVR1_b \tag{3.2}$$

where $OVR2_t$ = new customers in year t
$\quad OVR1_t$ = total customers in year t
$\quad BVR1_b$ = total customers in year b

In equation 3.3, the number of appliance units associated with new customers is determined by multiplying the number of new customers by an appliance-penetration rate. The penetration rate defines the fraction of new customers who will own the appliance.

$$OVR3_t = OVR2_t \times IVR3_t \tag{3.3}$$

where $OVR3_t$ = number of appliance units purchased by new customers in year t
$\quad OVR2_t$ = new customers in year t
$\quad IVR3_t$ = fraction of new customers who own the appliance

Equation 3.4 forecasts the number of appliance units purchased in year t by existing customers who did not previously own the appliance. These subsequent purchases, which are typically the result of improvements in economic status, are predicted as a function of the number of existing customers who do not own the appliance.

$$OVR4_t = IVR4_t \, (BVR1_b - BVR2_b) \tag{3.4}$$

where $OVR4_t$ = number of net new appliance units purchased by existing customers in year t

$IVR4_t$ = fraction of existing customers who purchase net new appliances in year t

$BVR1_b$ = total customers in year b

$BVR2_b$ = stock (total number) of appliance units in year b

Equation 3.5 forecasts the number of appliance units that will be replaced in year t because of deterioration or obsolescence. The number of replacements is calculated by multiplying the existing stock by an appliance-replacement rate. The replacement rate is the reciprocal of the appliance lifetime. For example, if the lifetime of a room air conditioner is 10 years, then the replacement rate is 0.10.

$$OVR5_t = IVR5 \times BVR2_b \tag{3.5}$$

where $OVR5_t$ = number of appliance units replaced in year t

$IVR5$ = appliance replacement rate

$BVR2_b$ = stock of appliance units in year b

Equation 3.6 calculates the total number of new units purchased in year t by summing the new units associated with new and existing customers.

$$OVR6_t = OVR3_t + OVR4_t + OVR5_t \tag{3.6}$$

where $OVR6_t$ = total new appliance units purchased in year t

$OVR3_t$ = number of appliance units purchased by new customers in year t

$OVR4_t$ = number of net new appliance units purchased by existing customers in year t

$OVR5_t$ = number of appliance units replaced in year t

Equation 3.7 calculates the stock of appliance units in year t by adding net appliance purchases in year t to the stock of appliance units in the preceding year b. Net purchases do not include those units acquired as replacements, since the effect of a replacement is merely to substitute a new unit for an old unit.

$$OVR7_t = SVR2_b + OVR3_t + OVR4_t \tag{3.7}$$

where $OVR7_t$ = stock of appliance units in year t

$SVR2_b$ = stock of appliance units in year b

$OVR3_t$ = number of appliance units purchased by new customers in year t

$OVR4_t$ = number of net new appliance units purchased by existing customers in year t

Equation 3.8 calculates the stock of existing appliance units in year t by subtracting new unit purchases from the total stock.

$$OVR8_t = OVR7_t - OVR6_t \qquad (3.8)$$

where $OVR8_t$ = stock of existing appliance units in year t
$OVR7_t$ = stock of appliance units in year t
$OVR6_t$ = total number of new appliance units purchased in year t

Equation 3.9 forecasts the electricity use associated with existing units by multiplying the existing stock by a unit-electricity coefficient.

$$OVR9_t = OVR8_t \times SVR3 \qquad (3.9)$$

where $OVR9_t$ = electricity use associated with existing appliance units in year t
$OVR8_t$ = stock of existing appliance units in year t
$SVR3$ = unit-electricity coefficient for existing appliance units

Equation 3.10 forecasts the electricity use associated with new units by multiplying the number of new units purchased in year t by a new unit-electricity coefficient.

$$OVR10_t = OVR6_t \times IVR6_t \qquad (3.10)$$

where $OVR10_t$ = electricity use associated with new units in year t
$OVR6_t$ = total number of new appliance units purchased in year t
$IVR6_t$ = unit-electricity coefficient for new units in year t

Equation 3.11 calculates total residential electricity sales by summing the electricity use associated with existing and new units.

$$OVR11_t = OVR9_t + OVR10_t \qquad (3.11)$$

where $OVR11_t$ = total electricity use in year t (that is, total residential sales)
$OVR9_t$ = electricity use associated with existing appliance units in year t
$OVR10_t$ = electricity use associated with new appliance units in year t

For the base year, the user inputs the unit-electricity coefficient used in equation 3.9 to calculate the electricity use of existing stock. In other years, the model calculates the unit-electricity coefficient for the existing stock by rolling in the new units purchased in the preceding year. The equation that performs the function is written as follows:

$$OVR12_t = OVR11_t \div OVR7_t \qquad (3.12)$$

where $OVR12_t$ = unit-electricity coefficient to be applied to existing stock in year $t + 1$

$OVR11_t$ = total electricity use in year t

$OVR7_t$ = stock of appliance units in year t

The preceding discussion has indicated that electricity use is calculated by multiplying the number of appliance units by a judgmentally derived unit-electricity coefficient, where the coefficient is equal to the annual kilowatt-hours per unit. This, in fact, is the procedure used for clothes dryers, ranges, and other non-weather-sensitive loads. However, for air conditioning and space heating, such a procedure is unwarranted because it ignores the year-to-year fluctuations in load that occur in response to variations in the weather. The residential sales model consequently employs a somewhat different approach to forecast space-heating and air-conditioning loads. For example, in the case of air conditioning, the forecast equation for existing units is written

$$OVR9SH_t = OVR8SH_t \times SVR3SH_t \times IVR7HDD_t \qquad (3.13)$$

where $OVR9SH_t$ = electricity use associated with existing air-conditioning units in year t

$OVR8SH_t$ = stock of existing air-conditioning units in year t

$SVR3SH_t$ = coefficient defining kilowatt-hours per cooling degree day per air conditioner

$IVR7HDD_t$ = number of cooling degree days expected in year t

In equation 3.13, the air-conditioning load is calculated by multiplying the number of units ($OVR8SH_t$) by a kilowatt-hour per unit per cooling degree day coefficient ($SVR3SH_t$) and by the expected number of cooling degree days ($IVR7HDD_t$). The air-conditioning units are expressed on a central equivalent basis, with three-room units considered the equal of one central unit. *Cooling degree days* (also referred to as *degree day excess values*) are a construct designed by engineers to reflect the relationship of space-conditioning energy use to weather. They are calculated as the excess of the mean daily temperature over a base temperature (for example, a day with a mean temperature of 80° would constitute 8 heating degree days if the base is 72°, and a month with 20 such days would contain 160 heating degree days). The base-year coefficient for air-conditioning use ($SVR3SH_t$) is derived econometrically, as is the coefficient for heating use. A regression equation for each year relating monthly electricity use to degree days is fitted. In the regression equation there is no income or electricity price variable because, during a given year, income and price are essentially constant and so the only reason for electricity use to fluctuate on a month-to-month basis is weather. The form of the regression equation is presented next. Because it is an econometric equation, a different format is used to present it. The endogenous (dependent) variable is denoted by Y and the exogenous (independent) variables by X.

$$Y1 = a1 + (b1 \; X1) + (c1.X2) \tag{3.14}$$

where $Y1$ = monthly electricity use per customer in kilowatt-hours
$\quad\quad X1$ = monthly heating degree days
$\quad\quad X2$ = monthly cooling degree days

In equation 3.14, the estimated intercept $a1$ identifies the electricity use per customer at zero degree days, and as such, it is an approximation of non-weather-sensitive load per customer. The coefficient $b1$ is a measure of heating use and is interpreted as the kilowatt-hours per customer per heating degree day. The coefficient $c1$ is a measure of cooling use and is interpreted as the kilowatt-hours per customer per cooling degree day. The coefficient $c1$ is divided by an air-conditioning saturation ratio to get kilowatt-hours per unit per cooling degree day.

Appliance-Saturation Submodels

The appliance-saturation inputs entered into an end-use model can be analytically derived. The type of modeling analysis used will depend on whether or not alternative fuels are available. Air conditioning provides an example of an application that is essentially dedicated to electricity (although some central gas units are in fact available).

To predict the air-conditioning saturation ratio, a linear or double-logarithmic function cannot be used. This is so because such functional forms could result in forecasts of the saturation ratio that exceed 1. The appropriate specification is the logit, because it constrains the saturation ratio not to exceed 1. This equation is written as follows:

$$\ln \frac{ASCAT}{1 - ACSAT} = q + vINCM + wEPRICE \tag{3.15}$$

where $ASCAT$ = air-conditioning saturation ratio in central equivalents
$\quad\quad INCM$ = real per household income
$\quad\quad EPRICE$ = real electricity price

In equation 3.15, the air-conditioning saturation ratio is expected to depend positively on income and negatively on price. A rise in income will encourage the acquisition of an air conditioner, while a rise in price will have the opposite effect. The precise relationship between the saturation ratio and the explanatory variables can be determined by taking the first derivative of equation 3.15. The derivative with respect to income is as follows:

$$\frac{\partial ASCAT}{\partial INCM} = vASCAT\,(1 - ASCAT)$$

According to the preceding derivative, the change in saturation resulting from a change in income depends on the level of saturation at that time. If everybody has a central air-conditioning equivalent (that is, the saturation is 1.0), then the first derivative becomes 0, indicating that an increase in income can cause no further increase in saturation.

The pattern exhibited by the derivative is highly symmetrical. The maximum value for the derivative occurs when the saturation is 0.50; at this point a rise in income causes an increase in saturation equal to $0.25v$. At points equidistant from 0.50, the derivative takes on the same value. For example, if the saturation is 0.75 or 0.25, the first derivative is $0.19v$.

Electric space heating is the most important application where alternative fuels are available. The factors affecting the choice of a fuel for a space-heating system include fuel availability, service performance, initial cost, and operating cost. Models to predict future electric space heating would ideally take into account all the factors affecting fuel choice. In practice, most models have assumed that fuel choice is based entirely on relative fuel prices. This is so because data on the other factors are not consistently available.

A number of formulations have been proposed to model fuel split; presented here is the version developed by the Oakridge National Laboratory.[5] The Oakridge Model is written as follows:

$$\ln\frac{ELECSAT}{OILSAT} = a1 + b1\ln EPRICE$$
$$+ c1\ln GPRICE + d1\ln OPRICE \qquad (3.16)$$

$$\ln\frac{GASSAT}{OILSAT} = a2 + b2\ln EPRICE$$
$$+ c2\ln GPRICE + d2\ln OPRICE \qquad (3.17)$$

where $ELECSAT$ = electricity space-heating saturation ratio
  $OILSAT$ = oil space-heating saturation ratio
  $GASSAT$ = gas space-heating saturation ratio

EPRICE   = electricity price
GPRICE   = gas price
OPRICE   = oil price

Equations 3.16 and 3.17 are estimated simultaneously subject to the constraint that the three saturation ratios *ELECSAT, GASSAT,* and *OILSAT* sum to 1. Because the equation is estimated subject to the constraint, the coefficients of the two equations provide sufficient information to estimate all three shares.

Equation 3.16 expresses the ratio of electric share to oil share as a function of energy prices. The coefficient $b1$ attached to electricity price will be negative, indicating that high electricity prices will reduce the relative electric share. However, the share of electricity is not determined solely by the coefficients of equation 3.16. Because the system is estimated simultaneously, the sensitivity of the electricity share also will depend on the estimated coefficients of the other equation. It can be shown that the change in electricity share caused by a change in electricity price is as follows:

$$\frac{\partial ELECSAT}{\partial EPRICE} = \frac{EPRICE}{ELECSAT}[b1\,OILSAT + (b1 - b2)\,GASSAT]$$

The change in electricity share caused by a change in natural-gas price is

$$\frac{\partial ELECSAT}{\partial GPRICE} = \frac{GPRICE}{ELECSAT}[c1\,OILSAT + (c1 - c2)\,GASSAT]$$

Appliance-Efficiency Improvements

A fundamental parameter in end-use analysis is the rate at which appliance-efficiency improvements will occur. On 30 June 1980, the Department of Energy (DOE) published in the *Federal Register* proposed rules for efficiency standards for refrigerators, freezers, clothes dryers, water heaters, ranges and ovens, room air conditioners, and central air conditioners.

These appliance-efficiency rules are designed to require manufacturers to produce, and consumers to purchase, significantly more efficient products. The efficiency of the rules should be enhanced by the development of a labeling program requiring manufacturers to label covered products with energy-cost or energy-consumption information that will assist consumers in making purchasing decisions. The Federal Trade Commission (FTC) has the responsibility for developing the labeling rules and administering the labeling program. The final rule for labeling only included room air conditioners, furnaces, clothes washers, dishwashers, water heaters, refrigerators and refrigerator-freezers, and freezers and appeared in the *Federal Register* of 19 November 1979. Labeling requirements are expected to be issued for central air conditioners and heat pumps in the near future.

The authority for DOE to promulgate mandatory appliance-efficiency standards was established by the National Energy Conservation Policy Act of 1978 (Pub. L. 95-9619). The proposed rules promulgated by DOE were based on an engineering analysis conducted by Arthur D. Little, Inc. and an economic analysis performed by other contractors.

The standards, among other things, define the minimum-efficiency standard that all appliances must meet by 1986. This minimum-efficiency standard corresponds to what has been determined to be technologically feasible and economically justifiable. It is, of course, expected that many of the appliances available in 1986 will, in fact, surpass the standards.

Refrigerators. By definition, an electric refrigerator is a cabinet designed for the refrigerated storage of food at temperatures above 32°F and having a source of refrigeration requiring an electric-energy input only. It may include a compartment for the freezing and storage of food at temperatures below 32°F, but it does not provide a separate low-temperature compartment designed for the freezing and the long-term storage of food at temperatures below 8°F. It has only one exterior door, but it may have interior doors or compartments.

The efficiency of a refrigerator is measured by an energy factor (EF) calculated as cubic feet per kilowatt-hour per 24 hours. In 1978, a new 18-cubic-foot top-mount automatic-defrost refrigerator had an average EF of 4.5 according to sales data supplied by appliance manufacturers. According to the proposed rules, by 1986, all units of this type would have a minimum efficiency of 8.2 EF. Thus all refrigerators (of this type) sold in 1986 would require 45 percent less electricity than those sold in 1978. As a result of the greater efficiency, the purchase price of the refrigerator is expected to increase by 5.3 percent.

Freezers. A freezer is defined as a cabinet designed as a unit for the storage of food at temperatures of 0°F or below, having the ability to freeze food, and having a source of refrigeration requiring an electric-energy input only.

The efficiency of a freezer is also measured by an energy factor (EF) calculated as cubic feet per kilowatt-hour per 24 hours. In 1978, a 15-cubic-foot chest freezer with manual defrost had an EF of 11.8. By 1986, all units of this type would have an EF of 18.7, which means that they would use 37 percent less electricity than units sold in 1978. The imposition of the standard is expected to increase the purchase price of the freezer by 3.1 percent.

Water Heaters. An electric water heater is defined as an automatically controlled thermally insulated vessel designed for heating water and storing heated water that utilizes electricity as the fuel or energy source for heating the water and is designed to produce hot water at a temperature of less than 180°F.

The efficiency of a water heater is determined by the amount of energy that is transferred to the hot water. In 1978, the average 52-gallon electric water heater installed had an efficiency of 77 percent. By 1986, all water heaters of this type must have an efficiency of at least 93 percent. This means that the 1986 units will use 17 percent less electricity than the 1978 units. The effect of the standards will be to raise the purchase price of the water heater by 13.3 percent.

Clothes Dryers. An electric clothes dryer is defined as a cabinet-like product designed to dry fabrics in a tumble-type drum with forced air circulation. The heat source is electricity, and the drum and blower(s) are driven by an electric motor(s).

The energy factor (EF) of a clothes dryer is defined as pounds per kilowatt-hour. In 1978, the typical unit sold had an EF of 2.65; by 1986, all units must have an EF of at least 2.98. This means that there will be a 11 percent reduction in electricity use. The increase in purchase cost resulting from the improved efficiency is expected to be 9 percent.

Cooking. Electric ranges and ovens are defined as consumer products that are used as the major household cooking appliances. They are designed to cook or heat different types of food by electricity or microwave energy. Each product may consist of a horizontal cooking top containing one or more surface units and/or one or more heating compartments.

The average 3.9-cubic-foot oven-cavity electric oven sold in 1978 had an EF of 11.3. The standards mandate that all units of this type sold in 1986 have an EF of 14.2, which will produce electric-energy savings of 20 percent. The resulting cost increase is 8 percent.

Room Air Conditioner. A room air conditioner is defined as a consumer product powered by a single-phase electric current that is an encased assembly designed as a unit for mounting in a window or through the wall for the purpose of providing delivery of conditioned air to an enclosed space and is not a "packaged terminal air conditioner." It includes a prime source of refrigeration and may include a means for ventilating and heating.

The efficiency of an air conditioner is measured by an energy-efficiency ratio (EER) that indicates the Btu's of heat removed per Btu of electricity used. In 1978, the typical 8500-Btu/h unit had an EER of 6.5. By 1986, all units must have an EER of 9.5, which implies a 32 percent savings in electricity. The purchase price of the air conditioner is expected to increase by 18 percent because of the incorporation of the technology to enhance efficiency.

Central Air Conditioners. A central air conditioner is defined as a consumer product powered by single-phase electric current that is rated below 65,000 Btu/h and is not contained within the same cabinet as a furnace with a rated capacity above 225,000 Btu/h and is either a "heat pump" or a "cooling only unit."

The EER of the central unit calculated over the season (SEER) averaged 7.0 for 30,000 Btu/h units sold in 1978. The standards mandate that such units must have at least a 11.1 SEER by 1986. The standards will reduce electricity use by 37 percent and the purchase price will rise 29 percent. Table 3-10 summarizes the efficiency improvements discussed in the preceding text.

Building Efficiency Improvements

On 28 November 1979, the Department of Energy published in the *Federal Register* proposed building energy performance standards (BEPS) as mandated by the Energy Conservation Standards for New Buildings Act of 1976.

DOE's initial analyses also show that the proposed standards will result in greater conservation than existing buildings standards, as well as recently revised standards such as a draft version (April 1978) of the Department of Housing and Urban Development (HUD) Minimum Property Standards and the American So-

Table 3-10
Proposed Mandatory Appliance-Efficiency Improvements
(*percentage reduction in electricity use of 1986 models over 1978 models*)

	Minimum Standards	*Best Available*
Refrigerators	46	57
Freezers	37	47
Ranges/ovens	20	20
Clothes dryers	11	13
Water heaters	17	45
Central air conditioners	37	50
Room air conditioners	32	46

Source: "Energy Conservation Program for Consumer Products," *Federal Register* (June 30, 1980): 43976–44001. The final rules are likely to be different from the proposed rules.

Notes: The minimum standards must be met by all units sold after January 1, 1986. This means, for example, that all refrigerators sold in 1986 will use at least 46 percent less electricity than the average unit (of the same model) sold in 1978. The best unit available in 1986 is likely to considerably surpass the standards. For example, the most efficient refrigerator available in 1986 is likely to provide 57 percent savings.

ciety of Heating, Refrigerating and Air-Conditioning Engineers, Inc. (ASHRAE) proposed Standard 90-75R (November 1977).

For example, single-family residential buildings designed to comply with the proposed standards might use between 22 and 51 percent less energy than current practice, and commercial and multifamily residential buildings might use between 17 and 52 percent less energy, depending on the type of building and the climate.

Studies assessing the probable costs and benefits to individuals show that the total cost of owning and operating a building designed in compliance with the proposed standards (that is, the capital cost of the building and the energy costs for heating, cooling, ventilation, lights, vertical transportation, and domestic hot water) will decrease compared with current practice.

The proposed standards are applied during the design of a building and regulate its design energy-conservation potential. They do not regulate the operation, maintenance, or energy consumption of the building once built. The standards thus take advantage of the opportunity to save energy and to increase the use of renewable resources by requiring that buildings be designed to be energy-efficient. The efficient operation and maintenance of the resulting energy-efficient buildings provide opportunities to save even more energy.

The proposed standards regulate the design of a whole building rather than prescribing requirements for its individual parts. This approach is markedly different from existing component performance standards, which specify the minimum energy-related performance of a building's parts, components, or subsystems. Component-based standards do not consider that the same set of building components assembled in different ways can result in varying levels of design energy consumption for the whole building. Whole-building performance standards take this into account by permitting a designer to meet an overall energy goal for a building by considering not only the efficiencies of parts of the building, but also the tradeoff among building components or among design strategies.

The proposed standards consist of three elements. First, *energy budget levels* must be set for different classifications of buildings in different climates. The energy budget levels are stated in terms of thousands of Btu's per square foot of gross area of the building design per year.

Second, the proposed standards provide the method for applying the energy budget levels to a specific building design to obtain an annual rate of energy consumption, which is its *design energy budget.*

Third, the proposed standards establish a method for calculating the estimated annual rate of energy consumption of a building design, which is referred to as its *design energy consumption.* Accordingly, the standards can be reduced to the simple requirement that the design energy consumption of a new building design may not exceed its design energy budget.

In calculating energy budgets, DOE has proposed to use a weighting-factor approach. The weights applied to a specific fuel are based on the relative price. Natural gas has a weight of 1, oil has a weight of 1.22, and electricity has a weight of 2.79. The weighting factors are used as a way of expressing the design energy budget of a building design. Application of the weighting factors is straightforward. The designer first calculates the energy requirements by fuel type. The energy requirement for each fuel type, expressed in thousands of Btu's per square foot per year is then multiplied by the appropriate weighting factor for the fuel type. These weighting figures are then summed over all fuels to arrive at the design energy consumption of the building. The value of the design energy consumption must be less than or equal to the design energy budget for the building design to be in compliance with the standards.

The impact of the weighting-factor approach is to discourage the use of electricity and promote the use of oil and gas. Such an approach has come under criticism in that oil and gas are scarce fuels, while electricity can be generated by abundant coal and nuclear resources.

The proposed energy budget levels for single-family residences contain three energy components: space heating, space cooling, and domestic hot water heating. The proposed energy budget levels for space heating and cooling vary to reflect regional changes in climate conditions; they also apply to each square foot of gross area of the residence, regardless of the size of the residence.

However, the proposed energy budget levels for domestic hot water heating are fixed quantities for all regions of the country; also, they are based on an average number of occupants per residence and do not vary with the size of the residence.

For the Omaha SMSA, for example, the heating/cooling energy budget for a single-family building is 50.0 MBtu/ft^2/yr for electricity, 49.2 MBtu/ft^2/yr for oil, and 41.6 MBtu/ft^2/yr for gas. The water heating budget is 54,600 MBtu/yr/unit for electric, 42,500 MBtu/yr/unit for oil, and 29,500 MBtu/yr/unit for gas.

In conclusion, it should be noted that action on BEPS has been deferred for a year and it is debatable whether BEPS will ever be enforced.

Commercial Sales Model

Factors Affecting Commercial Electricity Use

The discussion of commercial sales models will be brief because this sector has characteristics of both the residential and industrial sector. In 1978, the commercial sector accounted for 22.8 percent of U.S. electricity consumption. This sector is defined to include wholesale trade (SIC 50 and 51); retail trade (SIC 52-59); finance, insurance and real estate (SIC 60-67); services (SIC 70-89 not

Table 3-11
Historical Pattern of Commercial Electricity Use

	Unit-Electricity Coefficient (kWh/ft^2)	Commercial Floor Space (Billion Square Feet)	Commercial Electricity Sales (Billion kWh)
1960	7.6	15.8	120.0
1970	12.6	24.3	306.7
1973	14.4	26.9	388.3
1978	14.8	31.0	459.9

Sources: Energy Information Administration, *Statistics and Trends of Energy Supply, Demand and Prices* (Washington: U.S. Government Printing Office, May 1978), p. 103; Energy Information Administration, *Monthly Energy Review* (Washington: U.S. Government Printing Office, May 1980), p. 63; and Oakridge National Laboratory, *Commercial Energy Use: A Disaggregation by Fuel, Building Type, and End Use* (Oakridge, Tenn.: Oakridge National Laboratory, Jan. 1980), p. 36.

including SIC 88); and public administration (SIC 91–96). Associated with these SIC groups are stores, offices, hotels, warehouses, schools, hospitals, and other building types.

Table 3-11 presents data on commercial electricity use, commercial floor space, and electricity use per square foot. During the period 1960–1973, commercial electricity sales grew at a compound annual rate of 9.45 percent, but during the period 1973–1978, the growth rate was only 3.44 percent. The growth in electricity sales has outstripped that of floor space, indicating that kilowatt-hours per square foot has risen. In 1960, kilowatt-hours per square foot of floor space was 7.6, while in 1978, it was 14.8.

Electricity is used in commercial buildings for lighting, cooling, heating, ventilation, cooking, water heating, refrigeration, freezing, and the operation of office machinery. Table 3-12 disaggregates the kilowatt-hour-per-square-

Table 3-12
Commercial Unit-Electricity Coefficient
(in kWh/ft^2)

	Space Heat	Space Cool	Lighting	Other	Total
1970	0.9	4.8	5.3	1.6	12.6
1978	1.7	5.0	5.4	2.7	14.8

Sources: The 1970 disaggregation is based on Oakridge National Laboratory, *Commercial Energy Use: A Disaggregation by Fuel, Building Type and End Use,* pp. 8 and 12; the 1978 disaggregation is based on Energy Information Administration, *Annual Report to Congress for 1979, Volume Three* (Washington: U.S. Government Printing Office, January 1980), pp. 175 and 176.

Table 3–13
Fuel Shares of Commercial Building Inventory in 1975
(*percentage of total*)

	Space Heat	Space Cool	Lighting
Electricity	6	57	100
Gas	45	4	0
Oil	46	0	0
Other/none	3	39	0
Total	100	100	100

Source: Oakridge National Laboratory, *Commercial Energy Use: A Disaggregation by Fuel, Building Type and End Use,* p. 34.

foot coefficient according to application. In 1978, the coefficient of 14.8 kWh/ft² was distributed as follows: lighting 5.4; air conditioning 5.0; heating 1.7; and other applications 2.7.

The relatively low amount of electricity per square foot used for heating reflects the fact that only a small fraction of commercial buildings use electricity for space heating. Table 3–13 shows the contribution of oil, natural gas, and electricity to various commercial energy applications. As the table demonstrates, the space-heating function is dominated by oil and gas.

The amount of electricity used in the commercial sector is also sensitive to the type of building. Hospitals, for example, use 63 percent more electricity per square foot than commercial buildings on average, while warehouses use 58 percent less electricity than the average. Table 3–14 presents information on electricity intensity by building type.

A number of governmental programs have been instituted with the objective of decelerating the commercial demand for electricity. These include (1) grants

Table 3–14
Unit-Electricity Intensity Index, by Building Type, in 1975

	Index Value
All commercial buildings	1.00
Office	1.10
Retail-wholesale	1.34
Hospitals	1.63
Education	0.81
Warehouse	0.42
Religious	0.50

Source: Oakridge National Laboratory, *Commercial Energy Use: A Disaggregation by Fuel, Building Type, and End Use,* p. 36.

for energy audits in local buildings and public-care institutions, (2) grants to improve the energy efficiency of schools and hospitals, (3) a requirement that by 1990 all federal buildings should be retrofitted to ensure maximum efficiency, (4) a requirement for building efficiency standards, and (5) tax credits for investment in energy-saving equipment or solar-powered equipment.

End-Use Model Logic

The commercial end-use model takes the disaggregation of the residential end-use model a level further. While the residential model predicts electricity use by application, the commercial model predicts electricity use by both application and building type. Typical application categories are lighting, cooling, heating, and all other. Typical building categories are offices, stores, hotels, restaurants, warehouses, schools, and hospitals. For a given application in a given building type, the electricity usage is predicted by the following equation:

$$CKWH_{jk} = FLRSPC_j \times FRAC_{jk} \times EUC_{jk} \qquad (3.18)$$

where $CKWH_{jk}$ = commercial electricity use in application j in building k
$FLRSPC_j$ = floor space inventory of building j
$FRAC_{jk}$ = fraction of floor space of building j that uses electricity for application k
EUC_{jk} = electricity use per square foot (of floor space) for application j in building k

In practice, the commercial end-use model as defined by equation 3.18 must be extended to allow for vintaging. This vintaging will involve two extensions. First, separate electricity-penetration and electricity-utilization rates must be entered for buildings coming on-stream in each year of the forecast period. This is necessary because new buildings will have characteristics that differ markedly from those possessed by the existing stock. Second, allowance must be made for the possibility that because of retrofit programs, the electricity-utilization rate of some existing buildings will decline.

Industrial Sales Model

Factors Affecting Industrial Electricity Use

The high Btu cost of electricity makes its use uneconomical in such applications as steam raising, where fossil fuels can be applied. The chief industrial applications of electricity are for motive power and electrolytic process. The motive-power function refers to the operation of pumps, compressors, blowers, fans, machine tools, and other motors. Examples of electrolytic processes include the conversion of scrap to refined steel in the electric furnace and the conversion of alumina to aluminum by the Hall process. The provision of clean direct heat, air conditioning, and lighting are the remaining industrial electricity applications.

Conservation. About 75 percent of the electricity used in the industrial sector is accounted for by motors, and pumps consume about one-quarter of their output. The National Energy Conservation Policy Act of 1978 (Pub. L. 95-619) requires DOE to evaluate motors and pumps to determine if standards are necessary. DOE contracted Arthur D. Little, Inc., to undertake a study of this matter.[6] Summarized here are the principal findings from this study, along with some general facts pertaining to the subject, with a focus on motors. Table 3-15 contains general statistics.

There are two types of losses associated with electric-motor design and operation—intrinsic losses and extrinsic (system) losses. *Intrinsic losses* occur internally to the motor and determine the efficiency with which motors transform electric energy into mechanical energy; these losses can be affected only by motor-design changes. *Extrinsic losses* occur externally to the motor, but are

Table 3-15
Basic Comparison of Electric Motors and Pumps, 1977

Characteristics	Electric Motors[a]	Pumps[a]
1. Total number in use (millions)	720	191
2. Annual energy consumption (kWh $\times$ 10^9)	1,222	566
3. Maximum conservation potential (%)	2.3	4.2
4. Percent of population less than 1 hp	91.4	83.0
5. Size range of greatest consumption (hp)	>125	>125
6. Size range of greatest conservation (hp)	5.1–125	> 20
7. Manufactured in standard sizes	Yes	No
8. Efficiency data readily available	No	Yes
9. Efficiency in small sizes	Low	Low
10. Efficiency in large sizes	High	High
11. Load-matching losses	Low	High
12. Efficiency degradation with use	Low if any	Often high
13. Approximate number of manufacturers	50	400
14. Number of manufacturers accounting for 75% of market	8	11
15. Number of units sold (millions)	55	20
16. Value of units sold (million $)	2,022	1,875
17. Average value each	$36.77	$93.75
18. Percent of domestic purchases imported (units)	11.3	51
19. Percent of domestic purchases imported (dollars)	5	6

Source: Arthur D. Little, Inc., *Classification and Evaluation of Electric Motors and Pumps* (report to U.S. Department of Energy, February 1980), pp. 1–8.

[a]Over $1/6$ hp.

caused by factors inherent to motor design and operation that determine efficiency and power factor. These extrinsic losses can be affected by motor-design changes, as well as by application of power-factor correction capacitors or speed- and voltage-control devices external to the motor that essentially adjust the motor's peak power to the load.

The Arthur D. Little study focused on intrinsic losses, which are the determinant of motor efficiency. The level of such losses typically range between 5 and 36 percent of electric energy consumed, that is, motor efficiencies range between 95 and 64 percent.

The greatest potential for improving motor efficiency is in the 5- to 125-horsepower range (1 hp = 0.746 kW). Motors of under 5 hp have low average efficiencies (about 65 percent), but are not of interest because they account for only about 4 percent of motor electricity usage. Large motors of over 120 hp account for about 47 percent of motor electricity usage but already have very high efficiency levels (typically 94 percent).

Motors in the 5- to 125-hp range have average efficiencies ranging between 82.5 and 91.0 percent, with the higher efficiencies associated with the larger motors in the class. Significantly, more efficient motors are available for use; for example, in the 5- to 20-hp range, the average efficiency is 82.5 percent while motors of 88.5 percent efficiency are available.

The rate at which the average efficiency of the motor population will improve is likely to be very slow. With rebuilding the life of a motor in the 5- to 125-hp range can be about 20 years, which means that only 5 percent of the stock is replaced each year. In addition, efficiency is not a major criterion in the purchase of electric motors. Reliability is usually the single most important factor, since it is a critical requirement for the continuous process in which many motors are used. The price of the motor and the ability of the vendor to deliver on time are other important criteria. Recently, however, interest has been exhibited in energy-efficient motors, and purchasers have exhibited a willingness to pay the price premium associated with such efficiency.

With respect to existing motors, improvements in extrinsic efficiency may be possible. For example, NASA has licensed a technique to correct for the loss in efficiency that results when motors are not operating fully loaded. A solid-state electronic device is placed between the motor and power source so that it does not draw current it does not need.

The efficiency of electrolytic processes also can be improved. For example, a new smelting technique developed by Alcoa is claimed to use only 75 percent of the electricity required by the Hall process for the conversion of alumina to aluminum. In addition, the new process is environmentally cleaner.

Lighting loads also are amenable to conservation. More efficient light sources, such as sodium, can be used in place of mercury vapor. In addition, by using lighter colors on walls and keeping lighting equipment clean, loads can be reduced.

Interfuel Substitution. The major fossil fuel competing with electricity is natural gas. Where substitution does occur, it is likely to favor electricity. The cost of electricity is increasing at a rate much slower than that of the fossil fuels. Also, the supply of electricity, unlike that of natural gas or oil, is reliable.

The existence of substitution possibilities between natural gas and electricity is evidenced by an international comparison of industrial fuel-use patterns. In Mexico, the tendency is to rely on gas; in Norway, on electricity; and in the United States, on both.

In the food industry, electricity and gas compete as sources for providing clean direct heat. In the steel industry, different processes using alternative fuels are available. In primary steel production, the process chain involves coke ovens, blast furnaces, and basic oxygen furnaces (or open-hearth furnaces). In secondary steel production, scrap is converted to steel in an electric furnace. A move from primary to secondary production will involve the replacement of coke and natural gas by electricity.[7]

Cogeneration. Substantial amounts of oil, gas, and coal are used by industry to generate steam for process applications, while electricity is generally purchased from the utility. However, much of the steam is used in processes requiring only low-temperature heat. Significant fuel savings may be realized if the high-temperature steam is first used to generate electricity and the waste heat from such generation is then used for process steam. This configuration would constitute one example of industrial *cogeneration,* a term used to describe the simultaneous production of electricity and steam.

It should be noted that there are a variety of cogeneration schemes, each with different power-to-steam ratios (that is, the ratio of kilowatt-hours of electricity to millions of Btu's of process steam). Steam-turbine systems tend to have low power-to-steam ratios, while gas-turbine and diesel systems have high ratios. Because steam turbines can use coal, the economics favor their application.

It is extremely difficult to implement a cogeneration scheme using existing boilers. However, during the 1970s, because of uncertainty concerning fuel use and environmental legislation, industry tended to stretch out the life of boilers beyond the typical 30 years, and over the next few years, boiler replacements should rise. At the time of replacement, cogeneration is likely to be considered. It is estimated that cogeneration units of as little as 1 MW would be feasible.

Arthur D. Little, Inc., in conjunction with Westinghouse and Gibbs & Hill, performed a study for DOE relating to industrial cogeneration.[8] The study identified a significant potential for cogeneration, if institutional barriers were removed and appropriated incentives provided.

Recent legislation has created such incentives by requiring utilities to give extremely favorable treatment to cogenerators. Such legislation is particularly important because of the relationship between the utility and the cogenerator. The effect of such legislation is to make the utility sell electricity to the cogenerator at the standard industrial rate. However, the cogenerator is entitled to sell electricity to the utility at a rate that reflects the costs the utility can avoid by obtaining such electricity. Where the supply of electricity obtained from the cogenerator is of sufficient reliability, the avoided costs should include both variable and capacity-related expenses. Furthermore, the avoided costs should be of an incremental nature; that is, they should reflect theoretical displaced electricity generation and capacity.

The rules also provide that the cogenerator can buy all the electricity it needs from the utility and sell all the electricity that it produces to the utility. Because the price at which the cogenerator sells electricity will be higher than the price at which it buys it, this means that the cogenerator can obtain a net receipt from the utility for each kilowatt-hour it produces.

The rules imply a strong positive correlation between cogeneration and electricity price. A high price will encourage cogeneration and thus reduce the amount of electricity industry must buy from the utility. It should be noted, however, that the rules have not yet been fully clarified.

Trends. Table 3-16 presents data on industrial electricity sales, on manufacturing output (in constant 1979 dollars), and on the ratio of electricity sales to output. During the period 1960-1973, industrial electricity sales grew at an annual rate of 5.83 percent from 329 billion to 686 billion kWh. During the period 1973-1979, the growth rate slowed to 3.30 percent, and electricity sales grew from 686 billion to 834 billion kWh. The growth in electricity sales has outstripped that of output, so that the electric-output ratio has risen from 1.12 kWh/$ of real output in 1960 to 1.43 kWh/$ of real output in 1979.

Legislation. The government has instituted a number of programs designed to accelerate the trend toward industrial energy efficiency. Many of these programs

Table 3-16
Historical Patterns in Industrial Electricity Sales

	Electric-Output Ratio (kWh/1979$)	Manufacturing Output (Billions of 1979$)	Industrial Electricity Sales (Billions of kWh)
1960	1.12	294.7	328.6
1970	1.32	431.3	570.9
1973	1.32	518.0	686.1
1975	1.47	458.6	675.3
1979	1.43	582.6	833.7

Sources: Energy Information Administration, *Statistics and Trends of Energy Supply, Demand and Prices* (Washington: U.S. Government Printing Office, May 1978), p. 103; Energy Information Administration, *Monthly Energy Review* (Washington: U.S. Government Printing Office, May 1980), p. 63; Council of Economic Advisers, *Economic Report of the President* (Washington: U.S. Government Printing Office, January 1979), p. 184.

are embodied in the National Energy Act of 1978 (NEA). The relevant provisions of the NEA include (1) the requirement that all companies that consume at least 1 trillion Btu's per year in each of the ten most energy-consuming industries must report their energy usage to DOE each year and show that actions are being taken to conserve energy, (2) a directive to the Department of Energy (DOE) to evaluate if efficiency standards are required for pumps and motors, and (3) an additional 10 percent investment tax credit for investment in equipment designed to improve the heat efficiency of existing industrial processes or recycle waste materials.

Modeling Approaches

Background. It is possible to develop an end-use model of industrial electricity sales. Such a model would take into account (1) the distribution of motors according to horsepower, (2) the average hours of operation for each horsepower class, and (4) the percentage improvement in efficiency of new motors over existing motors for each horsepower class.[9] However, the application of such a model is difficult because of the limited amount of date on motor population and usage. Consequently, the discussion here will focus on econometric models.[10]

Theoretical Background. The aim of any firm within an industry is to maximize profits over the life of the firm. In order to maximize profits in the long run, a firm generally attempts to minimize its costs of production. This procedure entails determining the least expensive set of inputs over the long term that can produce the firm's product(s). The relative prices of the various inputs to the firm's production process determine the mix of inputs, subject to technological constraints on the substitution of inputs for one another.

This process of cost minimization is relatively simple in the short run where machinery is in place and the relative shares of the various inputs (capital, labor, materials, and energy) are fixed within very limited bounds. Over the long run, however, there is much more latitude for substitution among inputs.

The manager of the firm makes decisions concerning the quantity of each input used in the production process based on the expected relative price of the inputs. If, for instance, energy costs are expected to rise, but not as rapidly as the cost of new more energy-efficient machinery, more energy may be used per unit of output in the future. This means that firms seek to attain an economic optimum rather than a thermodynamic optimum. The thermodynamic optimum is the combination of inputs—labor, capital, materials, electricity, fossil fuels— that minimizes the energy content per unit of output. The economic optimum is the combination of inputs that minimizes the cost of producing a given level of output.[11]

Given two inputs, nonelectricity and electricity, the firm's economic objective function is written as follows:

$$TC = (PZ \cdot Z) + (PE \cdot E) \qquad (3.19)$$

where TC = total cost
PZ = price per unit of nonelectricity input
Z = nonelectricity inputs
PE = price per unit of electricity
E = electricity inputs

The issue arises as to the combination of Z and E that will minimize the total cost of producing a given level of output. To answer this, it is necessary to refer to the production function, an equation relating output to inputs. There are a number of production functions, one of the simplest of these, the Cobb-Douglas, is as follows:

$$Y = A \cdot Z^b \cdot E^c \qquad (3.20)$$

where Y = output
Z = nonelectricity inputs
E = electricity input

In the preceding function, the parameters A, b, and c define the relationship between production and the inputs. The equation is actually linear in logs and so the parameters b and c are elasticities. The parameter b shows the percentage increase in output resulting from a 1 percent increase in nonelectricity inputs, and the parameter c defines the percentage increase in output resulting from a 1 percent increase in the use of electricity. Because parameters b and c are constrained to sum to 1, it can be shown that a doubling of both inputs will double output.

The precise combination of inputs Z and E that will minimize the cost of producing a given level of output, subject to the production function, will depend on the prices of Z and E. Other things being equal, as the relative price of an input increases, less of it will be used. An equation relating the cost-minimizing quantity of an input to the relative input prices can be derived. This is the input demand equation, and the demand equation for the input electricity is of direct interest. In the case of the Cobb-Douglas, the demand equation for the input electricity is written as follows:

$$\frac{E}{Y} = k1 \cdot \frac{PZ^{k2}}{PE} \qquad (3.21)$$

where E = electricity input
    PZ = price per unit of nonelectricity inputs
    PE = price per unit of electricity
    Y = output

Equation 3.21 incorporates the production function (equation 3.20) and the cost constraint (equation 3.19). Moreover, it can be shown that the coefficients of the electricity demand equation are related to the coefficients of the earlier equations in the following way:

$$k1 = A(c \cdot PZ/b \cdot PE)$$
$$k2 = b$$

Equation 3.21 can be rewritten by taking logarithms to both sides. This gives

$$\ln \frac{E}{Y} = \ln k1 + k2 \ln \frac{PZ}{PE} \tag{3.22}$$

According to equation 3.22, the electricity use per unit of output depends on the ratio of other input prices to that of electricity. The coefficient $k2$ is positive, indicating that the higher the price ratio (the lower the relative electricity price), the greater the electricity use.

Empirical Form. To put equation 3.22 into an empirically estimatable form, a measure of output must be selected and the prices for the input with which the electricity competes must be developed. Value added is generally regarded as providing the most accurate measure of the level of industrial activity with a region. *Value added* is defined as the excess of the value of shipments over the cost of materials and energy and reflects the contribution made by the local area's economic resources (mainly labor and capital goods) to the value of goods produced in the area. Value added is a good measure of production because it avoids the inclusion of externally purchased materials, which represent production already taken place elsewhere. To exclude the effect of inflation, value-added data are converted to "real" (constant dollars) terms.

The inputs most competitive with electricity are labor and natural gas. Therefore, it is appropriate to include the prices of these two inputs into the econometric specification. The empirical industrial electricity sales equation is thus written as follows:

$$\ln ELVAD = a + b \ln GASELEC + c \ln WAGELEC \tag{3.23}$$

where $ELVAD$ = electricity use per dollar of real value added
$GASELEC$ = ratio of natural-gas price to electricity price
$WAGELEC$ = ratio of wage rates to electricity price

Forecast Adjustments. The econometric forecasts of industrial electricity demand should be adjusted to incorporate factors that were not built into the model. Among these factors is cogeneration. As industrial facilities generate more electricity inplant, this will reduce utility sales. Therefore, the econometric forecast must be reduced by an amount equal to the electricity that will be generated inplant.

Models to evaluate the feasibility of industrial cogeneration do exist. For example, the study performed by Arthur D. Little, Westinghouse, and Gibbs & Hill showed that a plant is most likely to cogenerate if (1) fossil prices are low, (2) electricity prices are high, (3) standby electrical power is available at a reasonable low rate, (4) surplus power can be sold at a high rate, and (5) a low hurdle rate is used to evaluate the investment. However, these models must be applied on a plant-specific basis, which makes their use impractical for a utility-forecast project. Hence, the factor defining future inplant generation must be decided on judgmentally rather than analytically.

A subjective increment to the econometric forecast also must be made to reflect the increased electrification concommitant with the uncertainties surrounding the supply of oil and natural gas. The shift to electricity is likely to be greater than would be expected as a result of relative price changes. Unlike oil and gas, the supply of electricity is reliable, so industry will tend to adopt electricity in new processes even if it involves a cost penalty.

Electric Peak-Demand Modeling Overview

Background

The 1 November 1979 issue of *Electrical World* reported the time of the 1979 system peaks for the different utilities; here are a few examples from that issue: (1) Consolidated Edison Co., of New York, August 2 at 3 P.M.; (2) Duke Power Co., Thursday, August 9 at 5 P.M.; (3) Indianapolis Power Co., Wednesday, August 8 at 4 P.M.; and (4) Pacific Gas and Electric Co., Tuesday, July 24 at 4 P.M.[12] The examples cited point to the fact that the peak tends to occur during business hours on a summer weekday. This is the result of abnormally high air-conditioning loads coinciding with normal commercial and industrial use. Figure 3-3 graphically depicts the daily load curve on a peak day. As the curve demonstrates, the greatest periodicity is evidenced by the residential and commercial sectors.

The peak-demand forecast is an important factor in justifying the need for additional capacity. Utilities have accepted the responsibility of always meeting

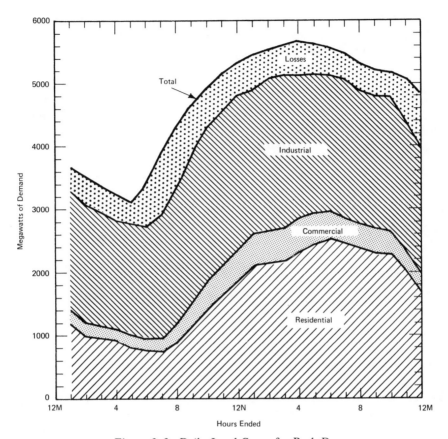

Figure 3-3. Daily Load Curve for Peak Day

the demands their customers place on them. This, together with the fact that electricity for the most part cannot be stored, means that utilities must have sufficient generation capacity to reliably meet the highest hourly demand expected to occur during the year. Electricity is a vital input to American life, and its sudden unavailability as manifested by "brownouts" or "blackouts," will create enormous socioeconomic dislocations.

Prior to 1973, peak-demand forecasting was a fairly routine activity in the United States. Demand increased each year with dependable regularity, and planners felt comfortable with extrapolating past trends. The oil embargo, the resulting energy-price rise, and the associated economic downturn disturbed the pattern in load growth. Noncoincident summer peak demand in the United States, which had grown at an annual rate of 8.0 percent over the period 1965-1973, grew at a rate of only 3.5 percent during 1973-1978, and the 1979 peak exceeded the 1978 peak by less than 1 percent.

The deviation of peak-demand growth rates from their preembargo trajectory interjected uncertainty into the load-forcasting area. Forecasters all over the country were now confronted with the task of designing peak-demand models that could incorporate the effect of rising real electricity prices, slowdowns in economic and demographic activity, the saturation of electric appliances, and the institution of governmental and utility policies to reduce electricity use and flatten the load-duration curve. Governmental policies include appliance-efficiency standards, building insulation standards, and conservation tax credits, while electric-utility policies include time-of-day pricing and load management.

The forces affecting peak demand are, if anything, more complex than those affecting electric energy. Nevertheless, while peak-demand models have undoubtedly become more sophisticated, they certainly do not contain the level of detail that is characteristic of electric-energy models. This phenomenon is attributable to the paucity of information on the composition of demand at the time of system peak. At peak, the loads created by specially metered industrial customers are known, but it is not possible to explicitly identify the loads of other customers, either individually or as a class.

Forecasting Methodologies

A basic taxonomy of peak-demand forecast methodologies (the term *methodology* is used to refer to a generic modeling approach) is according to their relationship to the energy forecasts.[13] In the *two-stage approach*, peak demand is forecasted as a function of the electric-energy projection. The energy projection (converted to an hourly basis) is multiplied by the reciprocal of the load factor to obtain a forecast of peak demand. For example, if the energy forecast is 20 million MWh and the load factor is 0.60 then the associated average hourly load is 2283 MW (20 million divided by 8760) and the peak demand forecast is 3813 MW (2283 multiplied by 1.67).

In the *one-stage approach*, peak demand is forecasted without direct reference to energy. A separate model of peak demand is developed in which peak demand (or its constituent elements) is expressed as a direct function of such variables as income, electricity price, temperature, insulation levels, and appliance efficiencies.

One-stage models can be further differentiated according to their level of detail. In the most primitive one-stage model, peak demand is forecasted in aggregate. The coefficients of the aggregative model are generally obtained by regressing annual system peak against temperature (on the day of peak), real electricity price, real income, industrial output, and other macroscopic economic or demographic variables. However, the forces affecting peak demand vary according to customer class, and as a consequence, the aggregative one-stage peak-demand model has been largely discarded as a forecasting tool.

The ideal one-stage approach is to forecast peak demand disaggregated by major class. Unfortunately, this idealized approach is very difficult to implement because data on the contribution to peak by customer class are not directly available except for specially metered industrial customers. Through the use of load research data and other specialized information, it is possible to approximate the nonindustrial contributions for selected historical years, but the data base so assembled is not of sufficient periodicity to permit time-series-based econometric (regression) analysis.

For the industrial class, the availability of reliable data does permit econometric modeling. It is possible to express the industrial contribution to peak as a function of electricity price and industrial output and to estimate the function by using regression analysis. Furthermore, it is possible to refine the industrial-demand analysis by grouping the customers according to SIC group and then apply regression analysis separately for each SIC group.

Two basic options are available to forecast the future contributions to peak of the residential, commercial, and other nonindustrial classes. In the end-use option, the historical contribution is forecasted as a function of appliance efficiency, building insulation, and other technical forces, using judgmental factors based on a review of engineering and legislative information. In the quasi-econometric option, the historical contribution is forecasted as a function of income and electricity price, using econometric elasticities derived in other studies.

Residential Peak-Demand Model

Factors Affecting Residential Load Shape

At the time of system peak, the residential load is considerably in excess of its load at other times. Electric utilities are therefore considering or testing policies designed to reduce the residential load at time of peak. These policies fall into two broad classes: time-of-day (TOD) pricing and load controls.

Time-of-Day-Pricing. Under a time-of-day rate structure, the price paid for electricity will depend on the time at which it is used. For example, electricity used during the peak season and during business hours will cost more than the same electricity consumed at other times. In principle, this should encourage consumers to postpone such deferrable loads as dishwashing to off peak periods.

The Public Utility Regulatory Policies Act (PURPA) of 1978 (Pub. L. 95-617) has required that the state commissions, who are responsible for the rates charged by the investor-owned utilities, investigate various innovative rate-structuring practices, including TOD. The commissions should require their adoption if it appears that such adoption would promote (1) the conservation of energy supplied by electric utilities, (2) the optimization of the efficiency of use of facilities and resources by electric utilities, and (3) equitable rates to electric consumers.

A number of utilities are already offering TOD rates on an experimental or limited basis. The degree of time differentiation varies by utility. In the simplest case, the rating periods are peak and off-peak, while in some instances a distinction is made between peak, shoulder, and off-peak. Moreover, in some instances, rates also are varied by season. However, the off-peak is almost invariably defined to include nighttime (10:00 P.M. to 6:00 A.M.).

Some of the utilities offering TOD rates have conducted experiments to quantify the degree of consumer response to TOC rates. For example, Northeast Utilities equipped two groups of customers with meters to record electricity use by time of day.[14] One group was subject to a TOD pricing regime and the other group remained under the conventional pricing structure. A statistical comparison of the group load shapes was then performed to calculate the time-of-day price elasticity. There also was a follow-up survey of the TOD customers to identify which appliance groups had been shifted to off-peak.

In general, the evidence indicates that consumers respond to TOD rates, but the degree of response is quite low. To a considerable extent, the degree of response depends on the structure of the TOD rate tariff and the composition of the load. In general, load shifting is most likely to occur if, in the tariff: (1) the peak period is defined narrowly and (2) the peak price is many times in excess of the off-peak price. A narrowly defined peak period (say 4 P.M. to 8 P.M.) facilitates load shifting, while a broadly defined peak period (say 8 A.M. to 10 P.M.) makes it difficult to shift loads. The higher is the peak price relative to the off-peak price, the greater is the economic incentive to postpone or sacrifice electricity use. The efficacy of TOD rates is greatest where the customer load is made up of applications that can be deferred. Laundry, dishwashing, and cooking are examples of applications where TOD pricing is likely to induce the consumer to rearrange schedules to shift usage from a peak period to an off-peak period. Air conditioning is an example of an application where the consumer cannot shift loads, only sacrifice them.

Load Controls. The application of load controls provides a more reliable mechanism for load management than TOD pricing, since load controls act by directly reducing loads rather than by inducing customers to do so.

Air conditioners and water heaters are among the more commonly controlled devices. Air-conditioner interruptions usually occur in a cycling mode. For example, air conditioners may be controlled 10 minutes per hour under normal summer conditions and 30 minutes per hour under extreme demand conditions. On controlled water heaters, generally the lower element is controlled, so that some heat is continuously provided to the upper element. Some utilities control heaters for periods of 16 hours per day thus allowing only one full charging of the water tank, while other utilities effect control for as few as 4 hours per day.

Load control of the appliance is achieved by the utility through two basic types of mechanisms: (1) remote-controlled devices that link a receiver device on the customer premises with the utility control center via a communication system and (2) point-of-use, or non-remote-controlled, devices that operate without any utility input once they have been installed. The efficacy of a wide range of remote and point-of-use load controls were evaluated by Arthur D. Little, Inc. in a study for the Electric Power Research Institute (EPRI).[15]

Remote-controlled devices are triggered by radio signals, high-frequency impulses over power lines, low-frequency ripple signals over power lines, and telephone pulses. Remote control provides flexible and precise load-management control in that the utility can shed loads exactly when required. In the case of water heaters, for example, cutoffs of about 7 minutes can be achieved by injecting ripples over power lines or by transmitting a disabling signal over the radio. Service is automatically restored and the brief interruption is not generally disruptive to the water-heating service.

Point-of-use controls do not provide as flexible a load-management tool as remote controls. An example of a point-of-use control is provided by thermostat-clock control of air conditioners. At a predetermined temperature, the thermostat activates a clock that cycles the compressor off and on. The air-conditioner fan is not affected by the control.

Load management, both remote and point-of-use, imposes some inconvenience on the customer, and so, utility customers who agree to load controls are granted preferential electric rates. In the case of water heaters, for example, the nature of the preferential rate depends on whether or not the device is separately metered. If it is, then a relatively low charge will be levied on the separately metered consumption. When there is no separate metering, then the discount is built into the regular residential declining block structure. The discount is applied to the middle of the final kilowatt-hour block, with the size of the discount block corresponding to an assumption about monthly water-heater kilowatt-hour usage.

Two-Stage Residential Model

In the first stage, the average hourly load is calculated for each residential end-use sales category by applying the following equation:

$$ALOADq = \frac{RSALESq}{8760} \tag{3.24}$$

where $ALOADq$ = average hourly load for residential end-use category q
$RSALESq$ = annual residential sales in end-use category q

In the preceding equation, the average hourly load is calculated by dividing annual sales by 8760, where 8760 is the number of hours in the year. In the second step, the contribution to system peak of each residential sales category is calculated by multiplying the average hourly load by a peak-load multiplier. This step is given by the following expression:

$$RPEAKq = ALOADq \cdot PMULTq \qquad (3.25)$$

where $RPEAKq$ = contribution to peak of residential end-use category q
$PMULTq$ = peak-load multiplier for residential end-use category q

The only new variables required to implement the two-stage residential peak-load model are the peak-load multipliers, of which one must be derived for each residential end use. The peak-load multiplier is the ratio of load at system peak to average hourly load, and its value will depend on the nature of the end use. In the context of peak-load multipliers, end uses can be classified into three groups, each of which are examined next.

The first class of residential end uses are those which have a peak-load multiplier of zero and which consequently can be ignored. In a summer-peaking system, space heating is an example of an application that make no contribution to the peak. The second class of end uses are those for which the peak-load multiplier is stable. Appliances that operate continuously, such as refrigerators and freezers, have stable multipliers. The third class of end use are those for which the peak-load multiplier is subject to seasonal and secular changes. The manner in which these multipliers are determined will be described using air conditioning as an example.

Assume there are 50,000 air conditioners, the annual air-conditioning load is 40,000 MWh, and average wattage of a unit is 800 W. The assumptions imply that the average air conditioner is run 1000 hours (note, $50,000 \times 0.008 \times 1000 = 40,000$) and the average hourly load is 4.57 MW ($40,000 \div 8760 = 4.57$).

The value of the peak-load multiplier will depend on the proportion of air conditioners assumed to be turned on at the time. If 50 percent of air conditioners are on, the multiplier is 4.38. This is so because the load created by 25,000, 800-W air conditioners is 20 MW, and 20 MW divided by 4.57 MW is 4.38. Similarly if 100 percent of the air conditioners are on, the multiplier is 8.76. Thus the peak-load multiplier is proportional to the number of units in operation at the time of peak.

The proportion of air conditioners that are likely to be on at time of system peak can be approximated from load research programs. It is likely that this proportion will be highly correlated to weather conditions. The system peak usually occurs on a day characterized by extreme temperature and humidity conditions. However, weather changes vary from year to year and it is therefore appropriate to assume for forecasting pruposes that future peak weather conditions will equal the historical mean.

The proportion of air conditioners that are likely to be on at time of system peak can be reduced by policy actions. The effect of load-management options is known, since the exercise of ratio controls on the air-conditioning units is at the discretion of the utility. The effect of time-of-day pricing is harder to gauge. Studies of the price elasticity of demand at peak show that this elasticity is lower than at other times.[16] This is particularly true for air conditioning.

One-Stage Residential Model

In the one-stage model, the residential contribution to peak is forecasted by multiplying the number of customers by the per-customer contributions to peak. The base year (for example, 1978) per-customer contributions are identified from a statistical analysis of load research data, while the future per-customer contributions are forecasted by modifying the 1978 contributions by factors that correspond to appliance-efficiency improvements, tighter building insulation, and load shifting to off-peak periods. These factors take a value of 1.0 in 1978 and in subsequent years are adjusted to take into account legislative and technological developments. For example, the appliance-efficiency factor incorporates the effect of the appliance-efficiency standards mandated by the National Energy Conservation Policy Act of 1978.

The summer peak-demand forecast for the residential sector is disaggregated by air-conditioning customers and non-air-conditioning customers. The air-conditioning customer is represented by a central equivalent, which is calculated assuming the three window units equal one central unit. This concept creates the need to develop a "no-air-conditioner" saturation or number of no-air-conditioning customers, which is not required in the energy model. The sum of air-conditioning and non-air-conditioning customers does not add to total customers, because of the use of the central-equivalent concept.

To estimate the base year (1978) non-weather-sensitive and weather-sensitive contribution to system peak of a typical central air-conditioning customer, the data on the peak-hour diversified demand of central air-conditioning customers for the peak month (for example, July) of the base year are regressed against daily degree days. The intercept of the equation identifies the per-customer non-weather-sensitive load, at time of peak. To obtain the weather-sensitive contribution, the slope is multiplied by a design degree-day value. The design value represents average peak-day weather conditions which are likely to be exceeded 50 percent of the time. An analogous analysis is carried out to identify the base-year per-customer contribution of a non-air-conditioning customer. The analysis will, of course, indicate a very small weather-sensitive component for this class of customer.

Future per-customer contributions are forecasted by multiplying the base-year contributions by various factors, each of which take a value of 1.0 in the base year and in subsequent years are adjusted to reflect load modifications.

Table 3-17 lists the equations in the model and Table 3-18 defines the

Table 3-17
Residential Summer Model

Equation Number	Dependent Variable		Explanatory Segment
3.26	$P1_t$	=	$K1_b \times Z1_t \times Z2_t$
3.27	$P2_t$	=	$K1_b \times Z2_t \times Z3_t \times Z4_t$
3.28	$P3_t$	=	$K2_b \times Z5_t$
3.29	$P4_t$	=	$K2_b \times Z5_t \times Z6_t$
3.30	$P5_t$	=	$K3_b$
3.31	$P6_t$	=	$K3_b$
3.32	$P7_t$	=	$K4_b \times Z7_t$
3.33	$P8_t$	=	$K4_b \times Z7_t \times Z8_t$

variables (factors) used in the equations. As the tables show, the type of factor used to modify the base-year contribution depends on the type of load. To illustrate the principles involved, the equations pertaining to the weather-sensitive load of air-conditioning customers will be discussed.

The weather-sensitive load of the existing air-conditioning customer (that is, one who was on the system in the base year 1978) is forecasted by multiplying the base-year contribution by a thermal-integrity factor and a load-shift factor.

The thermal-integrity factor $Z1$ is an index that measures the reduction in cooling (and heating) load that results from insulation retrofits. The index has a value of 1.0 in the base year. In subsequent years, its value is reduced to reflect insulation-related savings that result as existing customer retrofit their homes.

The load shift factor $Z2$ is used to model the load that is shifted off the peak because of TOD pricing or load controls. Its value is 1.0 in the base year, and in subsequent years its value can be adjusted to reflect the effect of TOD pricing or air-conditioning controls on load shape.

The weather-sensitive load of a new air-conditioning customer (that is, one who joined the system after 1978) is forecasted by multiplying the base-year contribution by a load-shift factor, a thermal-integrity factor, and an appliance-efficiency factor.

The load-shift factor is the same as that used for existing customers, but the thermal-integrity factor is not. In the case of existing customers, the integrity factor is used to reflect the impact of insulation retrofits, while in the case of new customers, it is used to quantify the effect of tighter insulation of new homes resulting from mandated standards or consumer choice.

The use of the appliance-efficiency factor reflects the fact that the air conditioners of new customers will be more efficient than the average air conditioner of 1978. The factor is set at a value that corresponds to the efficiency standards mandated by the National Energy Conservation Policy Act (Pub. L. 95-619).

Table 3–18
Definition of Variables in Residential Summer Model

Dependent Variables

$P1_t$ = weather-sensitive load of existing air-conditioning customers in year t
$P2_t$ = weather-sensitive load of new air-conditioning customers in year t
$P3_t$ = non-weather-sensitive load of existing air-conditioning customers in year t
$P4_t$ = non-weather-sensitive load of new air-conditioning customers in year t
$P5_t$ = weather-sensitive load of existing non-air-conditioning customers in year t
$P6_t$ = weather-sensitive load of new non-air-conditioning customers in year t
$P7_t$ = non-weather-sensitive load of existing non-air-conditioning customers in year t
$P8_t$ = non-weather-sensitive load of new non-air-conditioning customers in year t

Base-Year Contribution Variables

$K1_b$ = base-year weather-sensitive contribution per air-conditioning customer
$K2_b$ = base-year non-weather-sensitive contribution per air-conditioning customer
$K3_b$ = base-year weather-sensitive contribution per non-air-conditioning customer
$K4_b$ = base-year non-weather-sensitive contribution per non-air-conditioning customer

Modifying Factor Variables

$Z1_t$ = thermal-integrity factor for existing air-conditioning customers in year t
$Z2_t$ = load-shift factor for weather-sensitive loads of air-conditioning customers in year t
$Z3_t$ = thermal-integrity factor for new air-conditioning customers in year t
$Z4_t$ = appliance-efficiency factor for air conditioners in year t
$Z5_t$ = load-shift factor for non-weather-sensitive loads of air-conditioning customers in year t
$Z6_t$ = appliance-efficiency factor for non-weather-sensitive loads of air-conditioning customers in year t
$Z7_t$ = load-shift factor for non-weather-sensitive loads of non-air-conditioning customers in year t
$Z8_t$ = appliance-efficiency factor for non-weather-sensitive loads of non-air-conditioning customers in year t

Industrial Peak-Demand Model

Factors Affecting Industrial Load Shape

The industrial load curve is considerably flatter than the residential load curve, because diurnal and seasonal variations are generally not as significant in the determination of industrial electricity demand. Nevertheless, there are measures that can further improve the industrial load factor, and these are discussed next.

Industrial customers are subject to both a demand charge and an energy charge. The demand charge is based on the maximum kilowatts recorded during a period, while the energy charge is based on the amount of kilowatt-hours used during the period. The imposition of a demand charge gives the industrial custo-mer a direct monetary incentive to reduce demand. The effect of a demand charge on load shape is enhanced under a TOD strategy. In an industrial TOD scheme, both the demand charge and the energy charge would be differentiated by time of day. Demand recorded during peak periods would cost considerably more than if recorded during shoulder or off-peak periods.

To minimize demand charges, some industrial customers install controllers to limit demand. The demand-controller concept is one of limiting the demand charge by periodically "shedding" and restoring selected electric loads. Controllable loads are generally equipment that can be shut down intemittently without affecting the manufacturing operation of a given facility. For industrial customers, sheddable loads typically include those devices whose uses are not the basis of the manufacturing process and can be moved between several of the demand intervals. Good examples are the recharging of compressed-air reservoirs, the use of circulating or exhaust fans, and the use of electric furnaces.

Conventional demand controllers utilize hard-wired-logic timers to avoid large coincident loads and typically monitor and defer new-load startup until other loads are reduced. Such equipment is often preset manually. More sophisticated demand controllers include load shedders that also allow the interrupted loads to be restarted in a particular sequence after the demand window has passed.

The more recent demand controllers, based on solid-state devices and microprocessors, are capable of forecasting energy usage on the basis of recent demand. These types of energy-management devices may further be defined by their approach to limiting demand: instantaneous, ideal rate, or forecasting.

Instantaneous devices monitor the rate of electric usage and shed loads when a predetermined rate is reached. *Ideal-rate devices* measure the accumulated energy usage during the utility's demand interval and shed loads accordingly; these loads are restored during the following demand interval and the process is repeated. *Forecasting devices* are capable of predicting whether the present demand will be exceeded during the remainder of any single demand interval and, if so, of taking appropriate actions.

Customers also can minimize demand charges by rearranging schedules or employing equipment to use off-peak electricity. This issue was investigated for EPRI by Arthur D. Little, Inc., for ten major industries.[17] In many industries, the 24-hour-a-day operating schedule made load shifting through rearranged schedules impossible. The economic feasibility of equipment for using off-peak electricity also was found to be limited. One of the few examples was in the chlor-alkali chemical group, where the Hooker Chemical Company has developed a diaphragm-cell process for producing chlorine designed specifically to use off-peak electricity.

The interruptible tariff is another rate strategy that permits peak shaving. Under an interruptible tarriff, customers who agree to have a portion of their load interrupted receive a preferential rate. The availability of interruptible customers is of advantage to the utility, because it can curtail service to these customers if it appears that demand is going to exceed available capacity. The method of interruptible control varies. In some cases, the customer is requested by phone to reduce load; in other cases, the utility may shed the load directly.

Model Logic

As a preliminary to modeling the industrial contribution to peak, it is necessary to identify for each Standard Industrial Classification (SIC) group, the historical noncoincident and coincident demands. The *noncoincident demand* identifies the maximum hourly demand recorded, while the *coincident demand* indicates the demand at time of system peak. The ratio of the coincident demand to the noncoincident demand is termed a *coincidence factor*, and because of system diversity, the coincidence factor is less than 1.

Given such a historical data base, the industrial contribution to system peak can be forecasted by SIC group, using a two-step procedure. In the first step, noncoincident maximum demand for each group is forecasted as a function of such variables as industrial value added (a proxy for output) and demand charge. Noncoincident demand is related to the explanatory variables through elasticities derived from an econometric analysis of the data. The price elasticity, for example, indicates the percentage decrease in noncoincident demand resulting from a 1 percent increase in real-demand charge.

In the second step, the forecasted noncoincident demands are multiplied by coincidence factors to obtain a projection of the contribution to peak. The coincidence factors used in the forecasts are the historical ratios of contributions to peak to noncoincident demand, and they are specific to each of the industrial groups.

Other Contributions to Peak Demand

The contribution to system peak of the remaining sales categories—commercial, railroads, agriculture, public authorities, and streetlights—can be forecasted using simple econometric methods. Alternatively, a qualitative assumption can be made regarding future peak values.

The load imposed by line losses and company use can be calculated as a direct function of the other contributions to system peak. The formula to do this is

$$PLOSSi = PLOADi \cdot LFACTi \qquad (3.34)$$

where $PLOSSi$ = loss at system peak associated with sales category i

$PLOADi$ = load at system peak of sales category i
$LFACTi$ = loss factor for sales category i

The loss factors are equal to the ratio of loss to sales. Their values are obtained by engineering studies. Typical loss factors are 0.10 for residential, 0.085 for commercial, and 0.065 for industrial. Residential losses are highest because such customers are served at low voltage, and the continuous voltage stepdowns create losses. Finally, system peak is determined by summing the contributions of the indivudual classes and losses.

4

Coal-Demand Analysis

The demonstrated coal-reserve base of the United States is estimated to be large enough to support production at existing rates for about 350 years. These enormous reserves make coal a major option in reducing the nation's dependence on imported oil. However, the period after the 1973 oil embargo has witnessed an increase in coal utilization that was less than hoped for. Environmental constraints, an economic slowdown, and the natural-gas bubble were among the factors that coalesced to inhibit coal demand.

Despite recent disappointments, it is generally agreed that the long-term prospects for coal are excellent. Even the Harvard Business School Energy Project, which received wide publicity for its conclusion that conservation and renewable energy are the best route to energy independence, admitted that coal will experience steady growth.[1] The conclusions of the highly publicized MIT World Coal Study (WOCOL) are far stronger.[2] According to the WOCOL team, even with highly optimistic assumptions regarding the contribution of nuclear power, other energy sources, and conservation, it is clear that coal must play an increasingly vital role in supplying the world's energy needs.

Although there is a consensus that in the long run coal will become more important, an examination of recent forecasts reveals a wide range of uncertainty concerning just how much coal will be consumed over the next 20 years. The purpose of this chapter is to describe and critically evaluate recent major studies of coal demand through the year 2000.

Major Recent Published Studies of Coal Demand

A number of studies were issued in 1979 and 1980 that analyzed coal demand. Some background on these studies is provided next.

Much publicity has been given to the World Coal Study (WOCOL) conducted at MIT. The WOCOL reports issued in the summer of 1980 represent the culmination of an international project involving 18 months of research by a team of over eighty people from sixteen countries and coordinated by Carroll Wilson of MIT.

The WOCOL team that prepared the U.S. forecasts included participants from MIT, coal-producing companies (for example, Amax), companies engaged in coal conversion (for example, Bechtel), electric utilities (for example, Commonwealth Edison), the Department of Energy, and the Electric Power Research

Institute. In preparing its projections, the team used qualitative (that is, non-modeling) approaches and is in this respect different from other studies.

The WOCOL forecasts were issued for six scenarios or cases. Reference case A corresponds to an assumed low level of electricity generation (and thus coal demand), while reference case B corresponds to an assumed high level of electricity generation. Case A-1 adds to reference case A an assumption of limited oil imports, and case A-2 adds to case A-1 an assumed slowdown in the nuclear program. Both assumptions act to increase the share of coal in electricity generation and other activities. Cases B-1 and B-2 are related to reference case B in the same way that cases A-1 and A-2 are related to reference case A.

The Energy Information Administration (EIA) is a somewhat autonomous group within the Department of Energy created by the Department of Energy Organization Act of 1977 (Pub. L. 95-91). The EIA is charged with the responsibility of annually reporting to Congress forecasts of U.S. energy demand, supply, and price. To this purpose, EIA uses two large-scale models—the Mid-Range Energy Forecasting System (MEFS) and the Long-Run Energy Analysis Program (LEAP). Both models contain detailed representation of the U.S. energy network, the parameters of which are developed through econometrics or engineering judgment. The MEFS Model is actually a revised version of the Project Independence Evaluation System (PIES) developed by the Federal Energy Administration in 1974 to evaluate President Nixon's energy strategy.[3] The LEAP Model is based on the Stanford Research Institute–Gulf model and was developed for EIA by an outside contractor.[4]

MEFS and LEAP are separate models and are used by EIA in a complementary manner. MEFS is used to prepare the congressional forecasts for 1985, 1990, and 1995, while LEAP is used to generate the congressional forecasts for 2000, 2010, and 2020.[5] The forecasts are issued corresponding to three world oil-price scenarios: low, medium, and high. However, the projections of coal usage do not vary perceptibly by scenario.

The Brookhaven National Laboratory, part of the Department of Energy, maintains a model—the Time-Stepped Energy System Optimization Model (TESOM)—that is used periodically to quantify the impact of new energy-using or energy-producing technologies. Most recently, the model was exercised for the Gas Research Institute, and the results were published in the spring of 1980.[6] The forecast results were issued for a base case and a case involving an accelerated and successful research-and-development (R&D) program. The level of coal demand does vary between the cases, but not significantly.

In June of 1975, the National Research Council (NRC) started a study of the nation's energy future. The NRC appointed a Committee on Nuclear and Alternative Energy Systems (CONAES) to perform the study. A report was issued in 1979.[7] The study presents actual 1975 values and forecasts for 2010. It is not reviewed here because it does not contain predictions for the period 1980–2000.

In 1978, the Ford Foundation commissioned its third independent study of energy problems. The study was administered by the Resources for the Future, and its members included professors from Harvard University, the University of Chicago, MIT, Princeton, and executives from the World Bank, IBM, and Mitre. The report issued in 1979 contained policy recommendations, not independent forecasts; consequently, it is not reviewed here.[8]

The highly publicized Harvard Business School Energy Report was published in 1979. The report was prepared by individuals associated with the Business School and the Kennedy School of Government. The report indicates the probable directions for the U.S. energy sector, but does not contain any actual forecasts.

Finally, it should be noted that a number of consulting companies and corporations have been engaged in preparing forecasts of coal demand. For example, Arthur D. Little Inc. has prepared detailed coal-demand forecasts for a number of private-sector clients.

Broad Context for Coal Demand

At the most basic level, the U.S. demand for coal depends on total primary energy consumption and the share of coal in such consumption. Consequently, in evaluating the various forecasts presented here, the reasonability of these two basic parameters must be critically examined.

The growth in total primary energy consumption will depend on (1) the growth in real GNP and (2) the energy-GNP elasticity. The *energy-GNP elasticity* defines the percentage increase in primary energy consumption corresponding to a 1 percent increase in real GNP. If the elasticity is 1, then primary-energy consumption will increase at the same rate as GNP. However, because of conservation and the contribution of end-use renewables, the elasticity is likely to be significantly lower than 1.

In 1979, the U.S. primary-energy consumption equaled 78.7 quadrillion Btu's (quads).[9] Assuming an annual 2.5 percent real growth in GNP, the nation's output would increase 68 percent by 2000. This in conjunction with an energy-GNP elasticity of 0.4 would imply that the U.S. primary energy consumption would increase by 27 percent to reach 100 quads by 2000.

For the long run, coal can be regarded as a swing fuel, which will be resorted to if cleaner and more convenient forms of energy are not available. This means that the share of coal associated with a given level of primary energy consumption will depend on the assumed contributions of oil, gas, hydropower, nuclear power, and renewables. If these other energy forms are readily available, this will hinder the penetration of coal.

Table 4-1 presents 1979 U.S. primary energy demand along with various forecasts for 2000. To facilitate a comparison of the forecasts, they have been

Table 4-1
U.S. Primary Energy Demand in 1979 and Forecasts for 2000
(*in quadrillion btu.*)

	1979	EIA	Brookhaven	WOCOL (A)	WOCOL (B)
Oil domestic	20.4	20.5	23.0	18.1	18.1
Oil imported	16.7	13.1	7.5	17.9	19.7
Gas domestic	19.8	16.4	17.6	15.0	15.0
Gas imported	0.7	0.7	1.5	2.0	2.0
Nuclear	2.8	11.3	8.3	8.3	16.6
Hydro	3.2	3.3	5.3	3.8	3.8
Cent. renewables	0.1	2.1	1.1	0.3	0.3
Coal	15.0	38.2	37.6	29.8	47.3
Total	78.7	105.6	101.9	95.2	122.8

Sources: The 1979 data are from Energy Information Administration, *Monthly Energy Review* (Washington: U.S. Government Printing Office, August 1980), pp. 5–6; the EIA forecasts are for the middle oil-price case as published in Energy Information Administration, *Annual Report to Congress, Volume Three* (Washington: July 1980), pp. 165 (the data are adjusted to exclude decentralized renewable use); the Brookhaven forecasts are for the base case as published in *A Long-Range Assessment of R&D Policy for Gas-Related Conversion Technologies* (Upton, N.Y.: Brookhaven National Laboratory, April 1980), p. 31; and the WOCOL forecasts are from MIT, *Future Coal Prospects: Country and Regional Assessments,* Vol. 2 (Cambridge, Mass.: Ballinger, 1980), p. 51.

adjusted to a consistent basis. In particular, the following conventions have been adopted:

The Btu contributions of solar water heating, boiler use of wood, and other "end-use" renewables have been excluded.

Domestic oil is defined to include shale oil and alcohol from biomass, but not coal liquids.

Coal consumption includes the coal used in gasification and liquefaction.

In 1979, the United States consumed 78.7 quads of energy, of which oil contributed 37.1 quads, natural gas 20.5 quads, nuclear power 2.8 quads, hydropower 3.2 quads, and coal 15.0 quads. About 45 percent of the oil consumed was imported, but the other resources consumed were almost exclusively indigenously supplied.

As table 4-1 shows, primary energy consumption is forecasted to grow quite slowly, but the growth in coal use is expected to be much stronger because of an increase in the share of coal in meeting the nation's energy needs. The forecasts presented in table 4-1 imply growth rates of coal use during 1979-2000 that range between 3.3 and 5.6 percent per year. (It should be noted, of course, that these forecasts exclude coal exports).

The WOCOL forecasts have been prepared by qualitative (nonmodeling), and highly aggregated approaches. Consequently, many key assumptions are not exactly specified. However, those assumptions which have been specified are in some instances subject to criticism. Both case A (low coal demand) and case B (high coal demand) are predicated on an unusually high level of U.S. oil imports. For example, in case B, WOCOL assumes that in 2000 the United States will import 19.7 quads of oil (about 9.3 million barrels a day). This implies that in 2000 the United States will be importing more oil than it currently does, a view many analysts disagree with. Another key assumption in WOCOL that appears unrealistic concerns the level of electricity generation. Case B assumes that electricity generation will grow at the extremely high rate of 4.4 percent per year during 1977-1985 and 4.0 percent per year during 1985-2000.

The WOCOL team presents forecasts of coal demand for various cases, but it does not indicate which case it considers to be the most likely to be achieved. The WOCOL forecasts in toto bound the probable future for coal. In case B, coal consumption is forecasted to grow from 15.0 quads in 1979 (679 million short tons) to 29.8 quads in 2000, which implies a compound annual growth rate of 3.3 percent per year. In case B, coal consumption in 2000 is set at 47.3 quads, which implies an annual growth rate of 5.6 percent per year.

EIA has developed forecasts for three scenarios, with each scenario corresponding to an assumed international oil price. However, coal consumption in the EIA model is largely insensitive to oil price. In the middle-oil-price scenario, coal consumption in 2000 is 38.2 quads, and in the high-oil-price scenario, coal consumption is 37.9 quads. This insensitivity to world oil price is somewhat surprising. A high oil price should encourage coal consumption.

The EIA forecasts are, in general, reasonable. According to EIA's middle-oil-price scenario, primary energy consumption will grow at a rate of 1.4 percent per year, from 78.7 quads in 1979 to 105.6 quads in 2000. EIA assumes a 2.8 percent annual growth rate in GNP, and so implicit in the primary-energy-consumption forecasts are a substantial improvement in energy efficiency, vigorous conservation, and accelerated use of renewable energy forms. However, the EIA forecast is, nevertheless, still perhaps on the high side. This may be due to the optimistic assumption that the United States will be able to import as much as 13.1 quads of oil.

The share of coal in primary energy consumption is forecasted to increase in the high-oil-price scenario from 19.1 percent in 1979 to 36.2 percent in 2000. Consequently, the forecasted growth rate in coal consumption is significantly higher than that of overall primary energy use. Coal consumption is forecasted to grow at an annual rate of 4.5 percent per year from 15.0 quads in 1979 to 38.2 quads in 2000.

The Brookhaven forecasts are similar to those of the EIA. According to the Brookhaven study, primary energy consumption in 2000 will be 101.9 quads, of which 37.6 quads will be coal. The individual elements of the Brookhaven forecast do, however, differ from those of EIA. For example, Brookhaven projects an unrealistically high level of hydropower usage (5.3 quads) in 2000.

Electric-Utility Sector

Background

In 1979, electric utilities accounted for 11.3 quads of the 15 quads of coal consumed in the United States. In contrast, in 1951, only 2.5 quads of the 13.2 quads of coal consumed in the United States was by electric utilities. Table 4-2 presents historical data on electric-utility and total coal consumption.

Coal is used by electric utilities to generate electricity. Alternatively, electricity can be generated from oil, natural gas, nuclear power, hydropower, and other resources. The amount of coal required to produce a unit of electricity is defined by a heat rate that expresses the Btu's of coal required to generate one kilowatt-hour of electricity.

The demand for coal by electric utilities is calculated as the product of three terms: (1) the amount of electricity generated, (2) the share of coal in such generation, and (3) the heat rate. For example, in 1979, 2247 billion kWh of electricity were generated, with coal-fired plants accounting for 47.8 percent or 1075 billion kWh. The heat rate for coal-fired plants in that year averaged 10,473 Btu/kWh, so that the generation of 1075 billion kWh necessitated the burning of 11.3 quads of coal. The future demand for coal will depend on the trajectory of these three parameters. In this section, the historical behavior of these parameters and forecasts of their future values will be discussed.

Table 4-2
Historical Patterns in Electric-Utility and Total Coal Consumption

	Electric-Utility Consumption (Million Short Tons)	Total U.S. Consumption (Million Short Tons)	Electric-Utility Consumption (Quadrillion Btu)	Total U.S. Consumption (Quadrillion Btu)
1951	105.8	506.6	2.5	13.2
1960	176.6	398.0	4.3	10.1
1965	244.8	472.1	5.9	11.9
1970	320.8	523.8	7.4	12.7
1973	389.2	562.6	8.7	13.3
1979	527.1	679.2	11.3	15.0

Sources: The statistics cover bituminous, lignite, and anthracite coal. The tonnage data for 1951 through 1970 are from Energy Information Administration, *Statistics and Trends of Energy Supply, Demand and Prices* (Washington: U.S. Government Printing Office, May 1978), pp. 79, 85, and 100; for 1973 and 1979, the source is Energy Information Administration, *Monthly Energy Review* (Washington: U.S. Government Printing Office, June 1980), p. 54.

Patterns in Electricity Generation

During the period 1960-1973, the amount of electricity generated by utilities increased at a compound annual rate of 7.2 percent because of declining electricity prices and rising incomes, which encouraged residential customers to acquire more electric appliances and industrial customers to substitute electricity for labor. During the period 1973-1979, the growth of electricity generated grew at a rate of 3.2 percent, or less than half the preembargo record, a slowdown that was attributable to rising energy prices, the associated economic downturn, and the already high saturation of electric appliances.

In the future, the factors that circumscribed electricity growth during 1973-1979 will be reinforced by a number of legislative initiatives. The National Energy Conservation Policy Act of 1978 (Pub. L. 95-619) required the promulgation of appliance-efficiency standards, the establishment of utility-conservation programs, and the provision of grants and low-cost loans for weatherization. The Energy Tax Act of 1978 (Pub. L. 95-618) provided for residential and business tax credits for designated investments in conservation or alternative energy sources. The Public Utility Regulatory Policies Act of 1978 (Pub. L. 95-617) contained provisions to measurably enhance the feasibility of industrial cogeneration, whereby a facility can simultaneously fulfill its internal requirements for process steam and electricity.

The factors depressing electric-sales growth will be partially offset by the growing competitiveness of electric energy with fossil fuels, which results from the relative stability of electricity prices and the reliability of electricity supply. However, the potential for substituting electricity for other fuels is limited in the industrial sector, while in the residential and commercial sectors, the continued availability of natural gas will inhibit the penetration of electricity.

Electricity demand also may be accelerated by governmental policies. Electrification is considered by some to be a good policy, since it indirectly promotes the use of coal, the preeminent fuel in electricity generation. (The term *electrification* is used here to denote any policy designed to increase the share of electricity in a given end-use application.) An example of an electrification policy is provided by the Department of Energy (DOE) Electric and Hybrid Vehicle Program designed to foster commercialization of electric cars. An electric car consumes about 0.4 kWh/mi, which amounts to 30 mi/gal at 1 kWh = 10,500 (note that 1 gal = 125,000 Btu). Thus the electric car does not reduce the amount of fossil fuel required, it merely substitutes electricity for oil.

However, the proposed DOE policy regarding building energy conservation circumvents the electrification principle. According to DOE's Building Energy Performance Standards (BEPS), which are currently in limbo, the design energy consumption of all new residential/commercial buildings must not exceed a DOE-specified design energy budget. In calculating the design energy consumption of commercial buildings, natural gas has a weight of 1.00, oil has a weight of 1.20, and electricity has a weight of 3.08. This means that a Btu of electricity is treated as the equivalent of about 3 Btu's of oil/gas, which makes it difficult for electrically heated buildings to satisfy BEPS and thus discourages the use of electricity in this application.

Table 4-3 presents forecasts of electricity generation as prepared by the EIA, Brookhaven, MIT, Electrical World, National Electric Reliability Council, National Coal Association, and the Economic Regulatory Administration.[10] The forecasts of electricity generation for 2000 range between 3736 billion and 5400 billion kWh. In 1979, electricity generated equaled 2247 billion kWh, so a forecast of 3736 billion kWh implies an annual growth rate of 2.45 percent per year, and a forecast of 5400 billion kWh implies an annual growth rate of 4.26 percent per year. A detailed end-use analysis of electricity consumption conducted by Arthur D. Little, Inc. indicates that the low forecast of 3736 billion kWh is, in fact, very reasonable. The Arthur D. Little analysis took into account demographic, housing, and economic trends, legislated improvements in appliance efficiency, penetration of electric space heat, electric-car use, industrial cogeneration, and other specific determinants of electric use.

Trends in the Share of Coal in Electricity Generation

Historical Patterns. The share of coal in electricity generation declined from 54.1 percent in 1965 to 45.6 percent in 1973. The decline resulted from (1) toughening air-pollution requirements in the late 1960s that caused a decline in the orders for new coal plants and the conversion of some existing coal units to oil; (2) the relaxation of import quotas on residual oil, which made this cheap energy form available to East Coast utilities, and (3) the accelerated pace of nuclear development that occurred after the favorable pricing policies instituted by General Electric in 1964. Table 4-4 presents historical data on the shares of electricity generation accounted for by various resources.

After 1973, the rising cost and reduced availability of oil and gas acted to reduce the joint share of oil/gas from 35.2 percent in 1973 to 28.2 percent in 1979. This process was expedited by the Energy Supply and Environmental Coordination Act of 1974, which set up a program to convert oil/gas-burning plants to coal. Nevertheless, the increase in the share of coal in electricity generation between 1973 and 1979 was quite marginal, from 45.6 to 47.8 percent, because during this period the share of nuclear power increased sharply from 4.5 to 11.4 percent.

The future share of coal in electricity generation will depend on the rate at which the use of oil and gas is phased out in base-load facilities, the nuclear build schedule, and the contribution of renewable resources.

Oil and Gas. The phasing out of oil and gas is the objective of the Powerplant and Industrial Fuel Use Act of 1978 (Pub. L. 95-620), which modifies and

Table 4-3

Comparison of Recent Forecasts of Electricity Generation

(*in billions of kWh*)

	1990	*2000*
Energy Information Administration (middle case)	3224	3869
Brookhaven National Laboratory	–	4107
MIT World Coal Study (low coal demand, case A)	3065	3736
MIT World Coal Study (high coal demand, case B)	3647	5400
Electrical World	3318	4542
National Electric Reliability Council	3492	–
National Coal Association (middle case)	3380	–
Economic Regulatory Administration	3509	–

Sources: Energy Information Administration, *Annual Report to Congress,* Vol. 3 (Washington, July 1980), pp. 108-109; the Brookhaven forecasts are from A.S. Kydes and J. Rabinowitz, *A Long-Range Assessment of R&D Policy for Gas-Related Conversion Technologies* (Upton, N.Y.: Brookhaven National Laboratory, April 1980); the MIT forecasts are from World Coal Study, *Future Coal Prospects: Country and Regional Assessments.* Vol. 2 (Cambridge, Mass.: Ballinger, 1980), p. 448; *Electrical World* (September 15, 1980); 66; the National Electric Reliability Council, *1980 Summary of Projected Peak Load, Generating Capability and Fossil Fuel Requirements* (Princeton, N.J., July 1980), p. 38 (the forecasts do not go beyond 1989, and the 1990 value reported in the table was derived by interpolation); National Coal Association, *NCA Economics Committee Long Term Forecast* (1980), Table 2; Economic Regulatory Administration, *Electric Power Supply and Demand for the Continuous United States* (Washington, 1980), p. 1-7) (the forecasts do not extend beyond 1989, and the 1990 values were derived by interpolation).

Table 4-4

Historical Shares of Electricity Generation, by Primary Resource

(*percentage share of total*)

	Coal	*Oil*	*Gas*	*Nuclear*	*Hydropower*	*Other*	*Total*
1960	53.5	6.1	21.0	0.1	19.3		100.0
1965	54.1	6.2	21.0	0.3	18.4		100.0
1970	46.1	11.9	24.3	1.4	16.2	0.1	100.0
1973	45.6	16.9	18.3	4.5	14.6	0.1	100.0
1979	47.8	13.5	14.7	11.4	12.4	0.2	100.0

Sources: The data for 1960 through 1970 are calculated from Edison Electric Institute, *Statistical Yearbook of the Electric Utility Industry* (New York, N.Y.: November 1979), pp. 18-22; the data for 1973 and 1979 are calculated from Energy Information Administration, *Monthly Energy Review* (Washington: U.S. Government Printing Office, June 1980), p. 58.

expands the coal-conversion program of the Energy Supply and Environmental Coordination Act. The new act also prohibits the use of oil and gas in new base-load facilities, but does permit exemptions for environmental and other reasons.

The Carter administration sent to Congress in 1979 a bill proposing $10 billion in direct payments to utilities to encourage conversion from oil and gas to coal or another alternative fuel. There are two major components to the proposed bill. First, up to $3 billion would be granted to the 107 plants at 50 stations that would be required by DOE to convert to coal by 1985. Second, $6 billion would be disbursed to utilities using more than 250,000 barrels a year of oil (or the equivalent amount of gas) to promote the voluntary reduction of oil and gas usage.

In certain regions, environmental factors may preclude the use of coal-fired power stations. Especially noteworthy in this context are the Clean Air Act of 1970 (Pub. L. 91-604) and the 1977 Amendments to the Clear Air Act (Pub. L. 95-95), which have set up air-quality goals that often conflict with the objectives of the Powerplant and Industrial Fuel Use Act. Under the Clean Air Acts, the nation is divided into air-quality control regions, each of which must meet nationally promulgated ambient air-quality specifications for various criteria pollutants, including sulfur dioxide and particulates (both of which are associated with coal use). Regions that violate the standards are declared to be nonattainment regions, and siting in such regions is especially onerous. Siting requirements are also restrictive in attainment regions, which have been designated as class I, a designation that includes, for example, wilderness areas. Thus coal-fired generation may be restricted in nonattainment and class I regions.

Nuclear Power. The role of coal will be enhanced by the problems besetting the nuclear industry. Since 28 March 1979, when the accident occurred at Three Mile Island, ten nuclear plants at various stages of development have been cancelled and numerous schedule delays have been announced. The cancellations include the Greene County Project in New York, in which $147 million had been sunk.

Table 4-5
Current Status of Nuclear Power and Capacity Plans, as of 31 March 1980

	Number of Reactors	Capacity (MW)
Operating	71	52,200
Permit granted: construction more than 10% complete	61	66,900
Permit granted: construction less than 10% complete	17	19,300
Permit granted: construction not started	10	10,500
Under construction permit	14	16,300
Ordered	3	3,500
Announced	0	0
	176	168,700

Source: Energy Information Administration, *Annual Report to Congress,* Vol. 3 (Washington, 1979), p. 111, based on a U.S. Nuclear Regulatory Commission, *Program Summary Report.*

Table 4-6
Forecasts of Nuclear Capacity
(*in gigawatts*)

	1990	*2000*
Brookhaven National Laboratory	–	177
Energy Information Administration (middle case)	128	180
Energy Information Administration (nuclear phaseout)	117	118
National Electric Reliability Council (for 1989)	140	–
Economic Regulatory Administration (for 1989)	143	–
Electrical World	146	–
National Coal Association	152	–
MIT World Coal Study (case A)	140	150
MIT World Coal Study (case B)	160	300

Nevertheless, a number of utilities are proceeding with their nuclear plans, and by 1990, the available nuclear capacity should be substantially higher than the current level. Table 4-5 presents the current and planned status of nuclear power as prepared by the Nuclear Regulatory Commission (NRC). Table 4-6 presents forecasts of nuclear capacity as prepared by various sources. The reactors in operation as of March 1980 represent 52.2 GW (gigawatts); the reactors under construction represent 86.2GW; and the permitted reactors represent 10.5 GW. It takes about 7 years to construct a reactor (after all permits are received), which means that nuclear capacity could increase from 52.2 GW as of 31 March 1980 to 148.9 GW by 1990. However, because of continued deferrals and cancellations, the actual capacity is likely to be lower, say, 125 GW. The 125-GW forecast assumes that all committed reactors (that is, construction more than 10 percent complete) will come on line, but only about one-third of the other reactors currently under construction will be completed by 1990. In summary, a reasonable assumption would put 1990 nuclear capacity at 125 GW and 2000 capacity at 160 GW. These assumptions correspond to an extremely modest ordering rate for new units. This is expected because of the Three Mile Island incident, the severe criteria for reactor siting, the lack of resolution on nuclear-waste disposal, social opposition, and other matters.

However, if the social and political negativism concerning nuclear power subsides, the pace of nuclear development could be much higher. A number of studies have been conducted to compare the economics of nuclear and coal-fired generation. Nuclear units have higher capital costs than coal-fired units, but because of their low fuel cost, the annualized costs (capital plus operating) of nuclear units may have a small cost advantage over coal units, especially in regions located at considerable distance from coal supplies. This is the conclusion of a study by the Electric Power Research Institute (EPRI), the utility industry's research arm.[11] In addition, reliance on nuclear power provides insurance against disruptions in coal supply.

It should be noted, however, that nuclear power is not always cheaper than coal. This is illustrated by a recent cost-of-service forecast prepared by Pacific Power and Light (PPL), a West Coast utility that provides service in six states.[12] PPL has adopted coal and nuclear power as its strategies for expanding its generating capability. PPL's new coal-fired units are expected to have unusually low fuel costs because coal will be supplied to PPL's plants by its own mining subsidiary (NERCO) and these units are mine-mouth located, thereby saving on transport costs, a major component of coal-utilization costs. The PPL analyses indicate that the cost of power from their planned coal units should be slightly lower than that from their nuclear units.

To translate nuclear capacity into electricity generation, an assumption must be made about the capacity factor. A kilowatt of capacity can produce 8760 kWh of electricity if the reactor is operated every single hour of the year. However, a reactor is shut down about 1 month per year for refueling; in addition, there may be outages because of equipment failures. The 1979 nuclear capacity factor nationwide was 0.58, which implies that 1 kW of capacity generates 5080 kWh (0.58×8760). It is likely that capacity factors will rise over time since as nuclear units mature, their capacity factors improve. A factor of 0.66 for 2000 is reasonable. This factor, in conjunction with a capacity of 160 GW, would imply 925 billion kWh of nuclear-generated electricity.

Hydropower and Renewables. Hydropower is currently the dominant renewable resource used in the generation of electricity. The rate at which hydroelectric production increases is expected to be slow for a number of reasons. There are a limited number of new hydropower sites available for base-load generation, and so this area is physically constrained. With respect to intermediate and peaking generation, unexploited hydropower resources are available; however, utilities will be reluctant to invest in new intermediate or peaking capacity because oil/gas units that have been phased out of base-load service are available for such a role at zero capital cost.

Various other renewable resources that are currently of marginal significance are expected to increase in importance over the next two decades, but their aggregate contribution will remain small. The list of new renewable options includes geothermal, solar thermal, wind, ocean thermal, and solar photovoltaic power. Geothermal power, wherein the thermal energy available in the earth's core is used to generate electricity, is the most immediately promising of the new technologies.

Coal Generating Capacity. Table 4-7 presents the current status of coal-fired capacity, along with capacity expansion plans. In December of 1979, there was 235 GW of coal-fired capacity, another 138 GW of capacity was expected to come on line by 1989, and 20 GW of conversion from oil/gas to coal was expected. However, the expected values, as presented in table 4-7, are not likely to be achieved. Because of lower than anticipated load growth, slippage in construc-

Table 4-7
Current Status of Coal-Fired Capacity along with Expansion Plans, as of
December 1979

	Capacity (MW)
Operating	234,599
Expected to come on-line by Dec. 1987	115,490
Expected to come on-line Dec. 1987–Dec. 1989	22,422
Mandated conversions from oil to coal 1979–1989	19,509
Mandated conversions from gas to coal 1979–1989	1,335
Total	393,355

Sources: The operating capacity is from Energy Information Administration, *Inventory of Power Plants in the United States, December 1979* (Washington, 1980), p. 525; the expansion plans are from National Coal Association, *1979 Survey of Electric Utility Capacity Additions* (1980), pp. 6, 12, 43–46; the mandated conversions are from Energy Information Administration, *Annual Report to Congress,* Vol. 3 (Washington, July 1980), pp. 108–109; the total figure does not make allowance for retirements or deratings.

tion schedules will undoubtedly occur, and 1990 coal capacity is likely to stand at about 360 GW.

Summary. Tables 4-8 and 4-9 present forecasted shares of electricity generation as prepared by various sources. The EIA (middle case) presents a reasonable scenario. According to the EIA, the share of coal in electricity generation will increase from 47.8 percent in 1979 to 56.9 percent in 2000; the nuclear share will increase from 11.4 percent in 1979 to 26.5 percent in 2000; the hydropower share will decrease from 12.4 percent in 1979 to 8.3 percent in 2000; the share of oil will decrease from 13.5 to 0.8 percent; and the share of gas will decrease from 14.7 to 2.3 percent.

The actual amount of coal-fired electricity generation is calculated as the

Table 4-8
Forecasted Shares of Electricity Generation, by Primary Energy Resource, in
1990
(*percentage of total*)

	Coal	Oil	Gas	Nuclear	Hydro-power	Other	Total
Energy Information Administration (middle case)	53.5	3.8	8.5	23.6	10.6	–	100.0
National Electric Reliability Council	49.0	12.6	3.3	27.2	7.4	0.5	100.0
MIT World Coal Study (case A)	45.6	15.4	5.1	23.9	9.7	0.3	100.0
MIT World Coal Study (case B)	52.5	12.6	4.2	22.4	8.0	0.3	100.0

Table 4-9

Forecasted Shares of Electricity Generation, by Primary Energy Resource, in 2000

(*percentage of total*)

	Coal	Oil	Gas	Nuclear	Hydro-power	Other	Total
Energy Information Administration (middle case)	56.9	0.8	2.3	26.5	8.3	5.2	100.0
Brookhaven National Laboratory	54.5	4.2	4.3	20.6	13.7	2.7	100.0
MIT World Coal Study (case A)	56.2	10.7	1.5	21.1	9.7	0.8	100.0
MIT World Coal Study (case B)	56.9	5.5	1.1	29.2	6.7	0.6	100.0

Source: The sources were cited in table 4-3.

product of electricity generated and the share of coal in such generation. According to EIA, 3809 billion kWh of electricity will be generated in 2000, of which 56.9 percent, or 2200 billion kWh, will be coal-fired.

In 1979, 1075 billion kWh of electricity was generated by coal-fired plants. Capacity in that year was 229 GW and the capacity factor was 0.54. If it is assumed that the capacity factor in 2000 is 0.57, a generation of 2200 billion kWh would require a capacity of 440 GW, a level-of-capacity increase that is very achievable, since it implies an addition of 80 GW over the 1990s.

Patterns in Coal-Fired Heat Rates

The coal-fired heat rate defines the Btu's of coal required to product 1 kWh of electricity. A kilowatt-hour of electricity contains 3412 Btu's, which means that a heat rate of 10,412 would imply that 7000 Btu's of energy are lost in the process of generation. Corresponding to the heat rate is the thermal efficiency; for example, a heat rate of 10,412 would imply a thermal efficiency of 32.8 percent (3412 ÷ 10,412). Electric utilities seek to improve the thermal efficiency of their generation, that is, lower the heat rate.

To forecast electric-utility coal demand, coal-fired electricity generation is multiplied by an average heat rate. At any given point in time there exists a wide variation in heat rates for coal-fired plants. For example, in 1978, the average heat rate for coal plants was 10,386 Btu/kWh while the Bull Run Plant (TVA), the most efficient plant in the country that year, recorded 8810 Btu/kWh.

Heat rates also vary over time. The average heat rate for coal-fired plants fell steadily until about 1965 and then leveled off at about 10,400 Btu/kWh. Similarly, the heat rate for the best individual unit in the country leveled off at about 8700 Btu/kWh. The decrease in heart rates resulted from increased steam pressure and steam temperature and other design improvements.

In the early 1970s, the requirement for scrubbers and other environmental controls acted to raise heat rates. Also, there occurred a decline in coal quality and consistency that impaired both heat rates and reliability.

In the future, an upward pressure on heat rates will be exerted by the environmental controls mandated for new plants by the Environmental Protection Agency (EPA). The EPA has published Revised New Source Performance Standards (RNSPS) that specify the allowable emissions levels from new coal-fired plants. The standards require that emissions from new plants per million Btu's (MMBtu) of coal burnt be substantially less than from existing plants. The EPA standards also contain a requirement for a percentage reduction in SO_2, which will mean that all new coal plants will have to install flue gas-desulfurization (scrubber) systems. These systems involve a substantial capital-cost outlay; in addition, their operation consumes electric energy, which increases the heat rate (in calculating the heat rate the electricity consumed by the generating facility itself is excluded). The standards also stipulate better nitrogen dioxides and particulate control, which also increases capital outlays and heat rates.

The upward pressure on heat rates may be reinforced by the regional shift in coal production. It is expected that coal output from Texas, North Dakota, and other western states will grow at a relatively rapid rate. However, heat rates for plants using Appalachian coal and Illinois Basin coal are lower than heat rates for plants using coal from Texas, North Dakota, and the western states. For example, the average 1990 heat rate for coal-fired plants using Appalachian coal is likely to be 10,300 Btu/kWh versus 10,800 Btu/kWh for plants using North Dakotan coal.

The development of new technologies to burn coal more efficiently (and also more cleanly) will exert a downward pressure on heat rates. Atmospheric fluidized-bed (AFB) boilers are expected to be commercially available during the 1990s. In an AFB boiler, ground coal is mixed with limestone and combusted with air at atmospheric pressure. Sulfur oxides react with the limestone to produce a dry material that is removed from the bed. The heat rate of an AFB system is expected to be about 9200 Btu/kWh.

Magnetohydrodynamics (MHD) is a process for the direct generation of electricity from coal. The MHD generator produces electricity by the interaction of a high-velocity electrically conducting gas with an intense magnetic field. The gas is produced by burning coal and adding potassium salt. The heat content left after passing through the MHD generator is used to fire a conventional steam power plant. The heat rate for such a system would be about 7500 Btu/kWh. MHD generators may become available by 2000–2010.

In addition to AFB and MHD, such technologies as combined-cycle coal units, fuel cells with coal gasifiers, and pressurized fluidized-bed combustion are expected to be commercially available by the end of the century.

The heat rate has been given scant attention in most studies of coal demand.

The MIT WOCOL study, for one, does not mention it. The EIA forecasts do address the heat rate. According to EIA, the heat rate for coal-fired plants will decrease from 10,508 Btu/kWh in 1979, to 10,358 Btu/kWh in 1990, and to 9736 Btu/kWh in 2000. The EIA forecasted heat rate for 2000 assumes a very rapid penetration of new, efficient coal-burning technologies. An informal analysis by Arthur D. Little, Inc. that took into account the changing regional mix of coals and the pollution-control requirements indicated that the heat rate should stabilize at 10,500 Btu/kWh through the end of the century.

The demand for coal is directly proportional to the heat rate. Other things being equal, a heat rate of 10,500 Btu/kWh would imply 7.8 percent more coal use than a heat rate of 9736 Btu/kWh. Thus the low heat rate used by EIA tends to bias their coal projections downward.

Electric-Utility Coal-Use Forecasts

Table 4-10 presents the forecasts of electric-utility coal use as issued by EIA, Brookhaven, and MIT. These forecasts, of course, reflect the assumptions on electricity generation, the share of coal in such generation, and the heat rate.

The EIA forecasts of coal usage (middle-oil-price scenario) by electric utilities indicates that consumption will increase from 11.3 quads in 1979 to 21.2 quads in 2000, which implies a compound annual growth rate of 3.0 percent. Brookhaven forecasts that electric-utility coal usage under the base case will equal 22.5 quads, implying an annual growth rate of 3.3 percent. The WOCOL forecasts indicate that electric-utility coal consumption in 2000 may range between 22.2 (reference case A) and 42.9 quads (reference case B-2). The higher estimate would imply an annual growth rate of 6.6 percent.

A reasonable estimate for 2000 would put electric-utility coal consumption between 22 and 24 quads. A much higher consumption level could result only if there was a severe constraint on nuclear development. For example, if nuclear capacity in 2000 is 125 GW rather than 160 GW, and if strict requirements lower the capacity factor from 0.65 to 0.60, nuclear-power outout would be reduced

Table 4-10
Forecasted Electric-Utility Coal Consumption
(*in quadrillion btu*)

	1990	2000
Energy Information Administration (middle case)	18.5	21.4
Energy Information Administration (nuclear phaseout)	–	23.6
Brookhaven National Laboratory	–	22.5
MIT World Coal Study (case A)	14.8	22.2
MIT World Coal Study (case B)	20.8	32.5
MIT World Coal Study (case B-2)	–	42.9

by 400 billion kWh. If this entire amount was made up by coal-fired generation, utility coal consumption would increase by 4.2 quads. Severe reductions in natural-gas supply also could increase coal use. Reduction in gas supply would encourage the application of electricity in various end uses, and this higher electricity use would raise coal requirements. A probable upper limit for electric-utility coal consumption would be about 30 quads.

However, an accelerated pace of nuclear development, such as envisioned before the Three Mile Island incident, could dampen coal demand. The dampening effect would be particularly severe if it coincided with improved natural-gas supply. A low estimate would placd utility coal consumption in the year 2000 at 18 quads.

A forecast of 18 quads in the year 2000 would imply a growth rate of 2.2 percent per year, a forecast of 23 quads would imply a growth rate of 3.4 percent per year, and a forecast of 30 quads would imply a growth rate of 4.8 percent per year.

During the period 1960-1979, electric-utility coal consumption grew at an annual rate of 5.2 percent per year. Thus the forecasted growth rate in utility coal consumption is not likely to achieve historical levels under most sets of circumstances.

Metallurgical-Coal Demand

Background

After electric utilities, coke plants constitute the most important market for coal. In 1978, of the 625 million short tons (MST) of coal consumed, 71 MST was accounted for by coke plants.[13]

Coke plants restrict their purchases to metallurgical coal, which is a specially selected blend with particular characteristics of sulfur content, volatile content, and coking properties. The coal is baked in coke-oven batteries at high temperatures with air excluded so that the coal does not burn but is transformed to a hard porous coke. It takes about 1.45 tons of metallurgical coal to yield 1 ton of coke.

Most of the coke produced is used in blast furnaces, where it acts as a reducing agent and source of heat in the conversion of iron ore to pig iron. To produce 1 ton of pig iron, about 0.58 tons of coke and 1.53 net tons of iron ore (and other materials such as fluxes) are used.

Pig iron is used chiefly in steelmaking. The open-hearth process for produced steel is being rapidly phased out, so that by 1990, it is likely that steel will be produced in electric furnaces or basic-oxygen furnaces. The electric furnace converts scrap to steel, while in the basic-oxygen process, the metallic charge includes scrap and pig iron. In 1978, 1 ton of steel produced in the basic-oxygen process required 0.83 tons of pig iron and 0.32 tons of scrap.

As the preceding discussion has shown, the future demand for metallurgical coke will depend on the demand for pig iron, and the demand for pig iron will in turn depend on the amount of steel produced in the basic-oxygen furnace.

To forecast metallurgical-coal demand (say, for 1990 and 2000), the approach used should recognize the derived nature of the demand for metallurgical coal. Ideally, the approach would involve

1. Forecasting for 1990 and 2000 the amount of steel that will be produced in the basic-oxygen and electric furnaces (open hearths are assumed to be completely phased out by 1990).
2. Estimating the amount of pig iron that will be associated with basic-oxygen steel production in 1990 and 2000.
3. Computing the coke required to produce the projected output of pig iron and determining how much of this coke will be domestically produced.
4. Calculating the metallurgical coal required to support domestic coke production.

The idealized approach has in fact been applied by Arthur D. Little, Inc., and the results indicate a stagnant demand for metallurgical coal. This stagnancy results from (1) the slow growth in domestic steel production; (2) the increasing penetration of electric furnaces, which do not use pig iron; (3) the introduction of scrap preheating and direct reduction, both of which permit a reduction in the amount of pig iron required to produce a ton of steel in the basic-oxygen process; and (4) a significant reduction in the amount of coke required to produce a ton of pig iron in the blast furnace.

There is, in fact, a possibility that metallurgical-coal demand may actually decrease. Some steel companies have indicated that if the government maintains the present trade policy, they will not invest in the steel business. Many are already diversifying into more profitable lines (for example, U.S. Steel into chemicals). This means that imports could rise substantially, to perhaps 40 percent of the market by 2000.

In this section, the various determinants of metallurgical-coal demand will be discussed, with particular emphasis on how these determinants will behave over the next 20 years. The discussion will utilize a top-down approach that corresponds to the derived-demand aspect of metallurgical coal demand.

Raw-Steel Production

Currently there are three processes for producing steel: the basic-oxygen furnace, the open-hearth furnace, and the electric furnace. In the basic-oxygen and open-hearth processes, a metallic charge of pig iron and scrap is converted to steel, while in the electric furnace, the metallic charge consists almost exclusively of scrap.

Table 4–11
Patterns in U.S. Raw-Steel Production
(*millions of short tons.*)

	1960	1970	1974	1978
Electric furnace	8	20	29	32
Basic-oxygen furnace	3	63	82	84
Open-hearth furnace	87	48	35	21
Total	98	131	146	137

Source: American Iron and Steel Institute, *Annual Statistical Report* (Washington, various issues).

Table 4-11 presents historical data on steel production by furnace type. As the table shows, during the period 1960-1978, raw steel production grew at an annual rate of 1.9 percent, but during the period 1970-1978, the growth rate was only 0.8 percent. The American Iron and Steel Institute (AISI), in a publication released in January of 1980, indicated that under an optimistic scenario, an annual growth rate of 1.2 percent could be achieved.[14]

The forecasted rate of 1.2 percent does not allow for a major increase in the share of imports in meeting consumption. During the period 1960-1978, U.S. finished steel consumption grew at a rate of 2.8 percent, while during that same period, U.S. raw-steel production grew at a rate of only 1.9 percent. The difference in growth rates is largely due to the enormous increase in finished-steel imports. In 1960, exports of finished steel actually exceeded imports, but in 1978, net imports of finished steel equaled 16 percent of consumption.

The growth in metallurgical demand will be slower than the growth in raw-steel production because of process shifts. In 1960, the production of raw steel was dominated by the open-hearth process, but by 1978, much of the open-hearth capacity had been phased out, so that open hearths produced only 15.3 percent of steel in that year, while the basic-oxygen process accounted for 61.3 percent and the electric furnace for 23.4 percent. The next decade will witness the continued phasing out of open-hearth capacity and the building of new electric furnaces and basic-oxygen furnaces. The AISI predicted that the basic-oxygen process would account for 52 percent and the electric furnace for 48 percent. In a recent study for the Department of Energy, Arthur D. Little, Inc. indicated that of the new capacity built, 62 percent would be basic oxygen and 38 percent would be electric.[15]

Pig-Iron Production

Of the 88 million short tons (MST) of pig iron produced in 1978, 84 MST was used in basic-oxygen and open-hearth furnaces to produce steel. In 1978, the

Table 4-12
Patterns in Pig-Iron Production

	Raw Steel Production (Excl. Elec. Furnaces) (Million Short Tons)	Hot-Metal Charge Rate (Tons of Pig per Ton of Raw Steel)	Pig-Iron Requirements (Million Short Tons)
1960	90	0.70	63
1970	121	0.72	87
1974	117	0.77	91
1978	105	0.80	84

Source: American Iron and Steel Institute, *Annual Statistical Report* (Washington, various issues).

production of 1 ton of steel in the basic-oxygen process involved 0.83 tons of pig iron and 0.32 tons of scrap, while in the open-hearth process, an average 1978 charge contained 0.63 tons of pig iron and 0.55 tons of scrap per ton of steel produced.

As the 1978 data show, the hot-metal charge rate (that is, the tons of pig per ton of steel produced) is much higher for basic-oxygen furnaces than for open hearths. This reflects the fact that the basic-oxygen furnace cannot accept a metallic charge in which scrap is more than 30 percent of the total, unless the scrap has been preheated.

Insofar as open-hearth furnaces are being phased out, future pig iron requirements will depend on the steel output of basic-oxygen furnaces and the associated hot-metal charge rate. Table 4-12 presents historical data on the hot-metal charge rate. As the table shows, the hot-metal charge rate has risen, a corollary of the replacement of open-hearth furnaces by basic-oxygen furnaces. It is likely that in the future the hot-metal charge rate will stabilize, so that pig iron production will grow at the same rate as basic-oxygen-furnace steel output.

Coke Requirements

Most of the coke consumed in the United States is used in blast furnaces as a reducing agent and source of heat in the production of pig iron. In the blast furnace, coke consumption is related to pig iron production by a *coke rate,* which defines the tons of coke per ton of pig. The coke rate has steadily decreased over time from 0.79 in 1960 to 0.63 in 1970 and to 0.58 in 1978, as table 4-13 shows.

The 0.58 coke rate of 1978 is an average, and in that year, coke rates varied from 0.45 to 0.70. During the next decade, the most inefficient blast furnaces will be retired and replaced by highly efficient units. The AISI predicts that the average coke rate will improve to 0.53 by 1988.

Table 4–13
Patterns in Coke Requirements for Blast Furnaces

	Pig-Iron Production (Million Short Tons)	Coke Rate (Tons of Coke per Ton of Pig)	Blast-Furnace Coke Requirements (Million Short Tons)
1960	66	0.79	52
1970	92	0.63	58
1974	96	0.60	58
1978	88	0.58	51

Source: American Iron and Steel Institute, *Annual Statistical Report* (Washington, various issues).

To forecast coke requirements for pig-iron production, the projected pig-iron output must be multiplied by a coke rate. However, U.S. coke production will not be the same as pig-iron coke requirements, because of other coke requirements (for example, by foundries), coke imports, and stock changes. Table 4-14 presents historical data on these elements. As the table shows, there has been a growing deviation between U.S. coke production and domestic requirements. In recent years, a number of coke ovens have been shut down because of environmental factors, and this has caused a significant increase in coke imports. For example, in 1978, 5.7 MST of coke were imported and 2.9 MST of coke inventories were depleted.

Coke Production

Coal is prepared for the coking ovens by screening and crushing. The coals are then blended into a mix suitable for coking. The coke-oven battery is a refractory structure consisting of many slot ovens. The oven is preheated by coke-oven gas, blast-furnace gas, or natural gas to high temperatures. The coal is

Table 4–14
Patterns in Coke Production
(*in millions of short tons.*)

	Blast-Furnace Requirements	Other Requirements	Net Imports and Stock Changes	U.S. Production
1974	58	6	–2	62
1978	51	6	–8	49

Source: Energy Information Administration, *Coke and Coal Chemicals in 1978* (Washington, November 1977), p. 9.

baked for between 16 to 18 hours. Since air is excluded from the ovens, the coal does not burn but is transformed into hard, porous coke. Volatile gases and liquids are produced during the coking process and these are conveyed to a by-product plant. The coke itself is cooled in a quenching station and later screened into blast-furnace coke and coke breeze. About 1380 pounds of coke and about 100 pounds of breeze are obtained per ton of coal.

Some of the coke breeze is used as fuel in agglomerating plants. The remainder is used in steam plants and in the production of elemental phosphorus from phosphate rock.

The byproduct gases and liquids produced during coking are rich in tars and oils but also contain noxious elements that must be removed. The valuable materials recovered include tar, naphthalene, ammonia, light oil, and coke-oven gas. The light oil is generally sold, and the tar and naphthalene are either sold or used as fuel. Each ton of coke yields substantial amounts of coke-oven gas, which are used to underfire the coke ovens.

The precise yields of byproducts from coal will depend on the type of coal and operating conditions. On average, about 6 MMBtu of coke-oven gas, 7.6 gallons of tars, 2.6 gallons of light oil, and 15.6 pounds of ammonia (expressed as ammonium sulfate equivalent) are recovered per ton of coal. On an energy basis, the byproducts recovered equal 8 MMBtu, or about one-third the Btu content of the coal.

Given a projection of coke production, the demand for metallurgical coal will depend on the amount of coal required to produce one ton of coke. Table 4-15 presents the historical coal-coke ratio. As the table shows, the ratio has remained stable, and 1.45 tons of coal are currently required to produce 1 ton of coke.

Research has been directed at improving the coke production process. However, the objective of the research has not generally been reducing coal requirements. Instead, the focus has generally been on conserving critical fuels or replacing metallurgical coal with abundant noncoking coals. Two key technologies are discussed next.

Table 4-15
Patterns in Metallurgical-Coal Demand

	Coke Production (Million Short Tons)	Coal/Coke Ratio	Coal Consumption by Coke Plants (Million Short Tons)
1974	62	1.45	90
1978	49	1.44	71

Source: Energy Information Administration, *Coke and Coal Chemicals in 1978* (Washington, November 1979), p. 9; Energy Information Administration, *Monthly Energy Review* (Washington: U.S. Government Printing Office, June 1980), p. 54.

The coal preheating system is a reliable and efficient technology that is currently in operation in the United States. In this system, the coal is dried and preheated prior to charging it in the coke oven. The preheated coal cokes faster and more evenly, reducing coking time from 16 to 18 hours to 12 hours. Published estimates of the possible savings in gas consumption resulting from coal preheating range to 17 percent, with 10 percent being a reasonable estimate. However, a small amount of steam and electricity will be required to operate the preheater.

The objective of formed-coke processes is to substitute abundant noncoking coals for metallurgical coals. This substitution is accomplished by sophisticated chemical processing of the coals and by mechanical forming of the coke product. An auxiliary advantage of the formed-coke processes is that they are totally enclosed, which facilitates pollution control, a major problem in coke production.

Two formed-coke processes have been developed in the United States and have been operated at a demonstration scale. The Consol-BNR process has been developed by a consortium of Consolidation Coal, Bethlehem Steel, and Republic Steel. The FMC process has been introduced by the FMC corporation.

Only very sketchy data are available about these processes. The FMC process can reportedly use almost any coal, while the Consol-BNR process requires the addition of some coking coal to the overall blend.

A problem with formed-coke processes is the nature of the byproducts they generate. Typically, the coke-oven gas associated with formed-coke processes has a much lower Btu content than the gas associated with standard processes. It would be difficult and expensive to retrofit steel facilities to use the low-Btu gas. Attempts are being made to improve the quality of the byproduct gases from formed-coke processes. If successful, this would improve the acceptance potential for such processes. In general, however, the feeling of industry experts is that formed-coke processes will not make a very significant penetration in the United States over the next two decades.

Metallurgical Coal-Demand Forecasts

As the preceding discussion has demonstrated, the demand for metallurgical coal is likely to show little or no growth. The factors leading to this conclusion are summarized as follows:

1. Raw-steel production is expected to grow at a relatively low rate, about 1 percent per year.
2. An increasing proportion of raw steel is likely to be produced by electric furnaces, which do not use pig iron.
3. Because of the preceding two factors, the demand for pig iron should grow by less than 1 percent per year.

Table 4-16
Comparison of Forecasts of Metallurgical-Coal Demand
(*in millions of short tons*)

	1990	2000
Energy Information Administration (middle case)	78	78
Brookhaven National Laboratory	100	110
MIT World Coal Study (case A)	96	107
MIT World Coal Study (case B)	96	118

4. The coke requirements will grow at a rate that is lower than that recorded by pig iron output because of the installation of new blast furnaces that use less coke to produce one ton of pig iron.
5. The penetration of (blast-furnace) coal-injection processes and the introduction of formed-coke processes should permit the replacement of metallurgical coal by steam coal.

Table 4-16 presents forecasts of metallurgical-coal demand. The forecasts are in general agreement that the demand for metallurgical coal will grow very little from the 1978 value of 71 MST. In my opinion, the Energy Information Administration forecast is the most realistic.

A Policy Note

The nation does not have a policy designed to promote metallurgical-coal demand (and correctly so). In fact, the major legislative initiative in this area, the National Energy Conservation Policy Act (NECPA) of 1978 (Pub. L. 95-019), will reduce coke use. The act required DOE to establish voluntary recycling targets. Among such targets is the percentage of steel that should be produced from scrap as opposed to pig iron. The effect of replacing pig iron by scrap is to directly reduce the demand for coke, since almost all the nation's coke is consumed in the production of pig iron.

Industrial-Fuel-Coal Demand

Background

In 1978, 1.6 quads of coal was consumed in nonmetallurgical industrial applications. Of this amount, 1.3 quads was as boiler fuel and 0.3 quads in other process applications (chiefly in the cement and lime industry). There is potential for coal to replace other fuels in these applications, and annual growth rates of between 4 and 10 percent have been predicted for coal in nonmetallurgical applications over the next two decades. This section reviews the factors affecting industrial nonmetallurgical demand and presents forecasts from various studies.

Policy Factors

To accelerate the use of coal in nommetallurgical industrial applications, the government has adopted a number of measures. Essentially these measures are aimed at raising the cost of using natural gas (the dominant industrial fuel) and at prohibiting nonpriority industrial uses of gas/oil. Some of the more important of these measures are summarized next.

The Natural Gas Policy Act (NGPA) of 1978 (Pub. L. 95-621) seeks to discourage the industrial use of gas. The act provides for a phased decontrol of natural-gas prices, and this is to be effected through the incremental pricing provision.

An incremental pricing threshold is to be computed on a March 1978 base rate of $1.48 per MMBtu plus an inflation adjustment. Amounts paid by the distribution company that exceed the incremental pricing threshold (or some other specified limit) and are associated with expensive imports, costly stripper-well gas, natural gas from Prudhoe Bay, increased state severance taxes, or surcharges paid by one interstate pipeline to another are subject to passthrough provisions. Under the passthrough requirements, amounts paid in excess of $1.45 per MMBtu would have to be placed in a special account. These excess amounts would then be passed through in the form of a surcharge to industrial users until such time as the delivered-gas price to these users equals the cost of alternative fuels.

The Energy Tax Act (ETA) of 1978 (Pub. L. 95-618) contains provisions designed to raise the effective capital cost of oil- and gas-fired boilers. According to ETA, new industrial oil- or gas-fired boilers will be denied the usual investment tax credit and will be limited to straight-line depreciation unless the use of coal at any such facility is precluded by federal air-pollution regulations or existing state air-pollution regulations. The credit and accelerated depreciation will, however, be allowed for new oil and gas boilers if they are applied in exempt uses (for example, farming).

The Powerplant and Industrial Fuel Use Act (FUA) of 1978 (Pub. L. 95-620) is designed to curtail the use of oil/gas in nonpriority industrial applications. According to FUA, new industrial boilers with a fuel-heat input rate of 100 million Btu's (MMBtu) per hour or greater are prohibited from using oil or natural gas unless an exemption is granted by DOE on grounds that the use of coal or an alternate fuel is precluded by environmental regulations, cost, site limitations, or for other reasons.

For existing industrial facilities, DOE may order individual coal-capable units with a fuel-heat input rate of 100 MMBtu/h or greater not to burn oil or gas, with exemptions granted for stipulated reasons. Units that are not coal-capable may be required, where feasible, to burn mixtures of oil and alternate fuels, using only the minimum amount of oil necessary to maintain efficiency.

Idealized Forecast Methodology

The approach used to forecast industrial coal use should explicitly separate the new and retrofit markets. In the case of boilers, the distinction should be between new boilers and existing boilers, while in the case of nonboiler applications, the distinction should be between new process heaters and existing process heaters. The distinction between *new* and *existing* is important because the retrofit potential is extremely limited.

In the case of boilers, the application of the idealized methodology involves the following steps:

1. Total boiler-fuel consumption (all fuels) is forecasted as a function of industrial production.
2. The total-consumption forecast is disaggregated according to whether it occurs in existing boilers (built prior to 1979) or new boilers (built after 1979). In determining the split between new and existing boilers, a key input is the average lifetime of a boiler.
3. Penetration rates are applied to determine the fraction of new boilers that will use coal, gas/oil, or biomass. The penetration rates will depend on the life-cycle cost of the various boiler alternatives. Coal-fired boilers have higher capital costs than oil/gas boilers, but the fuel costs are lower.
4. Coal boiler-fuel use is calculated by summing consumption in existing boilers and new boilers.

Total Requirements for Boiler Fuel

Estimates of the amount of energy currently consumed in industrial boilers vary widely. Resource Planning Associates (RPA) estimates 1976 boiler-fuel use at 13.1 quads; Resources for the Future (RFF), in its study, assumes a 1974 value of 10.1 quads; Energy and Environmental Analysis (EEA) estimates of 1974 boiler-fuel use are 6.8 quads; and the Energy Information Administration (EIA) reports 1978 boiler-fuel use at 6.5 quads.[17] However, the EIA estimate does not include fuel used for electricity generation, so that a reasonable 1978 estimate is 7.0 quads.

Table 4-17 presents 1978 boiler-fuel use disaggregated by energy form. Most of the coal is consumed in large boilers (over 100 MMBtu/h firing rate),

Table 4–17
Estimated Boiler-Fuel Use in 1978

	Quadrillion Btu	Percentage of Total
Oil	1.0	14
Gas	3.7	51
Coal	1.3	18
Other	1.2	17
Total	7.2	100

Source: Arthur D. Little, Inc. estimate based on various sources, especially Energy and Environmental Analysis, Inc., *Technical and Economic Feasibility of Alternative Fuel Use in Process Heaters and Small Boilers* (report to U.S. Department of Energy, Feb. 1980), pp. 3–4.

and the chemical and paper industries are important users. Most of the biomass consumption occurs in the pulp and paper industry in the form of bark, wood chips, shavings, and pulping liquors. Natural gas and oil are consumed in all industries and boiler types. Chemicals, petroleum refining, paper, food, and metals dominate the boiler-fuel use of natural gas and oil.

Boilers are used to produce steam for process applications and electricity generation. Process steam is an input in the production process, and therefore, the amount of process steam required should increase at the same rate as industrial output. However, because new boilers are likely to use 2 to 3 percent less energy per unit of steam output, the amount of fuel consumed to satisfy process-steam requirements is likely to grow somewhat slower than industrial output.

However, the trend toward industrial cogeneration may create a requirement for more boiler fuel than would otherwise be required. If a facility producing its own process steam but purchasing its electricity from the utility decides to cogenerate, it will need to produce more steam than would otherwise be required. However, if the facility is internally satisfying its process-steam and electricity requirements in separate units, then the implementation of a cogeneration scheme will reduce fuel requirements.

In general, the consensus seems to be that industrial boiler-fuel requirements will grow somewhat slower than industrial output. Industrial output is expected to grow at a rate of about 2.5 percent per year over the next two decades, and so boiler-fuel requirements should grow at between 2 and 2½ percent. The EIA, for example, forecasts a growth rate of 2.2 percent.

Share of Coal as Boiler Fuel

The potential for coal use is greatest in new boilers (although existing boilers designed to burn coal but using fuel oil/natural gas can switch back to coal).

Therefore, in projecting coal use in boilers, it is necessary to determine how much fuel will be consumed by existing boilers (that is, those built prior to 1979) and how much will be consumed in new boilers (that is, those built between 1979 and 1990).

The life of a boiler is typically in the range of 20 to 40 years, and a relatively high proportion of boilers were installed in the early postwar period, which means that a substantial amount of the boilers currently operating will be retired by 1990. The proportion of new boilers will, of course, be even higher by 2000.

The share of coal in meeting boiler-fuel requirements should increase significantly because of (1) the restrictions on oil/gas use in large boilers as stipulated by FUA, (2) the rapidly escalating cost of oil and gas in most regions, (3) the eventual resolution of the environmental uncertainties surrounding the use of coal, (4) the relatively favorable economics for coal-based steam topping turbine cogeneration systems when new process steam boilers are needed, and (5) the development of new technologies to burn and use coal.

There are, however, a number of factors that will inhibit the use of coal, especially in small boilers (that is, less than 100 MMBtu/h), that are not covered by FUA. The inhibiting factors include (1) the very high capital costs associated with coal-fired boilers, (2) the technical problems such as burner-size limitation and uncontrolled heat distribution that preclude the use of coal in some industrial facilities, (3) environmental constraints in certain regions, and (4) the improved supply prospects for natural gas.

The effect of the positive factors is expected to dominate, and the share of coal should rise significantly. Studies of coal demand indicate that the share of coal in boiler-fuel applications will rise from 18 percent in 1978 to between 35 and 55 percent by 2000.

Total Requirements for Nonboiler Fuel

The term *non-boiler-fuel requirements* is used here to exclude energy consumed in boilers, as petrochemical feedstocks, and in coking applications. It is also used to exclude process heat energy used in the petroleum-refining industry. It includes fossil fuel consumed in furnaces, kilns, and other process heaters in such applications as heating/melting in the metals industry, singeing/drying in the textile industry, baking/cooking in the food industry, and calcining/drying/melting in the stone, clay, and glass industry.

There is a paucity of data on non-boiler-fuel consumption. The EIA estimates that in 1978, 3.8 quads of energy were consumed in non-boiler-fuel applications (this estimate excludes petroleum-refining process heat applications). Presented in table 4-18 is a very crude estimate of non-boiler-fuel use in 1978.

Table 4–18
Estimated Non-Boiler-Fuel Use in 1978

	Quadrillion Btu	Percentage of Total
Coal	0.3	7.9
Oil	1.1	29.0
Gas	2.0	52.6
Other	0.4	10.5
Total	3.8	100.0

Source: Arthur D. Little, Inc. estimate, which excludes refinery process heat applications, based on Energy and Environmental Analysis, Inc., *Technical and Economic Feasibility of Alternative Fuel Use in Process Heaters and Small Boilers* (report to U.S. Department of Energy, Feb. 1980), pp. 3–4.

Non-boiler-fuel consumption is forecasted to grow at a rate distinctly lower than industrial production and also lower than the rate projected for boiler-fuel consumption. Non-boiler-fuel usage grows slower than boiler-fuel usage because (1) the potential for reducing energy use is generally greater in process heaters than in boilers, (2) steam raised by boilers can be substituted for direct process heat in some applications, (3) electricity can be economically applied in certain direct process heat applications, and (4) the life of a process heater is shorter than the life of a boiler, so the stock turns over more quickly. In summary, it is reasonable to expect that non-boiler-fuel consumption will grow at between 1 and 2 percent per year over the next two decades.

Share of Coal

In 1978, about 0.3 quads of coal was consumed in non-boiler-process applications. Most of this consumption occurred in cement and lime kilns, where the use of coal has risen sharply. In 1971, about 16 percent of cement production came from coal-fired kilns, while by 1979, about 72 percent of the capacity was coal-fired.

The use of coal in other process heat applications is limited by the problems involved in firing a solid fuel and the pollutants contained in coal. However, there are applications where the use of coal is technically feasible. According to a study performed by EEA, direct coal use is technically feasible in 29 percent of all new process heaters. Moreover, coal, gas, liquid-solvent refined coal, methanol from coal, and other coal derivatives can significantly enhance the penetration of coal.

The EEA study indicates that blast furnaces, iron cupolas, soaking pits, reheat furnaces, and aluminum rotary kilns are among the process heat applications where coal conversion is a possibility.

Because of the technological constraints involved, it is difficult to predict the general penetration rate for coal use in new process heaters. However, the fact that coal prices are rising slower than oil/gas prices should foster a greater use of coal. It is expected that the share of coal in non-boiler-fuel applications (which, it will be noted, again exclude feedstocks and refinery process heat) will increase from 8 percent in 1978 to between 14 and 22 percent by 2000. The share can rise much higher if coal derivatives (for example, methanol) become widely available.

Forecasts

Table 4-19 presents forecasts of industrial-fuel (boiler plus nonboiler) coal demand as prepared by various sources. According to the EIA, for example, industrial demand will increase from 1.0 quads in 1978 to 5.2 quads in 1990 and 8.2 quads in 2000. The EIA forecasts imply a growth rate of 10.3 percent per year for 1979-1990 and 4.7 percent per year for 1990-2000.

In my opinion, the EIA forecasts are predicated on an unrealistically high rate of coal penetration. I believe that the Brookhaven forecasts are more reasonable. According to Brookhaven, industrial coal demand will increase to 4.0 quads in 1990 and 5.9 quads in 2000. The Brookhaven forecasts imply a growth rate 7.9 percent per year for 1978-1990 and 4.0 percent per year for 1990-2000.

Synthetic-Coal Market

Background

In its solid form, coal is difficult and dirty to use. This limits or precludes its direct use in important energy applications in the residential, commercial, and industrial sectors. Thus there is considerable interest in converting coal into gaseous or liquid forms so as to permit its use in residential/commercial space

Table 4-19
Comparison of Forecasts of Industrial-Fuel-Coal Demand
(*in quadrillion btu.*)

	1990	*2000*
Energy Information Administration (middle case)	5.2	8.2
Brookhaven National Laboratory	4.0	4.9
MIT World Coal Study (case A)	2.4	3.4
MIT World Coal Study (case B)	3.1	6.1
MIT World Coal Study (case B-2)	–	7.8

heating, in motor transport, in industrial process-heat applications, and as a chemical feedstock.

Gasification of coal involves the reaction of the carbon (C) in the coal with steam (H_2O) to form carbon monoxide (CO) and hydrogen (H). This reaction requires high temperatures (900°C and above), which are provided by reacting some of the coal with oxygen.

If air is used as the source of oxygen in the heat-reaction process, a low-Btu gas with a heat content of between 100 to 250 Btu per cubic feet results. Low-Btu gas must be used at the site, and this limits its application to adjacent industrial facilities or power plants where it can be used as a boiler fuel.

When oxygen is used rather than air in the heat-generating reaction, a medium-Btu gas with a heat content of between 300 and 500 Btu per cubic feet is the output. It is possible to send this gas over moderate distances by pipeline. This gas can, among other things, be used as a chemical feedstock.

An additional step called *methanation* is required to produce high-Btu gas, or synthetic natural gas (SNG), with a heat content of 900 to 950 Btu per cubic foot (natural gas has a heat content of about 1030 Btu per cubic foot). High-Btu gas has good market potential because it can be transported in existing pipelines over long distances.

Several gasification processes have been developed including the Lurgi, the Winkler, and the Koppers-Totzek processes. The Lurgi process is the best known, and its application dates back to pre-World War II days.

There are three basic approaches to producing coal liquids: (1) indirect conversion, (2) hydrogeneration, and (3) pyrolysis. In indirect conversion, coal is first gasified, and then the gas is converted into liquid form. The Sasol plant, the only commercial-sized coal liquefaction facility in operation, is based on indirect conversion. Coal is gasified using a Lurgi gasifier and then converted to liquid using Fischer-Tropsch synthesis. The Fischer-Tropsch technology is not new and was extensively relied on by Germany during World War II to produce liquid fuels.

There are no commercial-sized hydrogenation facilities in operation. However, during World War II, Germany operated a number of hydrogenation facilities using the Bergius-Pier technology. Demonstration plants (about 6000 tons per day coal input) for the solvent-refined coal (SRC) process are being designed. SRC pilot plants have been successfully operated. Pilot plants (1 ton per day to 600 tons per day coal input) for other advanced hydrogenation techniques also are being constructed.

Pyrolysis involves the conversion of coal into char, tar, liquids, and gases by exposing the coal to very high temperatures in an inert or oxygen-deficient atmosphere. The char can be directly used as a fuel or further processed into other energy forms. Various pyrolysis processes (for example, Lurgi-Ruhrgas) are at demonstration or pilot stages, but there are no full-scale commercial facilities.

The Energy Security Act, signed on 30 June 1980, is designed to create a new synfuels industry. Title 1 of the act created the Synthetic Fuels Corporation, a special-purpose federal entity to provide financial assistance to the private sector in order to stimulate production of synthetic fuels. Preference is to be given to the following forms of assistance: (1) price guarantees, (2) purchase guarantees, (3) loan guarantees, (4) loans, and (5) joint ventures.

The Energy Security Act has a synfuel target of 500,000 barrels per day oil equivalent by 1987 and 2 million by 1992. The synfuels will include not only coal liquids and gases, but also such other "synthetics" as tar sands and shale.

Synthetic fuels represent a new market for coal. There are no historical data that can be used to provide a guide to the level of coal consumption that will accompany synfuel development. Consequently, the level of uncertainty surrounding synfuel coal-demand forecasts is particularly high.

With respect to future coal-synfuel demand, there are two broad areas that need to be investigated. The first area concerns technical feasibility; that is, does the nation have the process engineers, construction labor, materials, equipment, capital, coal supply, water supply, and other resources required to implement an accelerated synfuels program. The second area concerns economic feasibility; that is, can coal-based gases and liquids be produced at a cost that will be competitive with conventional energy forms and other synthetics such as shale.

It should be noted that the two areas are related. Technical feasibility defines the maximum level of coal synfuels that can be attained. Economic feasibility indicates how much coal-based synfuel production can, in fact, be expected given market forces.

Technical Feasibility

The DOE commissioned a study to assess to the feasibility of achieving a production rate of 1 million barrels per day oil equivalents of coal-derived liquids. The contractors for this study consisted of Bechtel National, Mechanical Technologies Inc., UOP/SDC, and Mound/Monsanto Research Corporation. The findings of these contractors are summarized as follows:[18]

Coal supply is not expected to be a constraint on achieving the synfuels target. The mining industry is found to have sufficient expansion capability to easily produce the coal needed to feed the liquefaction plants.

The target will create a substantial requirement for engineering expertise, but with the exception of chemical engineers, the engineering labor pool should not be excessively strained.

Pipefitters, boilermakers, electricians, and other categories of construction labor are likely to be in short supply. Reductions in the training period, the use of helpers in less skill-intensive tasks, and extensions of the work week are among the practices that could alleviate this problem.

Water supply will not generally be a deterrent to the coal-liquid's production goal, but there could be some problems in the western regions. Improved efficiency in agricultural water use could minimize this problem.

Certain categories of equipment may not be available in the requisite amounts. The list includes heat exchangers, compressors, distillation towers, and large pumps.

The availability of capital is not expected to be a constraint, despite the massive amounts required.

Permitting and licensing requirements could significantly delay the achievement of the target. State rather than federal regulations are expected to constitute the greater hindrance.

Economic Feasibility

If coal-based gases and liquids can be produced cheaper than oil, gas, or shale oil, then one can expect vigorous efforts by industry to exploit this investment opportunity. However, if coal-based gases and liquids are relatively expensive, the development will be slow, even with governmental incentives.

According to the Electric Power Research Institute (EPRI), in 2000, imported oil and gas will sell at $4.5 per MMBtu (in constant 1978 dollars) and coal-based synfuels will have a levelized cost of $5.4 per MMBtu.[19] The EPRI estimates indicate that without subsidies coal-based synfuels may not be economically viable.

A study prepared by the Engineering Societies' Commission on Energy Inc. for the DOE presents estimates of the levelized cost for alternative synfuel technologies.[20] The characteristics of synfuel products vary, and they are, therefore, put on a gasoline-equivalent basis. This involves using weights that reflect the ratio of the wholesale-market price of the synfuel to the wholesale-market price of premium gasoline. According to the study, levelized cost of coal liquids (indirect process) expressed in 1980 dollars will be $7.1 per MMBtu gasoline equivalent, the levelized cost of high Btu coal gas will be $8.3 per MMBtu gasoline equivalent, and the levelized cost of shale oil will be $7.8 per MMBtu.

According to the EIA, in 1995, the domestic wellhead price of natural gas (in 1979 dollars) will average $3.63 per MMBtu, imported Canadian gas will be priced at $6.72 per MMBtu, high-Btu coal gas at $6.33 per MMBtu, and middle-Btu coal gas at $6.02 per MMBtu.

Forecasts

According to the EIA, coal demand for synthetic purposes will account for 2.6 quads in 2000 (total U.S. coal production in that year is forecasted by EIA at 38.2 quads). In converting coal to liquid form, there are some losses, so for every 1 quad of coal consumed, only about 0.66 quads of liquids/gases is obtained. Thus a forecast of 2.6 quads of coal implies 1.7 quads of synfuels. Expressed in oil equivalents, 1.7 quads per year amounts to 0.8 million barrels per day.

The EIA forecast of 2.6 quads of synthetics is for a middle-oil-price case. In the high-oil-price case, the demand is 2.8 quads, and in the low oil price case, it is 2.2 quads. The high-oil-price case implies 0.86 million barrels per day oil equivalent of coal-synfuel production, and the low-oil-price case implies 0.67 million barrels per day.

The MIT WOCOL study forecasts that by 2000, the synfuels industry will account for between 1.39 and 5.56 quads of coal. The low forecast corresponds to a synfuel output of 0.43 million barrels per day oil equivalent, and the high forecast corresponds to 0.73 million barrels per day.

Given the constraints involved, it seems that the lower bound of the synfuels forecast (that is, 1.4 quads to 2.2 quads of coal) is much more likely. A reasonable forecast for 2000 of, say, 1.6 quads of coal would translate into 0.5 million barrels per day of oil equivalent.

Coal Exports

Background

Currently less than 10 percent of the world coal production is traded, and much of this trade is in metallurgical coal. The existing trade in steam coal is generally made up of movements between neighboring countries.

The United States is the dominant coal exporter, and in 1979, the United States exported 65 million short tons. Most of the U.S. coal exports, with the exception of shipments to Canada, were made up of metallurgical-grade coal. The chief importers of U.S. coal in 1979 were Canada (19.2 million tons), Japan (15.7 million tons), Italy (5.0 million tons), France (3.7 million tons), other EEC nations (9.4 million tons), and Brazil (2.8 million tons).[21]

Almost all the U.S. coal currently exported is mined in the Appalachian Region. Shipments to Canada occur through the Lake Erie ports of Conneaut, Ashtabula, Sandusky, and Toledo. Shipments to Western Europe and Japan are principally through the ports at Hampton Roads (Virginia) and Baltimore.

U.S. imports of coal are negligible. In 1979, the United States imported

2 million tons, of which 0.17 came from Australia, 1.12 from South Africa, and 0.70 from Poland.

Factors Determining Future U.S. Coal Exports

As noted earlier, U.S. coal exports are currently dominated by metallurgical coal, with some steam-coal shipments to Canada. Both these market areas are unlikely to show much growth. Factors that will act to stabilize metallurgical-coal exports include (1) the slow growth in the world steel industry, (2) the increasing efficiency of blast furnaces, (3) the introduction of methods to replace coking coals with other coals in steelmaking, and (4) the growth in electric-furnace capacity.

The anticipated stagnancy of both metallurgical coal exports and steam-coal exports to Canada imply that if the United States does not develop new international markets for its coal, it can expect little increase in exports. However, there is a strong likelihood that new markets for U.S. coal will, in fact, materialize. During the next two decades, Western Europe and Japan are likely to import large amounts of steam coal for electricity generation and other applications.

The rise in the price of oil and gas has made the substitution of coal for oil/gas extremely attractive, especially in the area of electricity generation, where such substitution is eminently feasible in the long run. The markets for steam coal are particularly great in the highly industrialized but energy-poor nations such as Japan and Italy. This is evidenced by the high proportion of electricity generated in these countries from oil/gas. Of the 317 billion kWh of electricity thermally generated by Japan in 1977, 300 billion kWh were from oil- or gas-fired units. Of the 115 billion kWh thermally generated by Italy in 1977, 110 billion kWh were from oil- or gas-fired units.[22]

It is clear that Japan, Italy, France, and other nations will minimize their reliance on oil- or gas-fired generators. It is also clear that the share of coal in electricity generation will rise in these countries. However, the extent by which the share of coal increases will depend on the growth of nuclear power. An accelerated nuclear program could result in a quite modest increase in coal-fired generation.

Nor does a rise in coal-fired generation automatically translate into an increase in U.S. steam-coal exports. The importing countries may choose to purchase coal from nations other than the United States. In general, importers will seek to identify the source with the best-quality coal (that is, low-sulfur, high-Btu, and so forth) located at the closest distance. However, for reasons of economy and security, importers will diversify their sources of supply. According to the MIT WOCOL study, Australia will be the source for about 25 percent of the European market; shares of between 15 and 20 percent will be attained by South Africa, Poland, the United States, and Canada, along with other countries, will provide the remainder. In the case of Japan, WOCOL indicates that Australia and the United States will each receive about a third of the market, with Canada and China accounting for most of the remaining imports.

Forecasts of U.S. Coal Exports

In 1979, the United States exported 65 million short tons of coal, which represented a calorific value of approximately 1.5 quads. Table 4-20 presents coal exports as prepared by different sources. For 1990, the projections range between 2.2 and 3.3 quads, and for 2000, the projections range between 3.4 and 5.6 quads. The average value of 2.5 quads for 1990 and 3.9 quads for 2000 represents a reasonable forecast. These average values would imply an annual growth rate of 4.8 percent per year for 1979-1990 and 4.6 percent per year for 1990-2000.

Table 4-21 presents WOCOL forecast of U.S. coal exports disaggregated by metallurgical and steam coal. According to this study, by 2000, exports of steam coal, which are currently negligible, will exceed exports of metallurgical coal. The share of steam coal in 2000 is expected to range between 52 (low coal case) and 65 percent (high coal case).

Table 4-22 presents a WOCOL forecast of U.S. coal exports disaggregated by importing region. According to WOCOL, the Canadian share of U.S. exports is expected to decrease from 30 percent in 1979 to 13 percent (low coal case) or 5 percent (high coal case) by 2000; the Japanese share is expected to increase from 24 percent in 1979 to 43 (low coal case) or 36 percent (high coal case) by 2000; and the European share is expected to change from 35 percent in 1979 to 34 (low coal case) or 51 percent (high coal case) by 2000.

Table 4-20
Projections of U.S. Coal Exports

	1990	*2000*
WOCOL low coal case A	2.2	3.2
WOCOL high coal case B	3.1	5.1
EIA middle oil price	2.4	3.7
EIA high oil price	2.4	3.7
NEP III best estimate	2.2	–
NEP III high supply	2.9	–
Average	2.5	3.9

Sources: WOCOL and EIA as cited earlier (WOCOL projections are reported net of imports); NEP III are as reported in U.S. Department of Energy, *NEP-III Base Case 1985 and 1990, U.S. Energy Projections* (Washington, Nov. 1980).

Table 4-21
WOCOL Disaggregation of U.S. Coal Exports, by Type, in 2000
(*in percentages.*)

	Low Coal Case A	High Coal Case B
Metallurgical	48	35
Steam	52	65
Total	100	100

Source: The forecasted shares are from MIT World Coal Study, *Future Coal Prospects: Country and Regional Assessments* (Cambridge, Mass.: Ballinger, 1980), p. 501.

Table 4-22
WOCOL Disaggregations of U.S. Coal Exports, by Importing Region
(*in percentages.*)

	1979	2000: Low Coal Case A	2000: High Coal Case B
Europe	35	34	51
Japan	24	43	36
LDC	11	10	8
Canada	30	13	5
Total	100	100	100

Sources: The historical shares are from Energy Information Administration, *Weekly Coal Report* (March 14, 1980): 9; the forecasts shares are from MIT World Coal Study, *Future Coal Prospects: Country and Regional Assessments* (Cambridge, Mass.: Ballinger, 1980), p. 501.

U.S. Coal Production

Total Production Forecasts

A forecast of U.S. coal production can be obtained by summing the individual elements of demand, which consist of (1) electric utilities, (2) metallurgical, (3) industrial fuel, (4) synthetic fuel, (5) miscellaneous domestic demand, and (6) exports. Table 4-23 presents historical values for U.S. coal production disaggregated by the preceding elements; table 4-24 presents various forecasts for 1990; and table 4-25 presents various forecasts for 2000.

These tables indicate that U.S. coal production on a calorific basis is expected to grow from 17.4 quads in 1979 to about 28 quads in 1990 and to about 41 quads in 2000. These forecasts imply a compound growth rate of 4.4 percent per year for 1979-1990 and 3.9 percent per year for 1990-2000. On

Table 4-23

Historical Market Patterns in U.S. Coal Consumption and Production

(*in millions of short tons.*)

	Electric Utilities	Metallurgical	Industrial	Transportation	Residential/ Commercial	Net Exports	Stock Adjustment	Production
1950	91.9	104.0	120.6	63.0	114.6	29.0	37.3	560.4
1955	143.8	107.7	110.1	17.0	68.4	54.1	-10.3	490.8
1960	176.6	81.4	96.0	3.0	40.9	37.7	-1.3	434.3
1965	244.8	95.3	105.6	0.7	25.7	52.0	2.9	527.0
1970	320.2	96.5	90.2	0.3	16.1	72.4	17.0	612.7
1975	406.0	83.6	63.6	—	9.4	65.9	26.1	654.6
1979	528.8	77.1	65.9	—	9.1	64.1	30.7	775.8

Source: Energy Information Administration, *Annual Report to Congress, 1979*, Vol. 2 (Washington: U.S. Government Printing Office, 1980), p. 111.

Table 4–24
Comparison of WOCOL, EIA, and NEP III Consumption and Production
Forecasts for 1990
(*in quadrillion btu.*)

	WOCOL: Low Case A	WOCOL: High Case B	EIA: Middle Case	NEP III: Best Estimate	NEP III: High Supply	Average
Electric utilities	14.8	20.8	18.7	18.0	19.6	18.4
Metallurgical	2.5	2.5	2.1	2.0	2.0	2.2
Industrial fuel	2.4	3.1	5.4	3.7	4.7	3.9
Synthetic fuel	0.1	0.1	0.6	1.1	1.6	0.6
Net exports	2.2	3.1	2.4	2.2	2.9	2.6
U.S. production	22.0	29.6	29.2	26.9	30.8	27.7

Note: Residential/commercial coal use is very small and is classified with industrial-fuel use.

Table 4–25
Comparison of Coal Consumption and Production Forecasts for 2000
(*in quadrillion btu.*)

	WOCOL: Low Case A	WOCOL: High Case B	EIA: Mid Case	Brookhaven	Average
Electric utilities	22.2	32.5	21.4	22.5	24.7
Metallurgical	2.8	3.1	2.1	3.7	2.7
Industrial Fuel	3.4	6.1	8.4	4.9	5.7
Synthetic fuel	1.4	5.6	3.6	–	3.2
Exports	3.4	5.6	3.7	–	4.2
U.S. production	33.2	52.9	38.2		40.5

a tonnage basis, the growth rates should be slightly higher because of the shift to low-Btu western coals.

Regionalized Production Forecasts

The United States can be divided into three major coal-producing regions: Appalachia, the Midwest, and the West. The Appalachian Region, the dominant coal-producing area, includes eastern Kentucky, West Virginia, and Pennsylvania; the Midwest Region is defined to include western Kentucky, Illinois, and Indiana; and the Western Region is defined to include Texas, the Rocky Mountain States, and the Great Plains States. In 1979, Appalachia produced about 50 percent of U.S. coal tonnage, the Midwest produced about 18 percent, and the West accounted for about 26 percent.

Table 4-26 presents state-specific data on coal production and demonstrated reserves. The demonstrated-reserve base is defined to cover all known inplace coals of all rank that are technically and economically minable at the time of evaluation. It is estimated that at least one-half the inplace coals can be recovered. Also presented in the table are the ratios of reserves to production. In the Appalachian Region the ratio averages 262, in the Midwest it averages 690, and in the West it averages 1135.

As table 4-26 shows, the United States has abundant coal reserves, which should be adequate to support high production rates. However, in the Appalachians, the *depletion effect* may become important. This effect refers to the rise in costs that occurs as high-grade, easily accessible deposits are used up, necessitating the recovery of less attractive deposits.

Table 4-26
Demonstrated Regional Coal Reserves and Reserve-Production Ratios

	Annual Current Production (Million Tons)	*Demonstrated Reserves (Billion Tons)*	*Reserve-Production Ratio*
Appalachia			
East Kentucky	100.6	13.5	134
Pennsylvania	86.9	30.8	354
West Virginia	112.7	38.6	343
Virginia	42.2	4.3	102
Ohio	45.6	19.2	421
Other	39.0	5.3	136
Total	427.0	111.7	262
Midwest			
West Kentucky	44.5	12.5	281
Illinois	59.1	68.0	1,150
Indiana	27.3	10.7	392
Other	11.2	7.4	661
Total	142.0	98.6	690
West			
Texas	25.3	3.2	126
New Mexico	12.3	4.6	374
Wyoming	70.9	55.4	781
Montana	32.4	120.6	3,722
North Dakota	14.1	10.1	716
Colorado	17.9	16.3	911
Other	28.0	17.8	636
Total	200.9	228.0	1,135
Total United States	770.8	438.3	569

Source: Reserve data are from Energy Information Administration, *Annual Report to Congress for 1979*, Vol. 2 (Washington: U.S. Government Printing Office, 1980), p. 121.

In determining the regional mix of coal production, the following factors are important:

1. The quality of coals in terms of Btu content, sulfur content, and other critical parameters.
2. The costs of production (on a Btu basis) of coal production in different regions.
3. The distances between the consuming and producing regions.

In terms of quality, Western coals generally have the advantage in terms of sulfur content. The bulk of Western coals are low-sulfur, while Midwestern coals are principally high-sulfur and Appalachian coals range in sulfur content. With

Table 4–27
OTA Regionalized Coal-Production-Share Forecasts
(*in percentage of total tonnage.*)

		1985		2000	
	1979	Low Coal Case	High Coal Case	Low Coal Case	High Coal Case
Appalachia					
East Kentucky	13.1	9.0	8.9	8.3	7.8
Pennsylvania	11.3	7.3	7.3	6.3	5.7
West Virginia	14.6	9.9	10.0	10.0	10.5
Virginia	5.5	2.9	3.0	2.0	2.3
Ohio	5.9	4.0	4.1	4.1	4.3
Other	5.1	4.3	4.4	3.2	1.7
Total	55.5	37.4	37.7	33.9	32.3
Midwest					
West Kentucky	5.8	4.3	4.4	4.0	3.6
Illinois	7.7	6.5	7.5	7.6	7.8
Indiana	3.5	2.6	2.9	2.1	2.7
Other	1.5	0.8	1.1	0.6	0.8
Total	18.5	14.2	15.9	14.3	14.9
West					
Texas	3.3	4.5	4.4	5.6	6.6
New Mexico	1.6	4.0	3.9	5.1	5.9
Wyoming	9.2	20.1	18.8	17.6	16.1
Montana	4.2	5.8	5.5	9.0	10.0
North Dakota	1.8	4.1	4.1	5.5	6.6
Colorado	2.3	4.1	4.1	4.6	4.5
Other	3.6	5.8	5.6	4.4	3.1
Total	26.0	48.4	46.4	51.8	52.8
Total United States	100.0	100.0	100.0	100.0	100.0

Source: Office of Technology Assessment, Congress of the United States, *The Direct Use of Coal* (Washington) p. 48.

Table 4-28
EIA Regionalized Coal-Production-Share Forecasts
(*in percentage of total tonnage.*)

		1990		1995	
	1978	*Low Oil Price*	*High Oil Price*	*Low Oil Price*	*High Oil Price*
Appalachia					
Northern Appalachia	24.5	21.5	21.4	21.1	20.7
Central Appalachia	27.9	14.1	13.6	9.7	9.0
Southern Appalachia	3.2	1.0	1.0	0.7	0.7
Total	55.6	36.6	36.0	31.5	30.4
Midwest/Central West					
Midwest	16.8	24.6	24.5	23.1	21.7
Central West	2.1	1.5	1.4	1.4	1.3
Total	18.9	26.1	25.9	24.5	23.0
West					
Gulf	3.1	5.5	5.3	4.5	4.2
Great Plains	14.9	22.5	23.7	30.9	34.5
Rockies	3.3	3.2	3.1	3.3	3.0
Southwest	3.2	5.0	4.9	4.5	4.1
Other	1.0	1.1	1.1	0.8	0.8
Total	25.5	37.3	38.1	44.0	46.6
Total United States	100.0	100.0	100.0	100.0	100.0

Source: Energy Information Administration, *Preliminary 1985, 1990, and 1995 Forecasts* (Washington, Spring 1980), pp. A-10, A-17, A-52, and A-59.

Table 4-29
WOCOL Regionalized Production-Share Forecasts for 2000
(*in percentage of total.*)

	Low Case A	High Case B
Appalachia/Midwest	48	43
West	52	57
Total	100	100

Source: MIT World Coal Study, *Future Coal Prospects: Country and Regional Assessments* (Cambridge, Mass.: Ballinger, 1980), p. 490.

respect to Btu content, Appalachian and Midwestern coals have the advantage in that they have much higher calorific values per ton than coals mined in the West.

Western coals are generally the cheapest to extract. However, on a delivered basis, Western coals are usually not competitive in the East because of the high cost of transport.

Table 4-27 presents historical and forecasted shares of coal tonnage as re-ported by the Office of Technology Assessment (OTA). According to OTA, the share of the Appalachian Region will decline from 56 percent in 1979 to about 33 percent by 2000, the share of the Midwest will decline from 18 per-cent in 1979 to about 15 percent by 2000, and the share of the West will increase from 26 to 52 percent.

Table 4-28 presents forecasts of regional coal shares as prepared by EIA. According to EIA, the share of Appalachia in 1995 will be about 31 percent, the share of the Midwest will be about 23 percent, and the share of the West will be about 47 percent. The EIA and OTA forecasts differ principally in their Mid-western forecasts. The OTA expects a relative decline for this region, while in the EIA forecast, this region registers a modest gain in market share. It is not un-reasonable to expect that the share of the Midwest will, in fact, remain at current levels.

Table 4-29 presents the regionalized production-share forecasts issued by WOCOL. In the WOCOL forecast, the share of the West in the year 2000 ranges between 52 and 57 percent.

A review of OTA, EIA, and WOCOL forecasts indicate that over the next two decades, the West is expected to become much more important as a source of coal. However, it is questionable whether the West will become as important as these studies indicate. A reasonable forecast would place the Western share of coal in the year 2000 at between 38 and 44 percent, which is still significantly higher than the current 26 percent share.

5   Energy-Supply Models

The U.S. primary energy supply is made up of oil, gas, coal, nuclear power, and hydropower resources. These resources are converted in refineries or utilities into secondary energy forms for delivery to the end-user. In 1979, oil and natural gas jointly supplied 73 percent of U.S. energy consumption, while coal supplied 19 percent. However, the ratio of currently economically recoverable reserves to current production is about 11 for oil and gas, while the demonstrated coal-resource base of the United States can support existing production rates for about 350 years. As a result, the next decades should witness a rebirth of the coal industry, as well as vigorous exploratory efforts to maintain the level of oil and gas reserves. In addition, new technologies such as geothermal, solar photovoltaic, biomass, coal gasification, and coal liquefaction will make increasing contributions to the nation's energy needs.

During the last few years, researchers have developed models to forecast U.S. energy supply. In the case of oil and gas, the focus of the models has been on the discovery of new reserves, while in the case of coal, the emphasis has been on identifying the future cost of extracting known reserves. Models also have been developed to optimize the conversion process at refineries and electric utilities.

This chapter will describe technical and econometric models to project oil/gas supply, optimize electricity generation, and evaluate new technologies. Methods to model other components of energy supply are covered in the case study presented in chapter 7.

Oil- and Gas-Supply Models

The methods for exploring, developing, and producing natural gas and oil are similar. Furthermore, significant quantities of natural gas are found in association with oil. Consequently, the methods used to model oil and gas supply are similar. This section discusses technological and econometric methods for forecasting oil supply, and these are also appropriate for forecasting gas supply.

Characteristics of Supply

Exploration for oil and gas takes place in regions where geological and geophysical criteria or past experience indicates there is a probability of oil occurring. To locate the oil and gas, exploratory wells are drilled into the structure to identify whether commercially recoverable reserves exist. To put the field into a production mode, developmental wells are drilled.

The number of wells drilled declined during the 1960s and 1970s.[1] During the 1950s, the number of exploratory and developmental wells drilled averaged 48,492, while for the period 1966-1975, the average annual number of wells drilled was 30,819. The decline is most evident during the 1970-1973 period (preceding the oil embargo), when the number of wells drilled averaged 26,963. Since 1975, drilling activity has picked up sharply; for example, during 1979, 49,816 wells were drilled.

Another measure of exploratory and developmental activity is the total footage drilled. This variable is the product of the number of wells and the average well depth. With the passage of time, the average well depth tends to increase, since the more accessible resources are likely to be located first. During the period 1970-1979, well depth averaged 4819 feet; in contrast, during the period 1950-1959, average depth was 4065 feet.

A certain percentage of the wells drilled are dry. In 1979, 31.3 percent of the wells drilled were dry. The dry-well ratio has not shown any time trend and has fluctuated between 30 and 40 percent of the exploratory and development wells drilled. It is important to note that the dry-well ratio is much higher when the data are restricted to exploratory drilling. For example, in 1977, of the 44,982 wells drilled, 9961 were exploratory; of these, 7275 were dry, which means that 73 percent of the exploratory wells were dry wells.

Over time, the breakdown between oil and gas wells has changed sharply. During the 1950s, of the exploratory and developmental wells drilled, the ratio of gas wells to oil wells was 0.161, while for the period 1977-1979, the ratio was 0.698.

The effect of exploratory and developmental activity is to add to the nation's oil and gas reserves. Meanwhile, of course, such reserves are being depleted by production. The U.S. reserves are at a relatively low level in relation to production, with recent oil and gas reserve-production ratios ranging around 11. In the case of natural gas, this represents a deterioration, but for oil, the recent ratios are not at variance with the postwar period. In 1947, the oil reserve-production ratio was 12 and the gas reserve-production ratio was 36. It should be noted that these reserve-production ratios refer to *proven reserves,* which are defined as those resources demonstrated by geological and engineering data to be recoverable from known reservoirs under existing economic and operating conditions.

Oil is produced from a reservoir by primary, secondary, or tertiary methods. *Primary recovery methods* utilize the natural pressure in the reservoir that is released when a well is drilled into it. This natural pressure causes the oil in the reservoir to flow toward the well. However, such pressure decreases with production, and only about 25 percent of the oil in the place is typically recovered by primary methods.

The recovery factor can be increased by 25 to 32 percent by the application of *secondary techniques.* These are artifical methods used to repressurize the reservoir to keep oil flowing toward the well. Pressure maintenance is accomplished by pumping water or natural gas into the reservoir.

Further recovery is possible by the application of *tertiary methods,* which by thinning the oil make it flow more easily. This is achieved by heating the oil by injecting steam or by diluting the oil by injecting solvents.

Workshop on Alternative Strategies Approach

The Workshop on Alternative Energy Strategies (WAES) was an international project centered at MIT that included participants from the United States, Canada, Western Europe, Japan, Mexico, Venezuela, and Iran.[2] The individual participants were chiefly associated with energy departments, energy companies, and research institutes and brought to the venture a wealth of practical experience. The purpose of the project was to generate forecasts of energy demand and supply for the "World Outside Communist Areas" (WOCA). The methods used by WAES to forecast oil supply are of interest because of their simple and straightforward nature. In the area of supply forecasting, sophistication is no guarantee of accuracy, and consequently, simplicity has considerable appeal.

The WAES analysis starts with the development of a historical series identifying the additions to proven oil reserves. There are two reasons why proven reserves increase in a particular year. First, new fields are discovered. Second, a reestimate is made of the reserves contained in a field discovered in a previous year. The second source of reserve addition can be very significant. For example, WAES reports that the 1950 issue of the *Oil and Gas Journal* estimated proven reserves of oil in the WOCA at 72 billion barrels, while current information indicates that reserves in fields discovered before 1950 were actually on the order of 300 billion barrels.

An examination of proven reserves indicates considerable year-to-year volatility. However, it appears that this is a result of the revision of estimates concerning previous finds. The WAES team states that the rate of new discoveries has been stable. The average new discovery rate in the WOCA was about 18 billion barrels during 1950–1970 and 15 billion barrels during 1970–1975.

Looking to the future, WAES concludes that the 15-billion-barrel new discovery rate is unlikely to be sustained. This conclusion is based largely on the belief that discoveries paralleling those that occurred in the Middle East (a region containing more than 60 percent of the WOCA reserves) are very unlikely to occur.

Revisions of estimates pertaining to previous finds may take the form of corrections or reassessments. In the past, improvements in seismic techniques have permitted a better estimate of reserves and led to upward correction of the initial conservative prediction. Reassessments occur as higher oil prices or improved technology permits more oil to be recovered from a field than was originally assumed.

The WAES team assumes that future revisions will be strictly in the nature of reassessments that will occur as higher prices make the application of secondary recovery techniques more universal. The contribution of such revisions is calculated by multiplying proven reserves (plus half the cumulative production) by the assumed percentage improvement in the recovery factor. The result of such calculations indicate that between 1975 and 1985, the contribution of enhanced recoveries will equal 33 percent of new discoveries, and by 2000, enhanced recoveries could equal new discoveries.

Given estimates of new discoveries and enhanced recoveries, it is possible to project additions to *gross reserves,* which are defined as the sum of the two components. According to WAES, gross additions to reserves should vary between 10 billion and 20 billion barrels per year.

From the forecast of proven reserves, WAES generates projections of oil production using technical and political criteria. The maximum technical production is determined by the reserve-production ratio. WAES states that the maximum production rate corresponds to a 10:1 ratio. If this rate is exceeded, it will reduce the amount of oil that can eventually be recovered from the reservoir. The 10:1 ratio cannot be assumed to apply universally, especially since new discoveries will be under development. Therefore, the WAES team settled on a 15:1 reserve-production ratio as being the maximum rate for the proven reserves of the WOCA. Actual production, however, is not likely to correspond to the technical criteria, and the WAES team will adjust the forecasts to reflect political reality. In countries such as the United States, the reserve-production ratio is about 11, while in many Middle East countries it exceeds 50.

The WAES approach relies heavily on judgment, and most of the important parameters are exogenous inputs rather than analytical derivations. Clearly, the success of such an approach will depend on the experience of the team supplying the inputs.

MIT Energy Laboratory Approach

The oil-supply model developed at the MIT Energy Laboratory attempts to endogenize some of the variables that are exogenous in the WAES approach. The difference in approach reflects the orientation of the Energy Laboratory. The laboratory is closely associated with the university, and professors and students at the schools of engineering and management are integrally involved in the research conducted at the laboratory. The research is funded by organizations such as the National Science Foundation and the Department of Energy. The emphasis in the laboratory appears to be on developing generalized methodologies rather than on generating specific predictions.

The MIT oil-supply model is the outcome of the World Oil Project at the laboratory funded by the National Science Foundation. The model is described by Eckbo, Jacoby, and Smith in a 1978 article in which they also illustrate its application to the North Sea Region.[3]

The model forecasts oil supply using a logic that centers around three components: an estimate of oil discoveries, a characterization of the size of the discoveries, and a determination of whether the discoveries are of a size that is economically recoverable.

The number of oil reservoirs found is calculated by multiplying the number of exploratory wells by a find rate. For example, if 40 oil wells are drilled and the find rate is 0.25, this would imply that 10 discoveries are made and 30 wells are dry. In the MIT model, the number of wells drilled and the find rate are both exogenous variables. In the North Sea example, the authors base their estimate of exploratory wells drilled on announced drilling plans and set it equal to 46 for each year from 1976 to 1978. The find rate is a judgmental constant and it is set equal to 0.24. These two assumptions imply that 11 discoveries will be made each year from 1976 to 1978.

The size of the discoveries is characterized using a probability function embedded in which are assumptions about the nature of resource depletion and the process of oil exploration. Because of the geological and exploratory assumptions built into the function, successive discoveries result in progressively smaller finds.

As of June 1976, 60 discoveries had been made in the North Sea Region, and the authors apply the probability function to ascertain the finds located by subsequent discoveries. According to them, the sixty-first discovery is likely to locate 258 million barrels; the sixty-second discovery 253 million barrels; the sixty-third discovery, 249 million barrels; the sixty-fourth discovery, 244 million barrels; and so on.

Not all discoveries are immediately economically recoverable, and the model classifies discoveries into economic and submarginal categories. This classification is based solely on the size of the find, although the authors do admit that reservoir depth, water depth, and distance to shore are among the factors influencing cost. If the size of the discovery exceeds a minimum economic size, reservoir development is assumed to start in the year of the discovery. Otherwise, the discovery is assigned to a submarginal inventory.

The minimum economic size is determined by development costs, operating costs, capital costs, taxes, royalties, other costs, and oil price. A decrease in costs or an increase in oil price will lower the minimum economic size, and vice versa.

For example, according to the authors, at $6 a barrel (1976 dollars), a reservoir must contain 200 million barrels to be economic, while at $15 a barrel, the minimum economic size is 75 million barrels. As the example shows, the classification of a reservoir as economic or submarginal is not irrevocable. Rises in oil price can make previously submarginal discoveries economic.

The rate at which production occurs from an economic reservoir is determined using an exogenous time profile. The profile is not described, but apparently it is based on an assessment of data on individual reservoirs contained in a report prepared by a North Sea contractor.

The major innovation of the MIT Energy Laboratory Model is its use of a probability function to predict the size of a discovery. However, the accuracy of these predictions is subject to serious question. It will be recalled that the model predicts the size of the discoveries as decreasing from 258 million barrels (61st discovery) to 244 million barrels (64th discovery). Compare this to the actual discoveries, which vary in size from 34 million barrels (15th discovery) to 4960 million barrels (32nd discovery).

Econometric Models

The number of barrels of oil (and gas) discovered can be calculated as the product of three terms:

1. The number of wildcat wells drilled, that is, wells drilled in areas that have not previously produced oil.
2. The success ratio, that is, the percentage of wildcat wells that locate oil.
3. The discovery size, that is, the average number of barrels of oil contained in a successful wildcat.

Econometric models of oil discovery typically contain three equations—one for each of the terms just listed.[4] The number of wildcat wells drilled is forecasted as a function of oil price and drilling costs. The higher is the oil price, the greater is the drilling, while the higher is the costs, the lower is the drilling. This specification reflects the hypothesis that higher prices and lower costs by raising profits encourage drilling.

The success ratio is forecasted as a function of such variables as oil price and the percentage of drilling accounted for by the major oil companies. The a priori expectation regarding the relationship between the success ratio and oil price is not clear. On one hand, there may exist relatively sure drilling prospects, which a higher price will bring forth, thus causing a positive correlation between the success ratio and oil price. On the other hand, an increase in drilling may be focused on marginal prospects, which would cause a negative correlation between the success ratio and oil price.

The drilling behavior of the major oil companies differs from that of the smaller companies. The majors make the significant large discoveries. To do this they make risky investments, drilling deep wells in very new areas. Thus, if the participation of the majors (measured, for example, as the ratio of wildcats drilled by majors to total wildcats) increases, the success ratio should decrease. However, the majors tend to use geological information and other systematic decision processes that act to raise the success ratio.

Discovery size is also forecasted as a function of oil price and the percentage of drilling accounted for by the majors. Discovery size is positively related to the degree of participation by the majors, because, as pointed out earlier, the majors tend to make the large discoveries. To the extent that there exist small relatively sure prospects that are brought forth by a price rise, the discovery size is negatively correlated to price.

Econometric modeling has made a significant contribution to the debate surrounding oil-price decontrol. A key issue in the debate has been the effect of higher oil prices on oil discoveries, with the proponents of oil decontrol arguing that higher oil prices will significantly increase discoveries.

In economic terms, oil discoveries are related to oil price by a price elasticity. The higher is the elasticity, the greater is the responsiveness of discoveries to price. In the econometric model, oil price appears in the equations for wildcatting, success ratio, and discovery size. Thus, if the equations are logarithmic, the price elasticity is the sum of the price coefficients in the three equations. A high price elasticity would support the argument that decontrol will increase discoveries.

Electric-Utility-Supply Models

Background

Electric utilities play a pivotal role in the U.S. energy economy. In 1978 they consumed 73.7 percent of the total U.S. coal consumption, 16.5 percent of the natural-gas consumption, and 10.3 percent of the oil consumption. They used these fossil resources as well as hydropower and nuclear power to generate 2206.5 million kWh of electricity, of which 1999.5 million kWh were delivered to the consumer.

Electricity is generated by rotating a large electromagnet inside a coil, forcing the electrons in the coil to move. The generator is usually rotated by steam-driven turbines, with the steam produced by burning coal, oil, or gas or by nuclear fission.

After electricity has been generated, it is conveyed to the consumer via a transmission and distribution network. As the electricity leaves the station, it is transmitted through high-voltage lines. Power from these lines must be stepped down in voltage before it can be delivered to the consumer, and these stepdowns occur in substations.

Electricity is a premium energy form, and for every Btu of electricity delivered to the consumer, about 3 Btu's of energy has been consumed. Most of the losses occur during the generation stage. The measure of generation losses is the thermal efficiency of the plant, which depends on the heat rate. The *heat rate* is defined as the number of Btu's of primary energy required to generate 1 kWh of electricity. Typically between 9500 and 11,000 Btu of coal, oil, or gas is required to generate 1 kWh of electricity. A kilowatt-hour of electricity contains only 3412 Btu, and so the typical heat rates imply substantial losses. For example, the thermal efficiency corresponding to a heat rate of 10,000 is 0.34, which means that 66 percent of the primary energy is lost during generation.

Transmission and distribution losses occur as electricity is transmitted and stepped down in voltage. These losses, which account for about 9 percent of the electricity generated, vary positively with the distance the electricity is transmitted and negatively with the voltage at which it is transmitted and delivered. For example, an individual customer located close to the power site and receiving electricity at high voltage imposes proportionately lower losses than a residential customer, who receives electricity at low voltage.

There have been occasional calls to increase the electrification of our society. This may appear surprising given the substantial inefficiencies that characterize the generation and delivery of electricity. However, electricity has a great advantage; namely, it can be produced using a wide range of primary energy sources, in particular coal and uranium, which are abundantly available in the United States. To the extent that the expansions in electricity capacity involve coal-fired and nuclear stations, this will reduce the nation's dependence on foreign energy sources. Such a trend, however, has been inhibited by the growing environmental concern about the effects of increased nuclear and coal use.

An electric utility must make three basic and interrelated decisions with regard to the generation of electricity. First, it must decide how much capacity to maintain. Second, it must select the mix of units that will constitute the required capacity. Third, it must choose the operating rate for each unit.

Utilities maintain capacity that is somewhat in excess of peak demand. This is necessary because at a given point in time, all the capacity will not be available. Some units will be unavailable because of maintenance or repairs, other units may be unavailable because of failures. The percentage by which capacity exceeds the peak demand is called the *gross reserve margin*. A typical reserve margin is 25 percent.

At any given point in time, reserves can be classified as spinning or cold. Spinning reserves consist of those generating units connected to the bus and ready to take load, while cold reserves are those units kept idle. It is necessary to have spinning reserves because the startup times required would not allow idle reserves to be responsive to sudden surges in demand.

A utility typically uses a wide range of units to make up its capacity. Of the electricity generated in 1979, coal accounted for 47.8 percent, nuclear for 11.4 percent, hydropower for 12.4 percent, natural gas for 14.7 percent, and oil for 13.5 percent.

The wide range of units used by electic utilities reflects the fluctuating demand for electricity. Utilities rely on coal and nuclear units for base-load generation, and at times of peak demand, they also use gas turbines and other peaking units. Base-load units have high capital costs and low operating costs, while peaking units have low capital costs and high operating costs.

Oil and gas are used in peaking units and also in base-load steam units. The Powerplant and Industrial Fuel Use Act of 1978 was passed with the objective of minimizing the use of oil and gas by electric utilities in steam base-load units. The act prohibits the use of oil or gas in new base-load plants (except where environmental, technical, or economic factors make their use imperative), but does permit the use of gas in peaking units.

Many generating units have the capability of burning more than one fuel, and the act requires DOE to order the conversion of existing units from oil or gas to coal, if such conversion appears to be technically and economically feasible; exceptions are made for environmental or other factors. Units that are not capable of switching to coal may be required by DOE to use coal-oil mixtures or mixtures utilizing fuels other than oil or gas. Coal-burning units are not permitted to switch to oil or gas.

The switch to coal will involve expanded outlays on pollution-control equipment such as scrubbers. The act therefore establishes a loan program to assist utilities that cannot raise the necessary funds for the environmental-control equipment.

Reserve-Requirement Models

Electric utilities install capacity that is in excess of their anticipated peak demand. This reserve margin provides an insurance in case demand is greater than anticipated or capacity is unavailable. Capacity may become unavailable because of forced or scheduled outage. *Forced outage* refers to equipment failures, while *scheduled outage* refers to shutdowns for maintenance purposes.

The choice of a reserve margin is an important decision in that overcapacity or undercapacity carries substantial penalties. An excessive reserve margin means that the utility will have unnecessarily high fixed costs. Too low a reserve margin would result in frequent electricity curtailments, which would cause hardship to consumers.

There are three basic methods used by utilities in selecting a reserve margin. In the standard percent-reserve method, the reserve margin is set as a fixed percentage of the anticipated peak demand. The fixed percentage is based on convention or past practice. Such a method is simple, but it does not allow for factors that could cause optimal reserve-margin requirements to change.

In the loss of largest generator method, the reserve is set equal to the size of the largest generating unit. Thus, in the event of a forced outage of the largest unit, the utility is insured against having to curtail supply.

The probabilistic method is the appropriate approach to computing the reserve margin. In this method, the loss-of-load probability (LOLP) function is developed, which indicates the probability that load will exceed available capacity. Specifically, the LOLP is defined as the number of days in which a loss-of-load incident occurs divided by the number of days in the period. Weekends and holidays are normally omitted in computing the period, so that a year is defined to consist of 250 days. Hence, if a loss of load is expected 1 day in 10 years, the LOLP is 1/2500, or 0.0004. The higher is the reserve margin, the lower is the LOLP, so that if LOLP is plotted on the vertical axis and the gross reserve margin is plotted on the horizontal axis, the curve will slope down to the right.

To derive a LOLP function it is necessary to develop separate generation and demand probability distributions. A generation probability distribution is illustrated next assuming two generators, each with a rated capacity of 100 MW and each having a forced-outage rate of 4 percent. The outage rate implies that for each unit there is a 4 percent probability of it being unavailable and a 96 percent probability of it being available.

Since there are two generating units, there are four possible events: (1) both units are operable; (2) only the first unit is operable; (3) only the second unit is operable; and (4) neither unit is operable. The probability of each event is calculated and presented as follows:

Probability of 200 MW availability $(0.96)(0.96) = 0.9216$
Probability of 100 MW availability $(0.96)(0.04) = 0.0384$
Probability of 100 MW availability $(0.04)(0.96) = 0.0384$
Probability of   0 MW availability $(0.04)(0.04) = \underline{0.0016}$

Total of probabilities   1.0000

The load-demand distribution is based on an organization of load demands (as predicted by an economic model) into blocks. The distribution shows the probability of the load exceeding a given block level.

The generating and demand probability distributions can be combined to identify the probability that load exceeds capacity. The demand distribution indicates the probability that demand will exceed a certain level, and the generating distribution indicates the probability that such a level of capacity will be available. The product of the probabilities is the probability of a loss-of-load incident. Clearly for a given demand distribution, the greater is the capacity, the lower is the LOLP.

The question arises as to what is the optimal reserve margin, that is, by how much should capacity exceed anticipated peak demand. The advantage of a high reserve margin is that it reduces the LOLP. Of course, when a utility feels that a probability of a load loss is imminent, it can take steps to mitigate the event. First, it can purchase electricity from neighboring utilities; however, peak demand is usually weather-induced, so neighboring utilities are not likely to have much surplus power either. Second, it can curtail power to interruptible customers, reduce voltage, apply load controls to air conditioners and water heaters, and in other ways try to reduce demand. To the extent that these efforts are not fully successful, brownouts or blackouts will occur.

The costs created by a blackout cannot be easily measured, but they are certainly enormous. The consumption of electricity gives rise to great consumer surplus; that is, the price the consumer pays for electricity is far lower than the price he or she would be willing to pay. If electricity is curtailed, this consumers' surplus is lost, thus creating societal losses that far exceed the value of the curtailed electricity.

The consumers' surplus is the area under the demand curve, and in theory, this area can be calculated by integrating under the curve. However, it must be emphasized that the demand curve that we are dealing with here is the demand for electricity in the very short run, a period in which the consumer has few choices or options open to him or her. This means that the demand is highly inelastic, particularly for very small amounts. The value of electricity in such uses as refrigeration and lighting is very high, which contributes to the inelasticity of demand.

The disadvantage of a high reserve margin is that the utility is carrying substantial excess capacity. For example, if the utility has a peak demand of 10,000 MW and capacity of 11,000 MW, its reserve margin is 10 percent. To increase its reserve margin to 20 percent, it would have to add a 1000-MW unit. The cost of a new base-load 1000-MW unit, when constructed, will involve current dollar outlays in excess of a billion dollars. Of course, the reserve-margin increment could be achieved far more quickly and cheaply by adding peaking units, but in any event, the upgrading of the reserve margin will substantially increase fixed costs.

The effect of an increased reserve margin on variable cost depends on the manner in which the reserve increase was attained. If it came about by the addition of a base unit, total variable costs may actually decrease. The utility can operate the new base unit in place of existing peaking units, with savings in fuel costs that outweigh the increase in nonfuel operating and maintenance costs. However, if new peaking units are added, total variable costs will probably increase.

The optimal reserve margin corresponds to the point at which societal cost is minimized. The societal-cost equation is written as follows:

$$TSC_i = CSC_i + UC_i \qquad (5.1)$$

where TSC = total societal cost associated with reserve margin i
$\quad CSC_i$ = consumer-loss cost caused by brownouts/blackouts associated with reserve margin i
$\quad UC_i$ = utility fixed and variable cost associated with reserve margin i

As the reserve margin increases, the possibility of brownouts or blackouts increase and the consumer-loss cost falls. However, the increase in reserve margin will raise utility fixed costs. The optimal reserve margin is reached when the decrease in consumer cost is offset by an increase in utility cost. This rule, of course, is the analogue to the familiar marginal-analysis rule, which means that TSC_i is at a minimum when

$$MCSC_i = MUC_i \qquad (5.2)$$

where $MCSC$ = marginal consumer-loss cost at reserve margin i
$\quad MUC_i$ = marginal utility cost at reserve margin i

Optimized Generation-Planning Model

As discussed earlier, certain types of plants (for example, coal-fired units) have low operating costs and high capital costs, while other types of plants (for example, gas turbines) have high operating costs and low capital costs. This heterogeneity gives utilities considerable flexibility in deciding what mix of plants to employ in meeting a given pattern of electricity demand.

In the long run, utilities have to decide what particular selection of base-load, intermediate, and peaking units should be built. In the short run, utilities have to decide the rate at which such units will be operated.

The short-run policy is described by the principle of merit-order dispatch, according to which plants will be dispatched in order of their operating cost. Efficient, low-operating cost, base-load units will be used first, while high-operating-cost, peak-load units will be brought on line last. Because peak units are used only if demand cannot be satisfied by base and intermediate units, they have low capacity factors, while base-load units have high capacity factors.

Using a linear program (LP), it is possible to identify a strategy that will minimize both long-run and short-run costs; that is, the LP will indicate the optimal mix of plants and the optimal rate at which such plants should be operated. Described next is the LP approach formulated by Anderson and Turvey for electric-utility-supply planning.[5]

The objective function of the Anderson LP is to minimize the sum or discounted capital and operating costs over a future time period. This function can be written as follows:

$$\text{Min} \sum_{t=1}^{T} \sum_{j=1}^{J} C_{jv} \cdot X_{jv} \sum_{t=1}^{T} \sum_{v=-V}^{t} \sum_{j=1}^{J} F_{jvt} U_{jvt} \qquad (5.3)$$

where C_{jv} = capital costs per megawatt of capacity for plant type j commissioned in year v

X_{jv} = capacity (in megawatts) of plant type j (for example, coal-fired unit) commissioned in year v

F_{jvt} = discounted operating costs at time t per megawatt-hour of electricity generated by plant j commissioned in year v

U_{jvt} = electricity generation (in megawatt-hours) by plant j commissioned in year v

The objective function is optimized by identifying the capacities (X_{jv}) and operating rates (U_{jvt}) that will minimize cost, subject to the following three constraints.

The first constraint is that total electricity generated must meet demand, where demand is exogenously specified. Denoting demand as Q_t, this constraint is written as follows:

$$\sum_{j=1}^{J} \sum_{v=-V}^{t} U_{jvt} \geqslant Q_t \qquad (5.4)$$

The second constraint is that no plant can be operated above its available capacity. Available capacity is less than nameplate capacity because of scheduled and forced outages. The available capacity of a plant is calculated by multiplying nameplate capacity (X_{jv}) by an availability factor (A_{jv}). The availability factor, which lies between 0 and 1, indicates the percent of time the plant can be operated. The second constraint is written as follows (note there are 8760 hours in a year):

$$0 \leqslant U_{jvt} \leqslant A_{jv} \cdot X_{jv} \cdot 8760 \qquad (5.5)$$

The third constraint is that the reserve-margin target be met; that is, nameplate capacity should exceed peak demand by the specified reserve margin. Denoting peak demand by PQ_t and reserve margin by M, this constraint is written as follows:

$$\sum_{j=1}^{J} \sum_{v=-V}^{t} A_{jv} \cdot X_{jv} \geq (1 + M)PQ_t \tag{5.6}$$

The model described here is relatively simple. In practice, the planning models used by the electric-utility industry are highly complicated and contain procedures to deal with probabilistic factors (for example, outages) and the seasonal capacity variations associated with hydropower.

Evaluating New and Existing Technologies

The methodology of levelized cost provides a basis for comparing different publicly owned, funded, or regulated investments in new or existing technologies to produce energy. For instance, a public electric utility confronted with alternative technological investments can use levelized costing to identify which technology will permit it to offer electricity at the lowest price per kilowatt-hour. Or the Department of Energy (DOE) can use levelized costing to identify which investment technology for coal gasification is associated with the lowest price per million Btu's of gas.

The result of a levelized cost analysis is a constant or levelized price per unit of energy to be charged over the lifetime of the system. The levelized price will just recover all fixed and variable costs and also repay debtors and provide a return to stockholders. The levelized price can be viewed as generating that level of revenue that will create a net present value of zero.

This section discusses a methodology for levelized costing that was developed under a contract to the Energy Research and Development Administration (now part of DOE).[6] Similar methodologies have been developed at the Oakridge National Laboratory, also part of DOE.[7]

Capital-Recovery Factor

The capital-recovery factor is used to calculate the uniform annual payment that will amortize a loan over a given period of time. The formula for the capital-recovery factor is

$$CRF = \frac{i}{1 - (1 + c)^{-L}} \tag{5.7}$$

where CRF = capital recovery factor
    c = cost of capital
    L = period of loan

For a business or utility, the interest rate does not fully represent the cost of capital. The sources of capital include debt, preferred stock, and equity stock. Associated with each of these sources is a cost, and the weighted average of these costs (with the weights corresponding to the capital mix) is the cost of capital.

To illustrate the computation of the capital-recovery factor, let us asume that the lifetime of the investment is 30 years and the cost of capital is 12 percent. Then then the capital-recovery factor is

$$CRF = \frac{0.12}{1 - 0.033} = 0.1241$$

The capital-recovery factor is multiplied by the amount of capital to get the annual payments required for amortization. If the capital in the example is for $100,000, then the payment is $12,410 a year for 30 years.

Present Value of Capital Investment

The present value of capital investment is a metric used in the capitalization of the project. The calculation of present value is complicated by considerations of inflation and timing. There are two inflation rates: the general inflation rate and the rate of inflation in capital goods. There are three key years: the base year, the year of commercial operation, and the year (or years) of the investment outlay.

The following formula is used to calculate the present value of capital investment, expressed in current dollars, as of the year of commercial operation:

$$PVCI = (1 + n2)^P \sum_t \left[CI_t \left(\frac{1 + n2}{1 + c} \right)^j \right] \qquad (5.8)$$

where $PVCI$ = present value of capital investment in current dollars as of year of commercial operation
    $n2$ = rate of inflation in capital goods
    CI_t = capital investments in year t in base-year dollars
    j = period of years between investment outlay and the year after commercial operation starts
    c = cost of capital
    P = period of years between commercial operation and base year

In equation 5.8, the capital-investment values are costed as of base year. However, if the project is implemented, the actual outlays will be quite different because of inflation in capital costs. Hence the presence of the term $n2$.

To illustrate equation 5.8, let us assume that the inflation rate for capital goods is 15 percent, the cost of capital is 12 percent, the starting year of commercial operation is 1990, and the base year is 1978. Then the present value of an outlay of $50 million in 1983 is

$$PVCI\,83 = (1 + 0.15)^{12}\;50,000,000\;\;\frac{1 + 0.15}{1 + 0.12}^{\,-7}$$

$$= 5.350 \times 50,000,000 \times 0.831 = 222,292,500$$

Similarly, the present value of an outlay of $100 million in 1984 is

$$PVCI84 = (1 + 0.15)^{12}\;100,000,000\;\left(\frac{1 + 0.15}{1 + 0.12}\right)^{-6}$$

$$= 5.350 \times 100,000,000 \times 0.853 = 456,355,000$$

If 1983 and 1984 are the only years of the capital outlays, then the present value of the capital investment is

$$PVI = PVI38 + PVI84$$

$$= 222,292,500 + 456,355,000 = 678,647,500$$

Annualized Fixed-Charge Rate

To condense the various fixed costs into a single rate, the annualized fixed-charge rate is calculated. The formula is

$$FCR = \frac{1}{1-t}\left(CRF - \frac{t}{L}\right) + B1 + B2 \tag{5.9}$$

where FCR = fixed-charge rate
   t = effective income tax rate
   CRF = capital-recovery factor
   L = lifetime of investment
   $B1$ = property tax rate (as a ratio of the present value of the capital investment)
   $B2$ = insurance premium and other fixed-charge rate (expressed as $B1$)

In the previous illustrations, the capital-recovery factor was 0.1241, the effective income tax rate was 40 percent, and the lifetime of the investment was 30 years. Adding to these data the assumptions of a property tax rate of 1.5 percent and a miscellaneous fixed-charge rate of 0.5 percent, the fixed-charge rate is

$$FCR = \frac{1}{1 - 0.4} \left(0.1241 - \frac{0.4}{30} \right) + 0.015 + 0.005$$

$$= (1.67 \times 0.1108) + 0.02 = 0.205$$

Levelized Fixed Charge

The levelized fixed charge represents the constant annual payment that will recover all fixed costs including a return on capital. The formula to calculate the levelized fixed charge expressed in base-year dollars is

$$LFC = (1 + n1)^{-P} (FCR \times PVCI) \tag{5.10}$$

where LFC = levelized fixed charge in base-year dollars
$\quad\quad n1$ = general inflation rate
$\quad\quad P$ = period of years between commercial operation and base year
$\quad\quad FCR$ = fixed-charge rate
$\quad\quad PVCI$ = present value of capital investment in current dollars as of commercial operation

In equation 5.10 the levelized fixed charges are calculated by multiplying the fixed-charge rate by the present value of capital investment. This estimate is then deflated so as to put levelized charges on a base-year dollar basis.

Assuming the general inflation rate is 10 percent and applying the data from our previous illustrations, the levelized fixed charges are

$$LFC = (1 + 0.10)^{-12} (0.205 \times 222,292,500)$$

$$= 0.319 \times 45,569,962 = 14,536,817$$

Present Value of Variable Costs

The methods used to calculate the present value of variable costs are identical to those used to calculate the present value of capital costs. The formula is

$$PVVC = (1 + n3)^{P} \sum_{t} \left[VC_{t} \left(\frac{1 + n3}{1 + c} \right)^{j} \right] \tag{5.11}$$

where $PVVC$ = present value of variable costs in current dollars as of year of commercial operation

$n3$ = rate of inflation for variable costs
VC_t = variable costs in year t
P = period of years between commercial operation and base year
j = period of years between cash outlay and the year after the commercial operation starts
c = cost of capital

Variable costs consist of operation, maintenance, and fuel costs. These three elements escalate at different rates, and so it is appropriate to apply equation 5.11 separately for each element.

Levelized Variable Charge

The levelized variable charge represents the constant annual payment that will recover all variable costs. The formula to calculate the levelized variable charge is

$$LVC = (1 + n1)^{-P}(CRF \times PVVC) \qquad (5.12)$$

where LVC = levelized variable charge in base-year dollars
$n1$ = general inflation rate
P = period of years between commercial operation and base year
CRF = capital-recovery factor
$PVVC$ = present value of variable costs in current dollars as of year of commercial operation

Using data from our previous illustrations and assuming that the present value of variable costs is $180 million, the levelized variable charge is

$$LVC = (1 + 0.10)^{-12} (0.1241 \times 90,000,000)$$

$$= 0.319 \times 11,169,000 = 3,562,911$$

Levelized Charge and Levelized Price

The levelized charge represents the constant annual payment that just will recover all fixed and variable costs and provide the required return on capital. The formula to calculate the levelized charge is

$$LC = LFC + LVC \qquad (5.13)$$

where LC = levelized charge in base-year dollars
LFC = levelized fixed charge in base-year dollars
LVC = levelized variable charge in base-year dollars

Using data from our previous illustrations, the levelized charge is

$$LC = 14{,}536{,}817 + 3{,}562{,}911 = 18{,}099{,}728$$

To calculate the levelized price, the levelized charge must be divided by the expected output of the energy facility. Let us assume that the facility is a power plant. If so, its energy output is calculated as follows:

$$EO = RCAP \times CAPF \times HOURS \qquad (5.14)$$

where EO = energy output in megawatt-hours
$RCAP$ = capacity in megawatts
$CAPF$ = capacity factor
$HOURS$ = number of hours in a year

If the facility has a capacity of 100 MW and a capacity factor of 50 percent, then the energy output is

$$EO = 100 \times 0.50 \times 8760 = 438{,}000$$

The levelized unit price, which in this case is dollars per megawatt-hour or mills per kilowatt-hour, is calculated as

$$LUP = \frac{LC}{EO} = \frac{18{,}099{,}728}{438{,}000} = 41.32 \qquad (5.15)$$

where LUP = levelized unit price in base-year dollars per megawatt-hour
LC = levelized charge in base-year dollars
EO = energy output in megawatt-hours

If the facility charges a price of $41.32 per megawatt-hour for each of the 30 years of the facility's lifetime, it will just recover all fixed and variable costs and provide the required return on capital. Because of inflation, however, such a pricing policy will not be adopted. If it were, it would involve overcharges in the early years that would be compensated by undercharges in the latter years. Thus levelized costing is not a guide to pricing strategy.

The purpose of a levelized cost analysis is to aid in the selection of energy technologies. A comparison of levelized unit prices allows the policymakers to assess which energy option would provide society with the least-cost technology for a given energy output.

Tax Preferences

The methodology for levelized cost presented here ignores the availability of investment tax credits and accelerated depreciation schedules. The DOE study cited earlier presents formulas that explicitly incorporate these tax preferences.

The investment tax credit has the effect of reducing the capital required for the project. A tax credit of 10 percent would imply that the actual investment cost would equal only 90 percent of outlay, since 10 percent of the cost would be credited against due taxes. Certain energy investments get special credits under the provisions of the Energy Tax Act. The act provides an additional 10 percent investment tax credit for industrial conservation investments and investments in equipment designed to use solar or wind power to generate electricity. At the same time, new oil- or gas-fired boilers are denied the usual investment tax credit.

In the straight-line depreciation method, an equal amount of the asset's life is depreciated each year of its designated lifetime. In an accelerated method, a greater proportion of the asset's life is charged in the early years. Because depreciation is a deductible item, the effect of accelerated depreciation is to increase after-tax income in the early years and decrease it in the latter years by an equivalent amount. By shifting revenue from the later years to the early years, accelerated depreciation increases the net present value of the project, since the discount factor is higher in the later years.

6

Regulated Energy Pricing

For certain energy forms—in particular, electricity—price is not determined by the market, but is instead set by regulatory commissions using accounting and economic criteria. The need for regulatory pricing arises out of the presence of what are called *natural monopolies.* An industry is considered a natural monopoly if the presence of more than one supplier would involve a significant waste of resources. In the United States, telephone companies and electric utilities are examples of natural monopolies, and the government has accorded such companies the right to be the sole supplier of services in a region, thus allowing for a more efficient utilization of this capital. Concomitant with such a monopoly right, however, is the need for regulation. The company is not allowed to price its product at what the market will bear, but must instead charge what a regulatory body had decided is a just and reasonable rate.

With respect to regulatory pricing or ratemaking, there are two basic stages involved: (1) choosing a rate level and (2) formulating a rate structure. The rate level selected must satisfy the so-called revenue requirement; that is, it must generate revenues that are sufficient to cover the utility's costs as well as provide an adequate return to its stockholders. The formulation of a rate structure involves determining the percentage of the required revenues that will be supplied by each of the customer classes.

The purpose of this chapter is to review the issues involved in ratemaking. The chapter has been organized into five sections. The first two sections describe the theoretical and practical considerations involved in selecting a rate level. The third and fourth sections discuss conventional and innovative rate-structuring methods. The fifth section discusses a simple model to prepare long-run forecasts of electricity price.

Financial Theory and Utility Regulation

To satisfy the revenue requirement, ratemaking commissions must allow utilities to charge a price that will generate revenues sufficient to cover operating and fixed costs and provide a fair and reasonable rate of return on capital. General guidance as to what is fair and reasonable was provided by the Supreme Court in the 1944 *Hope Natural Gas* case.[1] The Court ruled that (1) the return on equity should correspond to return on other investments having equivalent risks and (2) the return should be sufficient to maintain the financial integrity of the enterprise so that it can attract new capital.

Recently, financial theorists have attempted to develop a formulary approach to quantifying what is a reasonable rate of return. This approach involves the use of the capital-asset pricing model (CAPM). This section discusses the CAPM and its use in electric ratemaking.

Portfolio Theory

Investors as a class are a risk-averse group in that they will buy more risky securities only if it appears that the returns are likely to be high. The objective of portfolio theory, as introduced by Markowitz, is to satisfy such risk aversion by identifying the mix of securities that will minimize the risk associated with earning a given level of return.[2]

A portfolio is characterized by its expected value and its variance. The *expected value* indicates the return the investor is most likely to earn, and the *variance* shows the manner in which the actual return could deviate from the expected value. The objective of the risk-averse investor is to minimize the variance corresponding to a given expected value, and this can be achieved by diversifying the portfolio to include securities with dissimilar variances.

If an investor places all his or her funds in a single security with an expected return of 15 percent and a variance of 3 percent, then these are the characteristics with the portfolio. If, instead, he or she divides the funds between two securities each with an expected return of 15 percent and a variance of 3 percent, then the expected value of the portfolio will still be 15 percent, but the variance will have most probably been reduced. The variance will still be 3 percent only in the extremely unlikely event that the two securities move in perfect tandem. Otherwise, the variance of the portfolio will be less than 3 percent, and if there is perfect negative covariance between the two securities, then the variance of the portfolio will be reduced to 0 percent.

Capital-Asset Pricing Model

The capital-asset pricing model (CAPM) was developed by Sharpe and others, and builds on portfolio theory.[3] The CAPM starts from the premise that the risk associated with a given security, as approximated by its variance, can be divided into unsystematic and systematic components. The unsystematic component is that part of the variance which is specific to the security. The systematic component is that part of the variance attributable to the general volatility in the security market.

Portfolio diversification reduces risk only to the extent that the portfolio contains securities with dissimilar variances. This means that only unsystematic risk can be eliminated by diversification. Systematic risk cannot be controlled, in that it reflects the tendency of security returns to fluctuate in parallel.

Because unsystematic risk can be eliminated, the proponents of CAPM assert that there should be no reward for bearing such risk. Premiums should, however, be paid for bearing systematic risk, and the premium should be proportional to the degree of systematic risk.

While almost all securities are subject to systematic risk, the degree of systematic risk is not constant across securities. To compute the degree of systematic risk associated with a given security, a metric known as *beta* is calculated. The beta indicates the volatility of that security vis-à-vis the overall security market.

A beta value of 1 is assigned to an aggregate measure of market return, such as the Dow Jones or the New York Stock Exchange indexes. The beta of a given security depends on its association with the market index. If every time the market index changes by 10 percent, the security changes by 5 percent, then its beta is 0.5 (5/10). Clearly, the higher is the beta, the greater is the systematic risk. If a security has a beta less than 1, it is relatively stable, while if its beta exceeds 1, it is more volatile than the overall market.

In the CAPM, the return on a given security is assumed to be determined by its beta, the overall market return, and the risk-free rate of return. The equation for computing the return on a given security is

$$R_j = R_f + b(R_m - R_f) \tag{6.1}$$

where R_j = return of security j
R_f = return on risk-free security
R_m = return on market index
b = beta for security j

In the preceding equation, the return predicted for a given security is proportional to its beta. A beta value of 0 would imply that the security should earn a risk-free return (such as on the U.S. Treasury bill). A beta value of 1 would imply that the return on the security should equal that of the overall market. A beta value of between 0 and 1 would imply that the return on the security should be greater than the risk-free rate but lower than the overall market return. A beta value of greater than 1 would imply that the return on the security should exceed that of the overall market.

Suppose that the market return is 18 percent and the risk-free return is 14 percent. Then a security with a beta of 0.0 should earn 14 percent, a security with a beta of 1.0 should earn 18 percent, a security with a beta of 0.5 should earn 16 percent, and a security with a beta of 1.5 should earn 20 percent.

The CAPM, while offering a powerful tool for assessing the relationship between rate of return and risk, is not without problems. Its premise that un-systematic risk should not be compensated is questionable. This assumes that all investors are sufficiently sophisticated to diversify to a level that eliminates all unsystematic risk. Even if such a situation prevailed, it is hard to believe that, other things being equal, investors would not demand a premium to hold securities with high unsystematic risk.

Another problem with the CAPM is that it becomes inapplicable when the risk-free return exceeds the market return. This situation is likely to occur in periods of "stagflation," when inflation drives up the risk-free rate while reces-sion dampens stock-market returns.

Application of the Model

A ratemaking commission can use the CAPM to ascertain what return the utility stockholders should earn. This involves determining a value for R_j in equation 6.1. To make this determination, three inputs are necessary: (1) a risk-free rate, (2) a market return, and (3) the beta value for the utility stock.

The risk-free return can be the yield on a Treasury bill, while the market return can be the sum of capital appreciation and dividends on an overall stock-market index. The beta for the utility stock can be calculated by the application of simple regression analysis. To do this, it is necessary to rewrite equation 6.1 as follows:

$$R_j - R_f = b(R_m - R_f) \qquad (6.2)$$

To estimate the b in equation 6.2, the time series $R_j - R_f$ is regressed against the time series $R_m - R_f$, with the intercept suppressed. The estimated regression value of b indicates the beta for security j.

The use of beta in regulatory proceedings is suitable only if the value of the beta for the utility's stock remains stable. However, empirical research has shown that beta is far from stable. Hyman and Egan calculated beta values for electric-utility stocks for each year from 1959 to 1978, and their calculations showed the beta varying from 0.139 (1959) to 0.952 (1965).[4]

Regulatory Practice

The question arises as to whether regulators use the CAPM or some other ap-proach in setting allowable rates of return for electric utilities. The answer is that the CAPM is considered an arcane and untested tool and is at this point applied by a minority of regulatory commissions. In 1979, Harrington sent questionnaires to fourteen states requesting information as to their position on CAPM.[5] Oregon required the use of CAPM; Missouri and Pennsylvania planned to use it; Illinois, Maine, and Minnesota were considering its use; and eight other states responded that its use was possible. None of the respondents ruled out its future application.

Hagerman and Ratcherford used regression analysis to identify the economic and political factors that influence the rate of return on equity for electric utilities allowed by regulatory commissions.[6] Among the economic variables tested was the beta coefficient. As expected, the allowed rate of return was positively related to the beta, but the relationship was statistically insignificant. The allowed rate of return also was positively related to the debt-equity ratio, another proxy for risk, and in this case, the estimate was statistically significant. Two political variables also were found to be statistically significant—the size of the utility and the length of the term of the commissioners. The allowed return was positively related to the size of the utility, implying that larger utilities have specialized expertise that enables them to win higher returns from the ratemaking bodies. The allowed return was positively correlated to the length of the term of the commissioners, implying that the longer the term, the less the concern about renewal and so the greater the tendency to allow high returns.

Rate-Level Issues

The choice of an adequate rate of return on equity is not the only controversial area in the determination of an adequate rate level. Other matters that affect rate levels are the subject of debate, and some of the more important of these are discussed in this section.

Timing of Revenues

It is well known that a dollar today is preferable to a dollar tomorrow. This is especially true in today's environment of high inflation and interest rates. Electric utilities have, therefore, actively campaigned for practices designed to increase current revenues at the expense of future expenses. These practices do not affect the total amount of revenues received during the period; they merely alter the timing.

From the utility's viewpoint, a transferral of revenues from future periods to more current periods is tantamount to an interest-free loan. However, the utility's customers who are, in effect, extending this loan through higher current electric rates are opposed to such measures. They are not receptive to the argument that higher current rates will be compensated by lower future rates. Such an argument is particularly unconvincing to those customers who expect to die or move away in the near future.

The manner in which the utility is allowed to treat the capital tied up in construction of new facilities has a direct bearing on the timing of revenues. If the value of the construction work in progress (CWIP) is included in the rate base, then the utility is allowed to raise its rates to cover the interest on the capital invested in the construction of new facilities. In the alternative method, the interest is added to the cost of the plant and recovered during the life of the facility.

The treatment of investment tax credits and accelerated depreciation also can alter the timing of revenues, with the nature of the alteration depending on whether the utility practices flowthrough or normalized accounting. In the flowthrough system, electric rates are based on actual taxes paid, thereby immediately passing on to the consumer the tax benefits of accelerated depreciation and investment credits. In the normalized system, the tax savings are placed in a deferred tax account, which is subtracted from the rate base, and so only a part of the current year's tax savings shows up in reduced rates. For the utility, normalized accounting is the preferred alternative.

Regulatory Lag

Electric rates are usually set on the basis of costs in a test year, where the test year is generally the year preceding the submission of the petition. It takes a year to proffer a rate case before a commission. These two factors imply that rates can be based on costs that are as much as 2 years out of date. This phenomenon is called *regulatory lag*.

Regulatory lag acts to squeeze utility returns below that which the commission intended. The effect of regulatory lag is most harmful during periods of rapid inflation. In these periods, the utility will be charging rates that are too low in light of actual costs.

To mitigate the effect of regulatory lag, some states have adopted a future test year as opposed to a historical test year. That is, rates are based on projected costs, not past costs. Many states, however, are reluctant to adopt a future test year because it is hard to verify projected costs.

A more common, albeit less comprehensive, solution to regulatory lag is afforded by the automatic fuel-adjustment clause. This clause allows the utility to pass on the increased fuel costs to the consumer without a regulatory hearing. The clause has become popular as a result of the continuous fuel-price increases.

The fuel-adjustment clause has been attacked by consumer groups, who point out that it removes the incentive for cost minimization. The utilities respond that they have little or no control over fuel prices, and so should not be expected to bear the burden of fuel-cost escalation.

The Public Utility Regulatory Policies Act (PURPA) of 1978 (Pub. L. 95-617) contains provisions to ensure that automatic adjustment clauses are structured in a manner that will give the utility an incentive to control costs. It states that no electric utility may increase any rate pursuant to an automatic adjustment clause unless (1) such clause is determined not less than every 4 years by the appropriate state regulatory authority, after an evidentiary hearing, to provide incentives for the efficient use of resources by the utility, and (2) such clause is reviewed not less often than every 2 years by the state regulatory authority to ensure the maximum economies in those operations and purchases which affect the rates to which such clause applies.

Conventional Rate Structures

In setting rate levels, the concern is with choosing a level that will generate revenues sufficient to cover costs and compensate capital. With respect to determining rate structure, the central issue is identifying the percentage of revenues that are to be contributed by various classes of customers.

Historically, utilities have followed a non-time-differentiated rate structure, which does not differentiate as to the time of day at which such electricity is consumed. Because the cost of generating power varies according to the time of use, the conventional non-time-differentiated rate structures have been criticized by economists and others as not adequately reflecting consideration of economic efficiency. Nevertheless, a review of the conventional structure provides a useful point of departure from which to evaluate the innovations proposed.

Rate and Cost Classification

Electric utilities have traditionally grouped customers into various classes, with each class subject to a different rate. A typical scheme would include such classes as residential, commercial, industrial, and public authorities. Such classification is necessary because the cost of service varies sharply according to the nature of the customers' electricity needs. For example, industrial customers, who are served at high voltage, impose smaller losses on the system than residential customers, who are served at low voltage. In setting up rate classes, the objective is to group customers with similar demand characteristics into a class. Conflicting with the requirement to have homogeneity within a class is the necessity of avoiding a multiplicity of rate classes. The actual rate classification reflects a compromise between these two objectives.

To set rates by customer class, it is necessary to allocate the costs by customer class. The costs of producing electricity are related to the number of customers, the amount of electric energy generated (measured in kilowatt-hours or megawatt-hours), and the amount of generating capacity (measured in kilowatts or megawatts). Each category of cost—customer, energy, and capacity (or demand)—must be allocated to each customer class according to its responsibility for creating that cost. Once this has been done, rates can set for each class at a level that will recover allocated costs.

Customer- and Energy-Cost Allocations

The *customer costs* include those cost elements which vary according to the number of customers served and which will be incurred by the utility even if the customer uses no electricity. Capital or fixed customer costs include investments in meters and those parts of the distribution system required to serve the minimum load to the customer. Operating customer costs include expenses related to meter reading and the maintenance of customer accounts.

Energy costs are those which depend on the amount of electricity generated and include expenditures on fuel and operating labor. A significant proportion of the energy costs are fuel costs, which are related to electricity generated by the heat rate (Btu/kWh) and the type of fuel. A peak-load generating unit, such as a gas turbine, has high fuel costs per kilowatt-hour because it has a high heat rate and uses an expensive fuel. A base-load coal unit, however, has low fuel costs per kilowatt-hour because it has a low heat rate and uses an inexpensive fuel.

There is not much debate about the manner in which customer and energy costs should be allocated to the different customer classes. Customer costs are allocated according to the number of customers in the class, with appropriate weights applied to reflect differences in the nature of the customer service. Energy costs are allocated in proportion to the electricity consumed by the class, with corrections made for differences in loss factors.

Demand-Cost Allocation

Demand costs are defined as those cost elements which depend on the amount of capacity in place, where capacity consists of generating and transmission facilities and that portion of the distribution system not classified as customer-related. Demand costs also include those operating expenditures which do not vary with electric energy generated or customers. The demand costs per kilowatt depend on the type of generating facility. Infrequently, used peak-load units, such as gas turbines, have low capital costs per kilowatt and can be brought on line quickly. Base-load units, such as coal and nuclear power plants, have high capital costs per kilowatt and take 10 years or more to bring on line.

If the electricity consumed by the different customer classes exhibited perfect parallelism, the allocation of demand costs could be in proportion to the electricity consumption. This, however, is not the case. The residential class shows considerable volatility, and its contribution to peak demand is much higher than its contribution to annual electricity sales.

In assessing demand patterns, it is necessary to distinguish between the class peaks and the system peak. The *class peak* refers to the maximum load imposed by a particular class on the utility. The *system peak* refers to the aggregate maximum load imposed on the utility. The different class peaks do not coincide, and so the sum of the class peaks is greater than the system peak, giving rise to diversity.

A number of methods, none entirely satisfactory, are available to allocate demand costs by customer class. In the peak-responsibility method, demand costs are allocated to customer class according to their contribution to peak demand. The justification for this method is that peak demand is the determinant of total-capacity requirement, and so costs should be allocated in proportion to peak. However, while the total capacity required is determined by peak, the mix of capacity is based on the shape of the load curve. If the load curve is relatively flat, most of the capacity will be made up of base units. If, instead, there is a sharp peak that is considerably in excess of base, then the utility will maintain a greater proportion of cheap peaking units. Thus capacity costs depend on factors other than peak demand, and an exclusive reliance on peak as a basis for cost allocation can produce inequitable results.

In the class-maximum demand method, costs are allocated in proportion to the class peaks. Thus each class is treated as it would be if it were the only class on the system. No preference is given to those classes whose demands do not coincide with the system peak. Instead, the benefits of diversity are distributed equally to the different classes. This is not a very satisfactory premise, and so this method is also not completely equitable.

Rate Structures

Once costs have been allocated by customer class, rates can be set at level that will recover such costs. In principle, the rate schedule must include three components corresponding to customer, energy, and demand costs. However, utilities have not generally levied customer charges and have levied demand charges only on large commercial and industrial customers. In the interest of simplicity, utilities have relied on the energy charge as the primary method for recouping all costs.

For the residential customer, the energy charge has been the exclusive pricing mechanism, and the typical residential electric bill depends solely on the amount of energy (measured in kilowatt-hours) used during the month. Residential energy charges are not constant per kilowatt-hour, but follow a declining-block pattern, with successive blocks having a lower cents per kilowatt-hour charge. For example, Boston Edison customers pay $1.94 for the first 15 kWh or less per month, 5.6 ¢/kWh for the next 35 kWh, 4.3 ¢/kWh for the next 50 kWh, and so on, with consumption in excess of 1000 kWh being billed at 1.4 ¢/kWh. The rationale behind the high charge for the first block is to implicitly cover customer charges. The arguments in favor of successive declining blocks is less clear in that it is not apparent that additional loads can be served at lower costs.

For large commercial and industrial customers, the tariff typically includes a separate demand charge (based on maximum kilowatts used) and energy charge. The demand charge is traditional among industrial customers because the level of their use warrants the use of special meters to record maximum demand. Both demand and energy charges are often subject to a declining-block structure, with successive blocks costing progressively less.

In practice, the monthly demand charge does not always depend on the maximum kilowatts used by the customer during the months. Many utilities have a ratchet clause whereby the billing demand is equal to the maximum demand imposed by the customer during the last 11 months or some percentage thereof.

The tariff of the Fall River Electric Light Company illustrates the conventional rate structure for commercial and industrial customers. The billing demand is based on the maximum 15-minute measured kilowatt used in the month, but not less than 50 percent of the maximum demand established during the preceding 11 months and not less than 25 kW. There is a $70 charge for the first 25 kW of demand or less, a $1.70 per kilowatt charge for the next 275 kW, a $1.45 per kilowatt charge for the next 300 kW, and a charge of $1.35 per kilowatt for each additional kilowatt of demand. With respect to energy, there is a 1.04 ¢/kWh charge for the first 30,000 kWh, a 0.64 ¢/kWh charge for the next 50,000 kWh, and a 0.44¢ charge for all additional kilowatt-hours of consumption. The customer is also subject to a fuel-adjustment clause, where the bill is increased or decreased to reflect changes in the cost of fuel used for generating power by the utility or its wholesale supplier of electricity.

Innovative Rate Structures

In the aftermath of the 1973 oil embargo, increasing attention was devoted to promoting a more efficient utilization of energy resources. In this context, the conventional rate structures employed by the utilities were criticized as inequitable and inefficient, and a number of innovative alternatives were suggested.

However, it is not apparent that these alternatives are practical or universally applicable, and at this time, evaluative research is still being conducted.

The Public Utility Regulatory Policies Act (PURPA) of 1978 (Pub. L. 95-617) has required that the state commissions, who are responsible for the rates charged by the investor-owned utilities, investigate various innovative rate-structuring practices. The commissions should adopt them if it appears that such adoption would promote (1) the conservation of energy supplied by electric utilities, (2) the optimization of the efficiency of use of facilities and resources by electric utilities, and (3) equitable rates to electric consumers.

In this section, a number of innovative rate-design concepts will be discussed. According to a survey carried out by Energy and Environmental Associates for the Department of Energy (henceforth referred to as the DOE survey), some utilities are already offering such rates to their customers on an experimental basis, and these offerings also will be described here.[7]

Time-of-Day Rates

The concept of time-of-day (TOD) rates is not unfamiliar to the average American. Long-distance daytime phone calls cost more than the same calls made after 5:00 P.M. Travelers willing to take "red-eye" flights realize significant savings. However, the concept of TOD electricity rates, where the price paid for electricity varies according to the time of use, is almost totally unfamiliar to the American consumer.

Yet there are strong arguments in favor of TOD rates for electricity. The cost of generating electricity is not constant over time. This variation in cost is especially apparent when we compare peak and off-peak periods. If the demand for electricity at peak rises, the utility will have to invest in new capacity. The same demand increase at an off-peak period would not create such a need. Thus the demand or fixed costs associated with demand at peak are greater than those associated with demand at off-peak. The energy or variable costs associated with peak demand are also greater because such demand is met by relatively inefficient peak units rather than efficient base units.

The use of TOD rates is equitable because it reflects the time dependency of electric generating costs. A kilowatt generated at a peak period is more costly than one generated off-peak, and it is fair that the consumer using peak energy pay more than the consumer using off-peak energy.

Use of TOD rates is efficient because it promotes a more intensive utilization of generating facilities. It shifts demand from peak periods to off-peak periods, thus minimizing the need for new units and allowing a better utilization of existing units.

There are, however, many practical problems associated with TOD rates.

To implement them, special meters that record the time of use must be installed at the customer's site. For small customers, it is debatable whether the cost of such meters is offset by the savings created by more efficient use of generating units.

There is also a question as to the extent to which TOD rates will actually shift loads from peak to off-peak periods. The demand for electricity at time of peak (for example, a summer weekday at 5 P.M.) is highly inelastic, and it is doubtful as to whether customers will, in fact, strongly respond to price signals at such a time.

In fact, the effectiveness of TOD rates in shifting load from peak to off-peak is significantly dependent on the structure of the TOD rate tariff and the composition of the load. In general, load shifting is most likely to occur if, in the tariff, (1) the peak period is defined narrowly, and (2) the peak price is many times in excess of the off-peak price. A narrowly defined peak period (say, 4 P.M. to 8 P.M.) facilitates load shifting, while a broadly defined peak period (say, 8 A.M. to 10 P.M.) makes it difficult to shift loads. The higher is the peak price relative to the off-peak price, the greater is the economic incentive to postpone or sacrifice electricity use. The efficiency of TOD rates is greatest where the customer load is made up of applications that can be deferred. Laundry, dish-washing, and cooking are examples of applications where TOD pricing is likely to induce the consumer to rearrange schedules to shift usage from a peak period to an off-peak period. Air conditioning is an example of an application where the consumer cannot shift loads, only sacrifice them.

The DOE survey identified a number of utilities that were offering TOD rates on an experimental or limited basis. The results of this survey are informative in that they indicate the likely form of future, more universal rates.

The degree of time differentiation varied by utility. In the simplest case, the rating periods were peak and off-peak, while in some instances a distinction was made between peak, shoulder, and off-peak. Moreover, in some instances, rates also were varied by season. However, the off-peak was almost invariably defined to include nighttime (10:00 P.M. to 6:00 A.M.).

For each utility, DOE obtained information on the ratio of peak to off-peak rates. For nonexperimental residential rates, the peak to off-peak price ratio ranged between 1.50:1 and 14.63:1. It should be pointed out that these price ratios were calculated ignoring fuel-adjustment clauses. Since these clauses generally apply to peak and off-peak rates, their application should narrow the price differential between peak and off peak.

The TOD offering of Boston Edison exemplifies the approach identified by the survey. It TOD rate schedule has a seasonal structure and distinguishes between peak, shoulder, and off-peak periods. During June to October, the peak period is 11 A.M. to 5 P.M., and the shoulder period is 9 A.M. to 11 A.M. and 5 P.M. to 10 P.M. The peak rate is 9.25 times the off-peak rate and the shoulder rate is 2.58 times the off-peak rate. During November to May, the peak period is 8 A.M. to 9 P.M. and all other times are considered off-peak. During winter, peak electricity is priced at 2.58 times the off-peak rate.

Marginal-Cost Pricing

There is some confusion as to the terms *TOD pricing, peak-load pricing,* and *marginal-cost pricing.* The terms *TOD pricing* and *peak-load pricing* are used interchangeably to describe rates that vary by time of day in a manner designed to improve the utility's load factor. The term *marginal-cost pricing* is used to describe a particular form of TOD pricing. Strictly used, a marginal-cost rate structure would price each kilowatt-hour at the incremental cost of supplying it at that moment. Since the costs of electricity generation vary according to the time of day, marginal-cost pricing is always TOD pricing, but the reverse is not true.

Some form of marginal costing has been advocated by economists on the grounds that its use will maximize welfare. The marginal cost indicates the additional cost created by producing another kilowatt-hour, and as long as the price is set equal to the marginal cost, resources are being properly allocated. If the price is lower than the marginal cost, then the consumer may be obtaining a good that costs more to produce than it is worth to him or her.

There are at least two problems with implementing a marginal-cost rate structure. The first problem is the difficulty of calculating marginal cost, an issue that is treated at some length in a multivolume report performed for the National Association of the Regulatory Utility Commissioners (NARUC) and sponsored by the Electric Power Research Institute (EPRI) and others.[8] The second problem is that if prices are set equal to marginal cost, the revenue so generated will not necessarily satisfy the *Hope* revenue requirement. According to that requirement, the rates must be set at a level that will cover costs and provide a return to stockholders that is commensurate with the risk involved. If marginal costing is followed, the revenue obtained will satisfy the *Hope* requirement only by coincidence.

Typically marginal cost exceeds average cost at point of production. This means that following the marginal-cost pricing rule will result in total revenues that are in excess of total costs. Since costs are defined to include "normal" or "fair" profit, this means that the utility will earn excessive profits. Protagonists of the marginal-cost approach have argued that this problem is not insoluble, in that rates can be adjusted down to eliminate the excess revenue. In making these adjustments, guidance is provided by the inverse-elasticity rule. The rule states that rates must deviate the greatest amount from marginal cost for those customers with the most inelastic demand. Because of the inelasticity of demand, these customers are least likely to raise their consumption above the optimal level in response to lowered rates.

Interruptible Rates

TOD pricing is not the only method available to the utility for shaving peak demand. One other option is to curtail the load of large industrial or commercial customers at those times when demand appears likely to exceed capacity. Many utilities already offer large customers an interruptible tariff, whereby in return for agreeing to have a portion of their load interrupted at the utility's discretion, the customers obtain a discount or some other monetary advantage.

Interruption may occur by the application of direct controls by the utility or the customers may be asked to reduce their loads. The customers whose curtailment is at request are often subject to financial penalties for noncompliance. In addition, the portion of their load classified as interruptible, as opposed to firm, may be redefined to the amount actually curtailed by the customer, and since interruptible electricity is priced cheaper, this penalizes the customer.

Many utilities place no restriction on the number of times they can interrupt service or on the duration of such interruptions. In other instances, restrictions are specified. According to the DOE survey, for example, Detroit Edison restricts its curtailments to 500 hours a year or 12 hours a day, while Metropolitan Edison will not interrupt power more than 20 times a year or 150 hours a year. Moreover, prior to the power interruption, some utilities are required to give the customer warning. For example, while Detroit Edison is not required to provide advance notice, Metropolitan Edison must give a 15-minute warning.

Interruptible service is offered as a rider to regular (firm) service or under separate contract. When it is offered as a rider, the customer is given a credit for each kilowatt of interruptible load. When interruptible service is priced under separate contract, the rates are lower than those charged for firm service. The credit per kilowatt will depend on the number of hours in the year for which the utility is allowed to interrupt the customers load. The longer the period is, the higher is the credit.

The relationship between the credit and the allowed period of interruption is illustrated in a National Association of the Regulatory Utility Commissioners (NARUC) study.[9] According to the example, a peaking unit has a fixed cost of $30.91 per kilowatt and is run 1000 hours a year. This implies that if a customer is willing to accept 1000 hours of interruption, he should be rewarded to the extent of $30.91 per kilowatt. By similar logic and using data on an intermediate-load unit ($53.86 per kilowatt of capacity) and a base unit ($62.57 per kilowatt), the study shows that a customer willing to accept 3000 hours of interruption should receive a credit of $53.86 per kilowatt and a customer willing to accept 4300 hours of interruption should receive a credit of $62.57 per kilowatt.

Load-Management Rates

Load-management rates, which are offered to residential customers, are the analog to interruptible rates. In the residential sector, indiscriminate load interruptions are not possible, because the curtailment of such end uses as lighting, cooking, and refrigeration would cause serious inconveniences. However, there are certain applications—water heating, space heating, and air conditioning—where interruptions do not create serious disruptions, and some utilities have implemented load programs to control the use of these applications.

Air-conditioner interruptions usually occur in a cycling mode. For example, air conditioners may be turned off 10 minutes per hour under normal summer conditions and 30 minutes per hour under extreme demand conditions.

Water heaters are by far the most commonly controlled device. Control is usually effected by an onsite time switch, with a minority of utilities using remote radio controls. On controlled water heaters, only the lower element is controlled, so some heat is continuously provided to the upper element. Some utilities control heaters for periods of 16 hours per day, thus allowing only one full charging of the water tank, while other utilities effect control for as few as 4 hours per day.

The control of air conditioners or water heaters is clearly an inconvenience to the customer, and so utility customers who agree to load controls are granted preferential electric rates. In the case of water heaters, for example, the nature of the preferential rate depends on whether or not the device is separately metered. If it is, then a relatively low charge will be levied on the separately metered consumption. When there is no separate metering, then the discount is built into the regular residential declining-block structure. The discount is applied to the middle of final kilowatt-hour block, with the size of the discount block corresponding to an assumption about monthly water-heater kilowatt-hour usage.

Residential-Demand Charges

As discussed elsewhere, the residential customer, unlike the industrial customer, is generally subject only to an energy charge. Some utilities have recently introduced voluntary tariffs that include energy and demand charges. Discussed here are some of these demand charges as identified by the DOE survey.

The first class of demand charge is typified by that available to electric space-heating customers of the Public Service Company of Colorado. In addition to a preferential charge based on the kilowatt-hours used during the month, the customers pay a demand charge based on the maximum kilowatt used during any 15-minute period of the month. The first kilowatt costs $6.85, and all additional demand is priced at $2.85 per kilowatt. This demand-based rate system is quite popular and is subscribed to by approximately one-quarter of the eligible customers. The percentage of subscribers is even higher for new customers, many of whom have demand-limiting devices in their homes that shut off low-priority circuits at times of high demand.

The second class of demand-charge system is based on demand above a certain level. For example, the customers of Metropolitan Edison pay $1.10 per kilowatt for every kilowatt by which their maximum demand exceeds 15 kW. There is a ratchet provision built into the Metropolitan Edison tariff, whereby the demand charge is always at least 50 percent of the maximum demand incurred during the last 11 months.

The third class of demand-charge system is designed to penalize customers with poor load factors. The Pennsylvania Power Company offers a discount for all energy in excess of 100 kWh per kilowatt of maximum demand.

The fourth class of demand charge system is differentiated by time of day and season. Wisconsin Public Services Corporation is offering such a system on an experimental basis to approximately seventy-five customers. The demand charge is based on the maximum 15-minute kilowatts recorded during the on-peak period, while demand during off-peak does not count. The charge is seasonally differentiated and costs $2.95 per kilowatt during winter and $3.42 per kilowatt during summer.

The fourth class of demand charge is the theoretically preferred approach. The rationale for a demand charge is that a customer's maximum demand imposes a capacity requirement on the utility. However, when such demand occurs off-peak, it does not impose a commensurate capacity requirement, in that the system is not utilizing all its available capacity.

Lifeline Rates

One of the primary objectives of PURPA is to make electric rates reflect cost of service. However, the act makes an exemption for lifeline rates. If any electric utility does not have a lifeline rate, the state regulatory authority having rate-making authority with respect to such utility shall determine, after an evidentiary hearing, whether such a rate should be implemented by such utility.

Under the usual residential declining-block structure, successive block of energy are priced at progressively preferential rates. Instead, under a lifeline structure, a first block of up to 500 kWh is offered at a minimum cost. The rationale for such an offering is that electricity is a necessity of life, of which a minimum amount must be made available to all consumers at a universally affordable rate. Thus the lifeline rate is motivated by considerations of social welfare rather than economic efficiency.

Because the lifeline block of energy is priced at a lower than normal rate, the rates on successive blocks will have to be raised to compensate for the loss of revenue. Thus the subsidy for the small electricity users is paid by the large electricity users.

Three major criticisms have been levied against lifeline rates. First, it is pointed out that small electricity users are not necessarily poor. For example, affluent singles might well constitute a group with low electricity consumption.

Clearly, subsidizing the electricity consumption of such a group violates social-welfare objectives.

Second, it is argued that subsidizing electricity consumption is inappropriate in this era of energy shortage. Low electricity rates will encourage electricity consumption and thus counterbalance efforts to promote conservation.

The third argument against lifeline rates is that they do not reflect cost of service and so violate one of the fundamental tenets of rate design.

These arguments are indeed valid, and it is highly questionable whether lifeline rates in their basic form effectively achieve their objective of guaranteeing electricity service to those who cannot afford it. However, when carefully structured, lifeline rates can more efficiently fulfill their objective of social welfare. An example of a well-designed lifeline rate is that offered by Duke Power, which is described in an article by Koger.[10]

The Duke lifeline rate is available only to recipients of Supplemental Social Security Income (SSI). To be eligible for SSI, the recipient must be 25% below the federal poverty line, 65 years or older, or handicapped. By restricting the lifeline rate to recipients of SSI, Duke ensures that the beneficiaries of the low electric rates are in fact economically disadvantaged, thus rebutting the first criticism against lifeline rates.

The second argument against lifeline rates, namely, that it promotes excessive electricity consumption, is not very serious as long as lifeline rates are restricted to the genuinely poor. The electricity demand of such consumers is very inelastic, and so low prices will only marginally increase their electricity usage. It is more likely that the monetary savings realized by lower electric bills will be directed toward the consumption of other goods.

In fact, lifeline rates may actually encourage electricity conservation. The corollary of lifeline rates for the poor is higher rates for other residential customers. Since the demand of these customers is likely to be elastic, reductions in overall electricity consumption should result.

The third criticism that lifeline rates are not cost-justified is also debatable. Many poor customers have no air conditioning and use fuels other than electricity for space heating. Their load is made up of refrigeration, lighting, and other base loads. This implies that they have high load factors and so impose relatively stable demands on the system. In contrast, customers with air conditioning have low load factors and contribute more than proportionately to system peak. Consequently, a lifeline rate is cost-justified to the extent that the subscribers to it have better than average load factors.

Cogeneration Rates

The term *industrial cogeneration* is used to refer to the joint production of steam and electricity so that the plant jointly satisfies its requirement for electricity and steam. A cogenerating facility cannot be sure of producing exactly the amount of electricity it requires, so it will need to buy or sell electricity to the utility.

A cogeneration facility will need to sell electricity to the utility if the internally generated electricity is in excess of its requirements. A cogenerating facility may need to purchase electricity from the utility for a number of reasons. Supplemental power will be needed if the amount of internally generated electricity is less than the total requirements. Maintenance power will be needed on those occasions when the cogenerator's facilities are shut down for maintenance. Backup power will be required during periods of unscheduled outage.

From industry's point of view, the economics of an investment in cogeneration are sensitive to the prices at which it buys and sells electricity. Section 210 of Title II of PURPA contains provisions designed to enable the cogenerator to obtain relatively high prices for the electricity it sells and to pay relatively low prices for the electricity it purchases. Pursuant to Section 210, the Federal Energy Regulatory Council (FERC) has recently adopted rules concerning transactions between utilities and cogenerators. While the rules contain numerous exemptions, their basic thrust should measurably enhance the economic viability of industrial cogeneration.

Under the FERC rules, the cogenerator is entitled to purchase electricity from the utility at the regular industrial rate. However, the cogenerator is entitled to sell electricity to the utility at a rate that reflects the costs the utility can avoid by obtaining such electricity. Where the supply of electricity obtained from the cogenerator is of sufficient reliability, the avoided costs should include both variable and capacity-related expenses. Furthermore, the avoided costs should be of an incremental nature; that is, they should reflect theoretical displaced electricity generation and capacity.

The FERC rules also provide that the cogenerator can buy all the electricity it needs from the utility and sell all the electricity that it produces to the utility. Because the price at which the cogenerator sells electricity will be higher than the price at which it buys it, this means that the cogenerator can obtain a net receipt from the utility for each kilowatt-hour it produces.

Electricity-Price Forecasting

The cost of producing electricity varies from utility to utility as a function of such factors as generation mix, reserve margin, load factors, and fuel contracts. The variation in electricity costs has important ramifications for any attempt to forecast electricity prices in that the price of electricity depends directly on the cost of producing it.

The purpose of this section is to describe a methodology that can be used to prepare long-term forecasts of the price of electricity to industrial customers.

Such a methodology is useful to industrial facilities in their energy-planning process. This same methodology also can be used to forecast residential and commercial electricity prices.

Industrial Electricity-Price Patterns

The price of electricity varies dramatically across the nation. Utilities such as Con Edison and Long Island Lighting Company, which are heavily dependent on oil, charge prices that are in some cases 500 percent of the prices charged by utilities such as Washington Water Power and Idaho Power, which are based on cheap hydropower. However, these regional variations in electricity price should narrow over time as limited availability of hydropower sites and restrictions on oil-fired generation propel utilities all over the country to an increasing reliance on coal-fired and perhaps nuclear base-load units.

In general, industrial customers pay a price for electricity that is about 65 percent of the price paid by residential and commercial classes and about 80 percent of the average system price. The industrial class, which accepts service at a high load factor and accepts it directly from the utility's high-voltage transmission lines, imposes a relatively low burden on the utility's generation and distribution capacity requirements in comparison with the residential class, which has a poor load factor and accepts service via an elaborate system requiring expensive stepdown transformers and low-voltage distribution lines. The industrial class also contributes proportionately less to operating and maintenance costs because of such factors as lower line-energy losses and the relatively small number of customer accounts. These savings in fixed and operating and maintenance costs are passed on to the industrial customer in the form of relatively low rates.

It should be pointed out, however, that the class-price differentials have narrowed. In 1973, the industrial price of 1.25 ¢/kWh was 64 percent of the average system price of 1.96 ¢/kWh, while in 1979, the industrial price of 3.02 ¢/kWh was 76 percent of the average price of 3.97 ¢/kWh.[11] This narrowing trend reflects the rapid escalation of fuel costs, which constitute a relatively larger share of the industrial price.

Projecting the Average System Price

The utility must be allowed to charge a price that will satisfy the revenue requirement. For example, if the utility expects to sell 200,000 million kWh, which will cost $10,000 million to produce, then the average system price should be 5 ¢/kWh.

As a prelude to projecting the revenue requirement, it is necessary to develop assumptions (or formal forecasts) about the future electricity-consumption patterns in the service territory of the utility and the fraction of that consumption which each generating unit will meet. These assumptions imply a relationship between electricity generation and capacity that directly affects the fixed costs per kilowatt-hour. For example, if a utility is operating with an excessive reserve margin, then future increases in electricity consumption should translate into improved unit capacity-utilization factors, which, of course, reduce the fixed costs per kilowatt-hour.

Next, the revenue requirements (that is, total costs) corresponding to the capacity and generation assumptions can be calculated. In mathematical notations, the revenue requirement is expressed as follows:

$$RR = OM1 + OM2 + DEP + TAX + r(GBV - AD + CA) \qquad (6.3)$$

where RR = revenue requirement

$OM1$ = fuel and purchase-power components of operating and maintenance costs

$OM2$ = other operating and maintenance costs

DEP = depreciation

TAX = taxes

r = rate of return (a percentage) on rate base

GBV = gross book value of plant

AD = accumulated depreciation on plant

CA = current assets

Each element of the revenue requirement is projected separately. Fuel costs, for example, are projected for each generating unit as the product of electricity generation, heat rate (Btu/kWh), and fuel price ($/MMBtu). The most complicated element to predict is the return on the rate base, where debate centers on the definition of the rate base (for example, the treatment of construction work in progress) and the allowable return on such base.

In the simplest case, the rate base consists of the excess of gross book value (that is, plant and service at original cost) over accumulated depreciation. To project the rate base, the value of new generating units coming on line is added to the gross book value. The time series on accumulated depreciated, which includes the depreciation on new units, is then subtracted from the gross book value to give the rate base.

While the rate base is an asset-based construct, the return allowed on the base reflects the utility's capitalization—that is, the mix of debt, preferred stock, and equity. The predicted rate of return is calculated taking into account (1) regulatory practice, (2) current capitalization, and (3) future sources and costs of capital.

Given the projected revenue requirement, the average system price is calculated by dividing the revenue requirement by the original assumption on electricity consumption. In projecting the average system price, the analysis is carried out separately for each cost element in the revenue-requirement list. Thus it is possible to identify not only price per kilowatt-hour, but also fuel costs per kilowatt-hour, other operating costs per kilowatt-hour, and capital costs per kilowatt-hour.

Projecting Industrial Price

The price of electricity to industrial customers is calculated as a function of average system price. In aggregate, industrial price is about 80 percent of average system price, but this ratio varies by cost element. For example, the industrial fuel costs per kilowatt-hour are almost the same as the average system fuel costs per kilowatt-hour, while industrial capital costs per kilowatt-hour are significantly lower than their average system counterpart.

Given the average system price, disaggregated by the three components, the industrial price, similarly disaggregated, can be calculated by multiplying each system component by a proportion factor. If, for example, the average system capital cost per kilowatt-hour is 2 cents and the proportion factor is 0.5, then the industrial capital cost per kilowatt-hour is 1 ¢/kWh.

A Numerical Example

The linkages between the different methodological steps are best illustrated by example. Let us assume the following values have been produced by the earlier steps of the modeling analysis:

Revenue requirement	= $10,000 million
Fuel costs	= $ 4,000 million
Other operating and maintenance costs	= $ 2,000 million
Fixed costs	= $ 4,000 million
Delivered electricity	= 200,000 million kWh

In the preceding example, the average price that satisfies the revenue requirement is 5 ¢/kWh, which is calculated by dividing $10,000 million by 200,000 million kWh. Of this price, fuel costs account for 2 ¢/kWh, other operating and maintenance costs for 1 ¢/kWh, and fixed costs for 2 ¢/kWh.

To go from average price to industrial price, let us assume the following industry proportion factors:

Fuel factor	= 1.0
Other operating and maintenance cost factors	= 0.5
Fixed-cost factors	= 0.5

These data imply an industrial price of 3.5 ¢/kWh. The fuel-cost component is 2 ¢/kWh (1 X 2 ¢), the other operating and maintenance cost component is 0.5 ¢/kWh (0.5 X 1 ¢), and the fixed cost component is 1 ¢/kWh (0.5 X 2 ¢).

To ensure that the methodology produces realistic forecasts, it must be calibrated for the most recent year for which data are available. This calibration ensures that in the starting year, industrial price is linked to costs in a manner that reflects actual utility conditions. To perform such a calibration, data on electricity generation, capacity, heat rates, fuel costs, other operating costs, and fixed costs are gathered from form 1, form 12, and other materials submitted by the utilities to the Federal Energy Regulatory Council (FERC) and from the cost-of-service studies performed by the utilities.

Representative Power Costs for New Base-Load Units

In forecasting power costs, it is often necessary to develop independent estimates of the costs associated with new generating units. This is especially true in the preparation of long-term rate forecasts. For medium-term forecasts, it is possible to rely on site-specific costs on planned generating facilities, which utilities are required to submit under section 133 of PURPA. This section develops a generalized estimate of the cost of power production from a coal-fired unit in the western United States coming on line in 1990. The estimate includes an allowance for transmission expenses, customer expenses, and the other costs incurred in serving large industrial customers. As such it represents the "incremental" cost of power of serving a new (1990) large industrial customer. The incremental cost associated with a new residential customer would be somewhat higher because of higher fixed generation costs and distribution costs.

Construction Cost per Kilowatt for a New Coal-Fired Unit in 1990

Constant (Real) Dollar Estimate. The construction cost for a coal-fired unit is sensitive to the region of construction, the size of the unit, whether it is a first unit or an addition to an existing site, the coal type the unit is designed to burn, and various site-specific factors. Consequently, generalized construction estimates may not realistically represent the costs that a particular utility will incur in building a new coal unit.

A number of groups have published construction-cost estimates for future coal units. According to EIA, the construction cost for a new plant (with scrubbers) burning subbituminous Wyoming coal is approximately $830 per kilowatt in constant 1979 dollars.[12] This DOE estimate is based on a two 500-MW unit station design and excludes the cost of interest during construction (IDC) and associated transmission.

The Electric Power Research Institute (EPRI) has published an estimate of the capital cost per kilowatt for a twin 1000-MW coal plant in the West (with scrubbers) burning 8020 Btu/lb, 0.5 percent sulfer coal.[13] The EPRI estimate includes an allowance for interest during construction (IDC) and is expressed in constant 1976 dollars. Adjusted to exclude IDC and expressed in 1979 dollars, the EPRI analysis would indicate a construction cost of between $630 and $827 per kilowatt.

For the purpose of analysis, a construction cost of $800 per kilowatt in 1979 dollars has been adopted. This value excludes the transmission required to connect the new unit to the grid.

Current (Nominal) Dollar Estimate. The conversion of constant-dollar construction estimates into nominal dollars is complicated by the fact that the construction expenditures are spread over a number of years. This means that it is necessary to develop a construction-cost profile showing how the real capital cost of $800 will be spread over the 6 years of actual construction. Based on a review of DOE and utility estimates, the following rough profile has been adopted.

Years	1984	1985	1986	1987	1988	1989	Total
1979 dollars per kilowatt	64	96	200	240	120	80	800

The annual outlays, as presented, can now be converted to nominal terms by using an index of construction costs. The index takes a value of 1.0 in 1979 and, after that, grows at 9 percent per year compounded. This result is as follows:

Years	1984	1985	1986	1987	1988	1989	Total
Inflation index	1.539	1.677	1.828	1.993	2.172	2.367	
Nominal dollars per kilowatt	98	161	366	478	261	189	1,553

The preceding analysis has indicated that the construction cost per kilowatt for a new coal unit in 1990 corresponding to a real 1979 estimate of $800 per kilowatt and an inflation rate of 9 percent per year amounts to $1,553 per kilowatt.

Interest during Construction per Kilowatt for a New Coal-Fired Unit in 1990

Background. Many states do not allow construction work in progress (CWIP) in the rate base. This means that interest on the funds tied up in construction cannot be included in the price of electricity charged to customers until the plant is completed and becomes part of the rate base. Therefore, utilities capitalize the interest during construction (IDC) and, when the plant is completed, add the capitalized interest to the construction cost. The summed capitalized interest and the construction cost represent the capital cost associated with the new unit, and it is this value that becomes part of the utility's rate base.

The actual calculation of IDC can become very complicated for a number of reasons. For example, the IDC is a deductible item and the question arises as to whether the tax benefit should be passed on to current or future customers. Another issue concerns the compounding of IDC, that is, the calculation of interest on the IDC itself.

For the purpose of this analysis, a highly simplified approach has been used. The application of this approach involves two steps. In the first step, CWIP is computed, and in the second step, the IDC is computed as a function of CWIP.

Construction Work in Progress. As a prelude to computing IDC, it is necessary to identify for each year of construction, the value of CWIP. The value of CWIP is determined by cumulating the nominal construction outlays. For the construction outlays presented earlier, the CWIP per kilowatt is as follows:

Years	1984	1985	1986	1987	1988	1989
CWIP dollars per kilowatt	98	259	625	1103	1364	1553

Interest during Construction. The IDC is calculated by multiplying the CWIP by an IDC rate calculated using a FERC-specified formula. For this analysis, an IDC rate of 10.5 percent is used. This gives the following result:

Years	1984	1985	1986	1987	1988	1989	Total
IDC per kilowatt	10	27	66	116	143	163	525

Total Capital Cost per Kilowatt for a New Coal-Fired Unit in 1990

Generation-Capital Costs. The total capital costs per kilowatt of generating capacity is determined by summing the construction costs and the interest during construction. Construction costs have been calculated at $1553 per kilowatt and IDC at $525 per kilowatt, which gives a capital cost of $2078 per kilowatt.

Transmission-Capital Costs. To connect the new unit to the system transmission grid, new transmission lines will have to be constructed. The requirements for such transmission will depend on the siting of the unit. For example, a mine-mouth coal unit will require relatively more transmission investment than a unit constructed close to the load centers. In addition to such generation-related transmission, there also will be investments in regular system transmission additions and improvements.

An examination of balance-sheet assets indicates that the value of a transmission plant in service is equal to about one-third the value of a generation plant in service. However, transmission investments have in recent years averaged only one-sixth of generation investments. For this analysis, transmission investment has been set at $249 per kilowatt, or 12 percent of the generation investment of $2078 per kilowatt.

Fixed-Charge Factor

Public Utilities. To calculate the annualized capital charge, the capital cost (construction plus IDC) is multiplied by a fixed-charge factor. The fixed-charge factor includes the cost of capital and other fixed costs, such as property tax and insurance. For a utility financed soley by debt and paying no taxes (for example, a public power district), the computation of the fixed-charge factor is relatively straightforward. First, a capital-recovery factor is calculated, which defines the constant annual payment that will repay the interest and principal on a $1 loan over a specific period. If the interest rate is 10 percent and the period is 35 years, the capital-recovery factor is 10.37 percent (or 0.1037). Other fixed costs expressed as a fraction of the investment value are added to the capital-recovery factor to give the fixed-charge factor. If these fixed costs amount to 2 percent of the investment value, then the fixed-charge factor would be 12.37%.

Private Utilities. For private utilities, the calculation of the fixed-charge factor is complicated by the variety of financing instruments available and the effect of income tax considerations. The major component of the fixed-charge rate is the pretax cost of capital, which is calculated as a weighted average of the costs for the different sources of capital. The weights reflect the utility's capitalization, with typical capitalization ratios being 55 percent for debt, 10 percent for preferred, and 35 percent for equity. The costs attached to the different sources of capital must be expressed on a pretax basis. The pretax cost of debt is equal to the interest rate (for example, 13 percent). To pay interest of x dollars, the utility need earn only a revenue of x dollars (since interest is a deductible item). However, to pay dividends of x dollars, the utility must earn $x/1 - t$ dollars, where t is the effective tax rate. It should be noted the effective tax rate is much lower than the statutory tax rate because of the investment tax credit and other provisions.

For a private utility, the fixed-charge factor, inclusive of such elements as property tax, averages about 20 percent.

Annualized Capital Costs per Kilowatt and Kilowatt-Hour

Annualized Generation-Capital Costs per Kilowatt. To annualize the capital costs, they must be multiplied by the fixed-charge factor. The total capital-generation costs are equal to $2078 per kilowatt, of which construction outlays account for $1553 per kilowatt and IDC for $525 per kilowatt. The fixed-charge factor for a public power district is set at 0.125 and for a private utility at 0.20. This implies an annualized capital-generation cost of $260 per kilowatt for a public power district and $416 per kilowatt for a private utility.

Annualized Transmission-Capital Costs per Kilowatt. Using a similar approach, the transmission-capital cost of $249 per kilowatt can be annualized. For a public power district, the annualized transmission-capital cost is $31 per kilowatt (249 × 0.125), and for a private utility, it is $50 per kilowatt (249 × 0.20).

Annualized Generation- and Transmission-Capital Costs per Kilowatt-Hour. To transform the capital-cost estimates from a capacity (kilowatts) to an energy (kilowatt-hours) basis it is necessary to make an assumption about the number of kilowatt-hours generated each year per kilowatt of capacity. For the purpose of this analysis, a capacity factor of 0.70 is assumed. Since there are 8760 hours in the year, a capacity factor of 0.70 implies 6132 kWh/kW. The annualized capital cost per kilowatt-hour is thus calculated by dividing the annualized capital cost by 6132.

Generation-capital costs amount to $260 per kilowatt for public power districts and $416 per kilowatt for private utilities. Dividing by 6132 gives 4.24 ¢/kWh for a public power district and 6.78 ¢/kWh for an investor-owned utility.

Annualized transmission-capital costs amount to $31 per kilowatt for a public power district and $50 per kilowatt for a private utility. Dividing by 6132 gives 0.50 ¢/kWh for a public utility and 0.82 ¢/kWh for a private utility.

Variable Costs per Kilowatt-Hour in 1990

Fuel Price. According to the DOE, the delivered cost of contract coal to electric-utility plants in Wyoming in June of 1980 averaged $0.55 per million Btu's. Assuming a 9 percent per year escalation rate, this would give a 1990 price of $1.30. A price of $1.70 has been used in the analysis, with the differential reflecting the expense associated with fuel handling, the effect of new contractual stipulations, and other contingencies.

Fuel Costs. To calculate the fuel cost in dollars per megawatt-hour, the price of coal in dollars per million Btu's is multiplied by the heat rate. A 1990 coal price of $1.70 per million Btu's in conjunction with a heat rate of 10,900 Btu/kWh gives a fuel cost of $18.53 per megawatt-hour or 1.85 ¢/kWh for 1990.

Other Generation Expenses. According to DOE, nonfuel operating and maintenance expenses for steam power averaged 0.23 ¢/kWh in 1978.[14] Assuming an 8 percent per year inflation rate, this category would account for 0.58 ¢/kWh in 1990.

Transmission Operating and Maintenance Expenses. According to DOE, in 1978 transmission operating and maintenance expenses amounted to 0.04 ¢/kWh. Assuming an 8 percent per year escalation rate, this would give 0.10 ¢/kWh in 1990.

Customer-Related Expenses. In 1978, DOE reported that customer-related expenses amounted to 0.08 ¢/kWh. The value allocated to large industrial customers, however, is likely to be much lower, and a 1978 value of 0.03 ¢/kWh is assumed. Assuming an 8 percent per year escalation rate, customer-related expenses would be 0.08 ¢/kWh in 1990.

Administrative and General Expenses. In 1978, administrative and general expenses amounted to 0.19 ¢/kWh. For large industrial customers it has been assumed that 0.08 cents is allocated per kilowatt-hour. An 8 percent per year escalation rate would give a 1990 value of 0.20 ¢/kWh.

Table 6–1
1990 Incremental Power Costs Based on New Western-Coal Unit in 1990
(*in nominal ¢/kWh.*)

	Investor-Owned	*Public Power District*
Annualized capital costs		
Generation	6.78	4.24
Transmission	0.82	0.50
Variable costs		
Fuel	1.85	1.85
Other generation	0.58	0.58
Transmission	0.10	0.10
Customer	0.08	0.08
Administrative	0.20	0.20
Required price on energy produced (¢/kWh)	10.41	7.55
Required price on energy sold (¢/kWh)	10.73	7.78

Required Incremental Price for a New Coal Unit in 1990

Required Revenue on Energy Produced. The required revenue on energy produced is calculated by summing annualized capital costs on generation and transmission and variable expenditures on fuel, other generation operating and maintenance expenses, transmission operating and maintenance expenses, customer-related expenses, and administrative expenses. This gives a required revenue per kilowatt-hour generated of 10.41 ¢/kWh for investor-owned utilities and 7.55 ¢/kWh for public power districts. The details are shown in table 6-1.

Required Revenue on Energy Sold. For every net kilowatt-hour generated, about 0.97 kWh is delivered to large industrial customers, with the residual accounted for by transmission-line losses. The required price on kilowatt-hour sold is therefore calculated by dividing the required revenue per kilowatt-hour by 0.97. This gives an incremental price of 10.73 ¢/kWh for investor-owned utilities and 7.78 ¢/kWh for public power districts.

7

Public-Sector U.S. Energy Modeling

Background

Probably the most important (and possibly also the most sophisticated) public-sector model of the U.S. energy system is the Mid-Range Energy Forecasting System (MEFS). The model currently resides at the Energy Information Administration (EIA), a group within the U.S. Department of Energy. It is used to generate detailed forecasts of the U.S. energy situation that are reported annually to Congress.[1] Additionally, MEFS is used on an ongoing basis to assess the effects of a wide range of national energy policies. For example, in response to a request from Senator Henry M. Jackson, Chairman of the Senate Committee on Energy and Natural Resources, MEFS was run to analyze the impact of three proposals before Congress concerning natural-gas regulation.[2]

The MEFs Model's antecedents date back to the oil embargo of 1973. In the wake of that embargo, President Nixon proposed the launching of a project to make the United States independent of oil imports. Concurrently, a model, the Project Independence Evaluation System (PIES), was assembled by the Federal Energy Administration to help in the formulation of appropriate policies. The ill-conceived notion of energy independence was soon discarded, but the PIES Model survived. Both the PIES logic and forecasts underwent considerable scrutiny. Noteworthy in this regard is the Resources for the Future Seminar, at which eleven papers evaluating various components of the model were presented.[3] The model has been modified to respond to some of these criticisms, and the current version is in many ways an improvement over the original. Because of the model changes, and also possibly to avoid some of the opprobrium attached to the original version, PIES was renamed MEFS in 1979.

Modeling the U.S. energy system has not, of course, been the sole domain of EIA. The econometric modeling firms, universities, and DOE's national laboratories have been quite active in this field. An excellent technical survey of U.S. energy models emerged from the Energy Modeling Forum (EMF) administered by Stanford University for the Electric Power Research Institute. The interested reader is urged to consult, in particular, the paper by Hogan and Parikh, which reviews the DRI-Brookhaven Model, the Wharton Annual Energy Model, the Hnyilicza Model, and the Pilot Model.[4]

This chapter is based on my article, "Mid-Range Energy Forecasting System: Structure, Forecasts and Critique," *Energy Systems and Policy Analysis* 1(1980):5-24. I thank the editors of the journal for their gracious permission to reprint the material.

MEFS has been singled out for discussion because associated with it are regularly disseminated, regionalized price forecasts for gasoline, residual, distillate, gas, coal, and electricity. Such forecasts can be very useful input to projects evaluating the feasibility of new energy technologies or to studies projecting fuel acquisition costs for utilities.

This chapter describes and evaluates both the model and its forecasts. The description is based on a set of documentation issued by the Federal Energy Administration, the original developers of MEFS, and on discussions with EIA personnel. The forecasts are from an analysis report issued by EIA.

Structure of the System

Overview of MEFS

MEFS forecasts the state of the nation's energy system with a snapshot of the energy economy on an average day at the end of 5-year planning horizons (for example, 1980, 1985, and 1990). The predictions are regionalized equilibrium values for the prices, production, consumption, and import of major fuels.

It should be emphasized that MEFS is predictive, not optimizing; it does not identify the optimal policy bundle. Instead, it predicts the likely effect on the U.S. energy system, given a user-defined scenario. Each scenario incorporates assumptions about GNP, oil and gas reserves, world oil price, and national policies. Therefore, varying the scenario can indicate how changes in GNP, policies, and so forth affect energy production, consumption, imports, and prices.

MEFS is not a single model, rather it is a system of integrated energy supply and demand models. On the supply side, there are models for the primary extraction of coal, crude oil, and natural gas, as well as for their conversion in refineries and/or utilities into secondary energy forms. In the refinery model, crude oil is converted to residual, distillate, gasoline, and other petroleum products. Part of the refinery output, and some of the coal and natural gas, is converted in an electric-utility model into electricity. The electricity and remaining amounts of the fuels are consumed in the residential, commercial, industrial, and transportation demand sectors. Demand not satisfied by domestic production is assumed to be imported.

Figure 7-1 contains a schematic overview of the MEFS logic. As the figure shows, the disparate supply and demand models are used to generate curves for each fuel type showing the quantities that would be demanded or supplied at different prices. The oil-supply curve is modified to be perfectly horizontal at the point corresponding to an exogenous world oil price. The curves are entered into an Integration Model, which solves for equilibrium demand, domestic production, imports, and prices.[5]

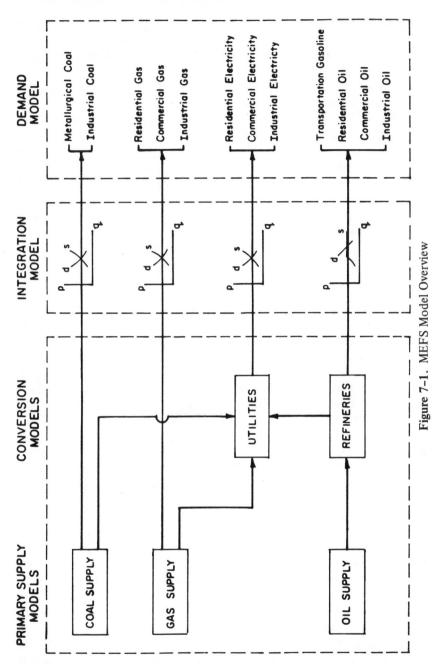

Figure 7-1. MEFS Model Overview

Integration Model

Because of its central importance, it is useful to start with the Integration Model. This model is regarded as a major innovation in terms of techniques for equilibrating demand and supply. It is the one component of MEFS that has remained largely intact over the years.

The premise on which the model is based is that the domestic energy market is workably competitive. Demand and supply curves are input to the model, and it locates the equilibrium by identifying the point at which demand and supply intersect. This equilibration is performed by the iterative use of a large-scale optimization program. The starting iteration involved:

1. Assuming initial demand prices and reading the quantities demanded at those prices off the demand curves
2. Using an optimization program in which the supply curves are imbedded to compute the least-cost method of supplying the quantity demanded
3. Reading the prices associated with the least-cost method off the supply curve
4. Adding mark-ups and taxes to the supply prices to give demand prices

The demand prices of step 4 will, in general, not be the same as those assumed in step 1. As a consequence, a second iteration will be required. The assumed price in step 1 of the second iteration will be the average of the prices in steps 1 and 4 of the first iteration. The iterative process will be stopped and equilibrium declared when the difference between the price in steps 1 and 4 is below a specified tolerance level.

Equilibration is performed separately for each year, and the inputs, that is, curves, also must be provided for each year of analysis. Currently, the model is run for the years 1985, 1990, and 1995. The solution of 1985 has no effect on those of 1990 and 1995, so the equilibration is, in effect, an exercise in comparative statics.[6]

Coal Supply Model

Coal has been assigned a central role in U.S. energy policy, and of all the fuels, by far the greatest increase in production is expected to come from coal. The higher costs associated with extracting this additional production will, however, mean a substantial rise in prices.

The curves generated by the Coal Supply Model trace out the price that must be paid to bring out various supply levels. The curves are of a long-run equilibrium nature and ignore the effect on production of such a temporary phenomena as strikes or excess inventories. These curves, which are derived for the years 1985, 1990, and 1995, are input to the Integration Model.

There is a curve derived for each class of coal in each region. Coal is classified by sulfur content and Btu's, so we have, for example, a supply curve for low-sulfur, high-Btu coal in the Northern Appalachia Region. The reason for the sulfur disaggregation is the Environmental Protection Agency regulations on the use of high-sulfur coal. The Btu disaggregation is prompted by the wide variation in heat content that exists among coals.

The supply curves show the production that will become available at different prices from existing mines or from as yet undeveloped mines. It should be pointed out that a mine is assumed to either produce at rated capacity or shut down. Thus supply is determined by the number of mines in operation and their capacity rather than at the rate at which they operate. For an existing mine to operate, the price must exceed its (unit) variable cost. For a new mine to come on stream, the price must exceed the sum of variable cost, fixed cost, and normal profit.

The basis for developing mine costs is a technological categorization framework developed by the modelers. There are 102 mine categories, with deep mines, for example, disaggregated by scale of operation, seam thickness, and seam depth. Associated with each mine category is a set of costs developed by deterministic accounting methods. All mines falling within a category are assumed to have the same set of costs.[7]

Oil and Gas Supply Model

Under any scenario, the U.S. production of crude oil and natural gas is expected to change only marginally over the next decade. That is not to say that the industry is expected to be stagnant; new sources must be developed to replace wells that will run dry. In predicting the new finds of oil and gas, the probabilistic element is much greater than was the case for coal. In the case of coal, the reserves are known; the question is whether the price is high enough to develop them. With respect to oil and gas, there is uncertainty about the level of drilling activity, as well as the reserves that are likely to be located by such drilling.

While the situations are very different, the end product of the Oil and Gas Supply Model must—because of the requirements of the Integration Model—be the same as the Coal Supply Model. Specifically, the Oil and Gas Supply Model must generate long-run equilibrium curves for the years 1985, 1990, and 1995 showing the quantities that would be available at different prices.

In MEFS, oil and gas supply from traditional sources is modeled using similar methodologies. Traditional sources are defined to consist of on-shore and off-shore production from the lower 48 states and the Alaskan outer continental shelf area. Supply from nontraditional sources are judgmental approximations made by technical experts. Nontraditional sources include oil from tar sands and shale, as well as production from the Alaskan North Slope.

The oil (and gas) supply curve for traditional sources is derived point by point. A point on the oil- and gas-supply curves is derived by estimating the production from new and old wells corrresponding to an assumed oil-price trajectory. By varying the price trajectories, a set of production estimates are traced out to give a production-price (that is, supply) curve. Estimating the production corresponding to a given price trajectory involves the following sequence of operations:

1. A level of drilling activity is selected, with the selection based on the assumption that drilling will continue up to the point at which the expected present value from drilling equals the costs. The expected present value is determined by the assumed oil-price trajectory and the size of the undiscovered oil-reserve base.
2. Finding rates are used to project the amount of oil located by the drilling activity
3. Recovery factors are used to estimate how much of the located oil will eventually be produced by each of three methods (primary, secondary, and tertiary). This cumulative production figure is added to existing reserves.
4. Decline rates are used to project the rate at which production will occur out of reserves.

It should be pointed out that the concept of a supply curve assumes deregulation of oil prices. With controls, the curve is a single point—namely, the quantity that will be supplied at the control price. In addition, the reader should note that the supply curve will become perfectly elastic at the world oil price, on the assumption that the United States can import as much as it wants at this price.[8]

Refinery Model

The refinery occupies a central position in the energy economy. It produces a variety of petroleum products from domestic and imported crude oil chief of which are gasoline, residual, and distillate. While refineries have some freedom in changing their input-output relationships, a particular refinery operates most economically when the attributes of its crude-oil input and the mix of its petroleum output reflects design-mode conditions.

The MEFS Refinery Model is based on the Refineries Petrochemical Modeling System (RPMS) developed by Bonner and Moore for use in the oil industry. Given demands for gasoline, distillate, residual, and other petroleum products, the Refinery Model selects the crude-oil supplies and mix of refinery modes that would satisfy these demands at minimum cost. Some of the identified modes reflect those at which existing refineries can operate; others reflect modes that could result from building new refineries or modifying existing ones. Each mode is itself an optimal state of a refinery's operation, and so not only do we have optimality between refineries, but also within a refinery.

In the model there is an intermediate step in going from crude oil to petroleum product. Crude oil is converted to a set of chemical attributes, and it is these attributes that are converted to petroleum products. Each refinery mode, of which there are twenty-six, requires fixed proportions of the chemical attributes and produces fixed proportions of the final products.

Each crude type available to a refinery is assumed to have a chemical composition that can be represented by ten attributes. The attributes include (1) gravity measured in pounds per cubic inch, (2) distillate measured as volume fraction, (3) reformer feedstock measured as volume fraction, (4) sulfur measured as pounds in the cut, and so on. There are a variety of crude types in the model. The list includes domestic crude types such as Oklahoma Mix, Pacific Offshore, and West Texas Mix and imported crudes such as Arabian Light, Algerian, and Venezuelan Mix. It should be noted that the list of domestic crudes includes oil extracted from shale and tar sands.

Electric Utilities Model

The MEFS Electric Utilities Model estimates the optimal generating capacity required to meet electricity demand. The complicating factor in the analysis is that utilities must provide service on demand. This demand, which is subject to diurnal, weekly, and seasonal periodicities, can be represented by a load-duration curve showing the demand for electricity in each of the 8760 hours of the year. The high point on the curve is the peak, and the utilities must have sufficient capacity to meet this demand. The area under the curve is equal to the total utility sendout.

In the MEFS Electric Utilities Model, the total electricity demand is partitioned into three segments: base (65 percent), intermediate (33 percent), and peak (2 percent). The model determines for each segment, the plants, existing and new, that will be required to satisfy demand. In making this determination, the objective function is to minimize the cost of meeting demand.

In identifying the required capacity mix, the model selects from a wide variety of generating plants. These plants are distinguished by type and include coal-fired steam turbines, residual-fired steam turbines, distillate-fired simple-cycle gas turbines, hydropower, nuclear, fuel gas, and geothermal.

Base-load facilities operate almost continuously, shutting down only for maintenance or repairs. They account for about half the system capacity but supply about 65 percent of demand. Because of their high rate of utilization, the MEFS Electric Utilities Model selects for base units those plant types (for example, nuclear) with low operating costs, even if they have high capital costs.

Intermediate and peak-load facilities often start up and shut down on a daily basis. These units have low utilization rates, and so the model selects for intermediate and peak load those plant types with low capital costs, even if their operating costs are relatively high. In the model, gas turbines may be operated only as peak-load units, while nuclear, fuel-gas, and geothermal plants may be operated only as base units.

Demand Model

In the MEFS Demand Model, demand curves are derived for eight major fuel types—distillate, residual, gasoline, other petroleum products, steam coal, metallurgical coal, natural gas, and electricity. These demand curves depict for the years 1985 and 1990 the quantities of these fuels that could be purchased at various prices. In developing the curves, economic, price, and technical factors are taken into account, as is the possibility of substitution between fuels.

The unusual characteristic of the MEFS Demand Model is that it must generate demand curves not point estimates of demand. The reason, of course, is that this is what the Integration Model requires. The derivation of a demand curve starts with the estimation of forecasting equations for each fuel. Next, assumed values for the exogenous variables and a specific price trajectory are entered into the equation to give a predicted demand value—that is, one point on the demand curve. This step is repeated continuously, each time with the same exogenous values but in combination with a different price trajectory, to give various points on the demand curve.

The MEFS analysis is disaggregated by sector as well as by fuel. The methodology used to predict energy demand in the residential, commercial, and industrial sectors involves two stages. In the first stage, total energy consumption is predicted, and in the second stage, it is distributed between the different fuel types. Total energy consumption is predicted using an econometric equation in which an energy-price index, sectoral activity, and a lagged dependent variable are the explanatory variables. The share of a particular fuel is an econometric function of the ratio of its price to the energy-price index and its own value lagged a year.

The second stage of fuel-share allocation in MEFS has been criticized for ignoring the symmetry and adding-up constraints.[9] This means that the fuel shares predicted by MEFS are not "theoretically pure," although purity, of course, is not synonymous with accuracy. In response to these criticisms, the residential- and commercial-sector methods described here are being dropped by EIA to be replaced by the Hirst model developed at the Oakridge National Laboratory.[10] This model uses a conditional-logit approach to predicting fuel shares and has the added advantage of incorporating, at various points in the analysis, engineering information on appliance-efficiency improvements, insulation retrofits, and so on.

In the transportation sector, simple technical methods are used to project the fuel consumed by the different transport modes. Fuel substitution is not generally possible in this sector, which considerably simplifies the analysis. Automobile gasoline consumption, for example, is predicted by dividing vehicle miles traveled (VMT) by the miles per gallon (mi/gal). The VMT is predicted as a function of disposable income, unemployment, and the cost of automobile travel. Miles per gallon is calculated from a vintaged automobile fleet; vintaging is necessary because of continuing improvements in vehicle fuel efficiency.[11]

World Oil Market in MEFS

In MEFS, world oil price is an exogenous input. The domestic-oil-supply curve is made horizontal at the value the user specifies for world oil price, on the unwarranted assumption that United States can import as much as it wants at this price. The source for world oil price is EIA's Oil Market Simulation (OMS) Model.[12] This is a small model—about thirty equations—that predicts oil demand and non-OPEC supply on a global basis. The excess of oil demand over non-OPEC supply is then compared with a user-entered value for OPEC production. If they are not equal, oil price is varied until such equality occurs. Price serves as an equilibrating mechanism in that a rise in it will depress demand and raise non-OPEC supply.

It should be noted that the OMS is not a stand-alone model. It is run in conjunction with the International Energy Evaluation System (IEES), a large-scale multifuel model that purports to do, although with less detail, for thirty-three global regions what MEFS does for ten U.S. regions.[13] IEES feeds OMS with various parameters, including demand and supply oil-price elasticities.

The latest OMS oil-price forecasts were released about the same time as those of MEFS, that is, the spring of this year.[14] EIA presented world-oil-price forecasts corresponding to five different scenarios—A,B,C,D, and E. These OMS forecasts are of relevance to this chapter in that a close connection has been established between MEFS and OMS. MEFS also has A,B,C,D, and E scenarios, with each MEFS scenario containing an exogenous oil-price input, that is, the output of its OMS counterpart. For example, the world-oil-price solution of OMS scenario A is the world-oil-price input of MEFS scenario A.

Governmental Forecasts

The latest MEFS forecasts from EIA (1979) were reported for a variety of scenarios.[15] Each scenario is a combination of assumptions that acts to affect

Table 7-1
MEFS Scenario Assumptions

Label	Demand	Supply	1985 World Oil Price (1978 Dollars)
A	High	High	$15 per barrel
B	High	Low	$21.50 per barrel
C	Medium	Medium	$15 per barrel
D	Low	High	$15 per barrel
E	Low	Low	$17 per barrel
C-high	Medium	Medium	$21.50 per barrel

Source: Energy Information Administration, *Energy Supply and Demand in the Midterm: 1985, 1990, and 1995* (Washington: U.S. Department of Energy, EIA Analysis Report EIA–0102/52, April 1979), pp. 8, 24, 37.

the demand or supply curve and thus price. A selection of a scenario is an important matter because prices vary quite significantly among scenarios.

Table 7-1 defines the assumptions associated with six of the seven MEFS scenarios. One of the MEFS scenarios—C-low—has not been included in the list because in the year 1985 it happens to be roughly equivalent to scenario C. Table 7-1 contains four columns: the first identifies the scenario label (A,B,C,D, E, and C-high); the second and third columns contain the associated demand and supply assumptions; and the fourth column contains the world-oil-price assumption. To take an example, scenario C assumes medium demand, medium supply, and a 1985 import price of $15 a barrel (in 1978 dollars).

Table 7-2 presents the 1985 price forecasts corresponding to the six scenarios. The energy forms covered in the table are gasoline, residual, distillate, natural gas, coal, and electricity. MEFS reports its projections in constant 1978 dollars.

Table 7-2
MEFS 1985 Price Forecasts
(in 1978 dollars.)

Fuel	Unit	A	B	C	D	E	C-High
Gasoline	$/gal	0.87	1.03	0.86	0.86	0.90	1.03
Residual[a]	$/barrel	17.84	24.20	17.85	17.08	19.99	24.35
Distillate[b]	$/gal	0.51	0.66	0.51	0.50	0.56	0.67
Natural gas[b]	$/million btu	3.37	3.71	3.47	3.38	3.49	3.62
Coal[a]	$/ton	35.09	42.26	39.07	35.03	41.24	39.79
Electricity[a]	¢/kWh	2.80	3.38	2.98	2.76	3.20	3.16

Source: Energy Information Administration, *Energy Supply in the Midterm: 1985, 1990 and 1995* (Washington: EIA Analysis Report EIA–0102/52, April 1979), pp. 24 and 37.
[a]Industrial delivered price.
[b]Residential delivered price.

Critique of Forecasts

Forecasts

It is appropriate to start the critique by appraising the forecasts reported in the previous section. A very relevant question is how reasonable do the 1985 price forecasts seem given what is known about current conditions and prospective trends. Most important, how reasonable are the scenario C forecasts, since it is this scenario that EIA considers to be most likely.

As far as oil is concerned, the projections are clearly too optimistic. It is hard to take seriously a forecast that has U.S. gasoline prices in 1985 at 86 ¢/gal, albeit 1978 cents. The low forecasts are a direct result of the MEFS scenario C assumption that 1985 world-oil prices will be $15 per barrel (1978 dollars). This assumption incidentally comes out of OMS scenario C, which EIA regards as the most likely to occur.

MEFS is far more buoyant when it comes to America's great resource, coal. Scenario C projects a significant increase in real coal price. This is probably a corollary of the sizable increase in coal production that MEFS predicts by 1985. To achieve such an increase, it is necessary to move up the supply curve and so to a higher price level. While the rationale behind the MEFS findings is clear, it is debatable whether they seriously considered the ramifications of the relative energy-price shift implied by their oil- and coal-price forecasts.

The low oil price and high coal production are indicative of the optimism that has persistently characterized MEFS forecasts. In fact, the 1979 forecasts are actually quite pessimistic when compared with those issued in previous years.

It is instructive in this context to look back at the world-oil-price scenarios associated with the first MEFS (or, as it was then called, PIES) forecasts.[16] These projections, released in 1974, were for the year 1985. They had three world-oil-price scenarios, all expressed in 1972 dollars, namely, $9 a barrel, $6 a barrel, and $3 a barrel. The $9-a-barrel assumption implied constant real world oil prices; and the others, a significant real decline.

It is amusing to examine just how wrong the modelers were. To do this, let us express their assumptions in 1985 dollars. The 1979 second-quarter GNP deflator was 164, and assuming a compound 7 percent inflation, the 1985 deflator will be 264.[17] Multiplying the three oil-price assumptions by 2.64 gives $23.76 a barrel, $15.84 a barrel, and $7.92 a barrel. Now compare this with the fact that the June 1979 meeting of OPEC compressed the price of member crudes to vary between $18 and $23.50 a barrel.

While the MEFS most likely forecast is not acceptable, this should not be cause for dismissing the model. The blame, it is important to note, lies not so much with the model as with the optimism of the scenarios fed into it.

A more substantive issue, with respect to the forecasts, concerns the relationships between the forecasts generated by the different scenarios. Are these relationships consistent with theory? In particular, do they agree with the laws of demand and supply? Most disturbingly, the answer is not always. To consider this, compare the forecasts generated by scenario C (medium demand, medium supply, $15 import price) with those of scenario D (low demand, high supply, $15 import). Both the demand and the supply conditions of scenario D are relatively more favorable to low prices, yet gasoline prices for scenarios C and D are exactly equal.

Methodology

When evaluating specialized models, it is conventional to discuss the specification of individual equations and the values of the parameters in them. The discussion of specification takes the form of identifying relevant explanatory variables that have been excluded or irrelevant ones that were included. The usual approach to appraising parameters has been to compare them with those of other studies or to indicate problems with the data or estimation techniques that would have led to biased estimates. The specification and parametric discussions are, of course, not independent, since a major cause of parameter bias is misspecification.

This sort of conventional critique is precluded by the size of MEFS. Instead, the emphasis here will be on identifying the major structural problems in MEFS. The reader interested in specifics is referred to the FEA documentation for a reasonably detailed, though not complete, discussion of the equations. The most important parameter values are listed in the document containing the price forecasts.[18]

The first criticism is more in the nature of a warning. MEFS contains a vast number of parameters, the great majority of which are judgmental. Because of this proliferation of essentially subjective parameters, the possibilities for significant errors in MEFS are impossible to isolate and the mechanism by which errors are propagated is a complete unknown. Thus the user has no analytical guide for bounding MEFS forecasts. This, by itself, need not be a matter of concern. By using a deterministic model to backcast, historical mean forecast errors can be computed. Unfortunately, MEFS has not been used to backcast, and as a consequence, one does not even have an empirical guide to the reliability of MEFS forecasts.

The second criticism has to do with the manner in which MEFS handles the interaction between the economy and energy prices. GNP, from the DRI Model, is an exogenous input to MEFS, where it is used to drive the energy-demand analysis. Now, of course, GNP is sensitive to energy prices, and the question arises whether the GNP projections driving MEFS are consistent with the energy prices coming out of MEFS. In the early version of MEFS, potentials for such inconsistency did exist. However, the current version adequately deals with this issue by iterating between the DRI and MEFS Models. The procedure can be described as follows:

1. The DRI Macroeconometric Model is run—with exogenous energy-price inputs—to give a GNP forecast.
2. The DRI GNP is entered into MEFS, which is solved to generate energy-price forecasts.
3. The MEFS energy-price predictions (aggregated into a suitable form) are entered into the DRI Model, which is rerun to give a new GNP forecast.
4. The new DRI GNP is entered into MEFS, which is rerun to give a new set of energy-price forecasts.

Unfortunately, while economic-energy interactions are now handled appropriately at the national level, serious regional inconsistencies still exist in MEFS. Before GNP can be used to drive energy demand, it must be apportioned to a regional level, because this is the level at which energy demand is predicted. The apportionment is performed in MEFS using ratios that define the regions' shares of the nation's GNP. These ratios are not varied during the iterative process and are thus assumed to be insensitive to energy developments.

The constancy of the regional shares is clearly incorrect. The regional shares of national GNP should be changed for at least two reasons. First, policies such as oil-price decontrol will cause a transfer of income to the energy-producing states. Second, industrial location patterns, especially for energy-intensive industries, are sensitive to relative energy costs, and therefore, states with relatively low energy costs should enjoy greater economic expansion. In summary, direct and indirect factors will cause the GNP share of energy-poor regions, such as New England, to decline, while the share of energy-rich regions, such as the Rocky Mountain Area, should increase.

The third structural problem with MEFS has to do with the existence of social, political, and environmental constraints on energy developments. By ignoring them, MEFS, in many instances, makes projections that, while physically realizable, are not attainable because of other limiting factors. This is particularly true of MEFS projections of increased Western coal production, which do not seem to have taken sufficient cognizance of the restraints imposed by labor shortages, community resistance, environmental legislation, and transportation bottlenecks. It should be pointed out that MEFS neglect of socioinstitutional constraints has been identified earlier.[19]

The final criticism is a rather unfair one, namely, that MEFS is not analytically complete. This is the sort of charge that can be levied against any model, and it must be noted that MEFS does contain a realistic and indepth representation of the everchanging U.S. energy scene. Nevertheless, the individual components of MEFS inevitably suffer by comparison with specialized models. This is most evident in MEFS's simplistic treatment of electricity demand. In MEFS, total electricity demand is deterministically apportioned into base, intermediate, and peak segments. An optimization model is then used to identify the least-cost manner of supplying these demand segments.

There are a number of developments in the electric-utility sector that make an arithmetic allocation of demand segments potentially dangerous. Time-of-day pricing and the use of load-control devices (for example, radio signals) are being increasingly adopted by utilities to flatten the shape of their load-duration curve. This flattening will, of course, mean changes in the base, intermediate, and peak ratios. Methodologies to take into account these policies, as well as other developments (for example, air-conditioning saturation) affecting the load shape, are described by DeSouza.[20]

At this point the reader might well ask: If MEFS scenarios are unrealistic, its forecasts internally inconsistent, its parameters subjective, and its logic simplistic, does it really make sense to adopt its price projections? The answer is a qualified yes. MEFS tackles a very complicated area in a reasonable and systematic manner, and while serious problems do exist, they are not irreparable. Most important, the model provides a regular and rich source of price forecasts, which, if used selectively, can be quite helpful. It is hoped that in the future EIA will issue forecasts corresponding to a set of scenarios that more reasonably bound the feasible future. This would give the selective user a better chance of finding a scenario that more closely corresponds to his or her preconceptions.

8 U.S. Energy Policies

Many of the models that have been discussed in this book are policy-oriented. They are structured to generate forecasts that take into account not only economic and demographic factors, but also legislative initiatives. There have been a number of acts passed relating to the energy area. This chapter reviews the omnibus National Energy Act (NEA), which is illustrative of the policy direction adopted by the country.

The objective of the NEA (which is made up of five separate acts) is to reduce the consumption of oil and gas, increase the consumption of renewable resources and coal, optimize the utilization of electric-generating facilities, and increase the production of natural gas. Each of these objectives, if realized, will contribute to the reduction of U.S. oil imports.

National Energy Conservation Policy Act

The National Energy Conservation Policy Act (NECPA) of 1978 (Pub. L. 95-619) seeks to promote the conservation of scarce energy forms (for example, oil and natural gas) and to encourage the use of renewable resources (for example, solar). To this purpose, a number of grants are to be provided for and various efficiency standards are to be promulgated. The act is directly primarily toward the residential sector, but contains programs affecting all sectors.

Residential Sector

Utility Conservation Program. This measure is designed to increase consumer awareness of conservation economics and to facilitate consumer adoption of appropriate conservation techniques. Governors are required to submit plans to the Secretary of Energy describing how utilities will inform customers of conservation and solar-energy options and the energy savings and costs associated with such options. A utility must inspect the customer's residence upon request to determine cost-effective options. The utility also must provide lists of lenders, suppliers, and contractors and to offer to arrange for financing if required.

Appliance-Efficiency Standards. The Department of Energy is required to set, within 2 years and 45 days from the date of enactment, energy-efficiency

179

standards for thirteen categories of appliances. The appliances covered include air conditioners, water heaters, clothes dryers, refrigerators, freezers, ranges, furnaces, dishwashers, and television sets. The efficiency standards are defined so that appliances can provide a given performance using less energy.

Conservation Financing Program. The Government National Mortgage Association (GNMA) is directed to purchase and sell energy-conservation loans of up to $2500, with priority given to elderly and moderate-income families. *Moderate income* is defined as equal to, or lower than, the median income for the area.

Two GNMA programs are to be established with a total authority of $5 billion. A $3 billion fund is provided to subsidize loans by offering them at reduced rates. A $2 billion standard fund is provided for supplying credit where it is not available.

Solar Financing Program. GNMA is authorized to purchase up to $100 million of reduced-interest loans to homeowners and builders for the purchase and installation of solar heating and cooling equipment in residential dwellings. Support for up to $8000 per unit will be provided with loan repayments due within 15 years.

Other Residential Financing Programs. The Department of Housing and Urban Development (HUD) is authorized to insure loans for energy-conserving improvements to multifamily housing and to make grants and establish standards for such improvements to federally assisted housing. HUD is also authorized funds to make energy-conserving improvements to public housing.

Low-Income Conservation Grants. The legislation extends a grant program for states to purchase and install materials to weatherize homes occupied by low-income families, particularly the elderly and handicapped. *Low-income families* are defined as families with incomes of 125 percent or below that of the federally established poverty level. Eligible materials include insulation, storm windows and doors, caulking and weather stripping, furnace-efficiency modifications, and clock thermostats. The maximum-grant expenditure for any dwelling unit is $800. Grants can be used for both owner-occupied and renter-occupied residences. Appropriations authorized for this program are $200 million in both fiscal years 1979 and 1980. A separate $25 million grant program under the Farmers Home Administration has been established to finance the weatherization of dwelling units of low-income families located in rural areas.

Commercial Sector

Conservation in Schools, Hospitals, and Public Buildings. Grants are provided to the states to help them assist eligible institutions to pay for energy audits and the installation of conservation and solar-energy measures. These grants will generally cover up to 50 percent of the costs. Institutions eligible for grants include public and private nonprofit elementary and secondary schools, colleges and universities, and hospitals. In addition, grants are authorized over 2 years to conduct energy audits of public buildings. Institutions eligible for these grants include buildings owned by units of local governments and nonprofit nursing homes, community health centers, neighborhood health centers, and orphanages.

Conservation in Federal Buildings. Energy audits are required of all existing federal buildings. Each federal agency must retrofit a certain percentage of its total square footage with energy-conservation measures or solar-energy systems so that by 1990 all federal buildings are retrofitted to ensure maximum efficiency. All new buildings must be designed to minimize their life-cycle energy costs. These provisions strengthen existing requirements for energy conservation in federal buildings.

Federal-Building Solar Demonstration Program. The federal government is authorized up to $100 million to demonstrate solar technology by undertaking a 3-year program for installation of solar equipment in federal buildings. The program is designed to stimulate the manufacture of solar equipment, help lower its costs, and thereby make solar-energy systems more attractive for widespread commercial use. In addition to this program, the federal government is authorized $98 million over 3 years to purchase photovoltaic-energy devices for use in federal buildings. The purpose is to stimulate the development of a permanent low-cost private photovoltaic-production capability.

Industrial Sector

Energy-Use Reporting Requirement. All companies that consume at least 1 trillion Btu's per year in each of the ten most energy-consuming industries must report their energy-consumption figures to the Department of Energy (DOE) each year and show that actions are being taken to conserve energy. Companies may report indirectly through third parties, such as trade associations, if DOE finds that such a reporting program is effective.

Recycling Targets. Targets are to be established by DOE defining the percentage of production that should be based on recovered materials (for example, scrap). Progress on the achievement of these targets is to be reported annually by DOE.

Motor and Pump Standards. DOE is directed to evaluate pumps and motors to determine if performance-efficiency standards are necessary and to propose test procedures and labeling requirements for any equipment covered.

Transportation Sector

Automotive Fuel-Efficiency Penalties. The Secretary of Transportation presently has authority to impose on automobile manufacturers civil penalties of $5 per car manufactured for every one-tenth of a mile per gallon by which the company's fleet average fails to meet the mandated fuel-efficiency standard in any given year. The Secretary would be authorized to increase the civil penalties up to $10 upon a finding that such an increase would result in substantial energy conservation for automobiles. Such an increase, however, could be imposed only if the Secretary found that it would not cause undue economic hardship, cause a significant increase in unemployment, adversely affect competition, or lead to significantly greater imports.

Off-Road Vehicle Study. The Department of Transportation (DOT) is directed to study the energy-conservation potential of recreational motor vehicles, including airplanes and boats used for recreation.

Energy Tax Act

The Energy Tax Act (ETA) of 1978 (Pub. L. 95-618) provides special tax credits for investments in energy-conservation equipment and technologies utilizing renewable sources of energy. The most important stipulations of the act are summarized here.

Residential Sector

Insulation-Investment Credit. A nonrefundable credit—up to $300—is provided for 15 percent of the first $2000 invested in qualifying equipment. Specifically, a credit is provided for investments in insulations, caulking, weather stripping, modified flue openings, storm or thermal doors and windows, automatic furnace-ignition systems, clock thermostats, and other items.

Solar-Investment Credit. A nonrefundable credit is provided for investments in solar, wind, and other renewable sources of energy in both new and existing residences. The credit would be 30 percent of the first $2000 and 20 percent of the next $8000 spent, for a maximum of $2200. The investment will be eligible if the equipment is used to heat or cool a home or provide hot water.

Commercial and Industrial Sectors

Conservation Tax Credit. Above the normal investment tax credit an additional 10 percent investment tax credit is provided for investment in equipment to improve the heat efficiency of existing industrial processes, including heat exchangers and recuperators. The credit is also available for equipment used in the recycling of waste materials.

Solar/Wind-Energy Tax Credit. An additional 10 percent tax credit is available for investments in equipment designed to use solar or windpower to generate electricity, to heat or cool, or to produce hot water.

Discouragement of Oil/Gas Boilers. To discourage the use of oil and gas, new industrial oil- or gas-fired boilers will be denied the usual investment tax credit and will be limited to straight-line depreciation unless the use of coal at any such facility is precluded by federal air-pollution regulations or existing state air-pollution regulations. The credit and accelerated depreciation will, however, be allowed for new oil and gas boilers if they are applied in exempt uses (for example, farming).

Transportation Sector

Gas-Guzzler Tax. Beginning in the 1980 model year, a tax would be imposed on cars whose fuel economy is far below the fleet-average standard set. The tax rate increases as fuel economy decreases to a minimum of $3850 on the most inefficient cars by 1985. The tax would not apply to light trucks, vans, recreational vehicles, vehicles with four-wheel drive, or other nonhighway vehicles or emergency vehicles.

Gasohol Tax Exemption. The act provides an exemption from the 4-cent federal excise tax on gasoline for fuels containing a mixture of at least 10 percent alcohol produced from agricultural products or waste. Alcohol produced from coal, oil, or natural gas is ineligible for the exemption. The act also provides for expedited consideration of applications to produce ethanol.

Vanpooling Exemption. The act provides that employer-furnished vanpool services will not be considered income to the employee, thus removing a potential obstacle to enhance vanpool usage.

Powerplant and Industrial Fuel Use Act

The Powerplant and Industrial Fuel Use Act (PIFUA) of 1978 (Pub. L. 95-620) is designed to severely restrict the use of oil and gas by electric utilities and large industrial boilers and to promote the use of coal.

Utilities

New Plants. The act differentiates between base, intermediate, and peak generating capacity. Base units are used to generate the bulk of the utility's electricity, and consequently, the requirements are the most stringent for these units, with the use of oil or gas prohibited in new base-load power plants. Permanent exemptions from this prohibition may be obtained, however, for specified environmental, technical, and economic reasons. The act permits construction of gas-fired or oil-fired peak-load power plants, and gas also may be used for intermediate-load facilities, but only where needed to meet environmental requirements.

Existing Plants. The DOE is authorized to require existing coal-capable units to convert to coal if it appears technically and financially feasible. Any such facility may be exempted for the same reasons as new power plants. For existing non-coal-capable units, DOE may require the use of coal-oil mixtures or mixtures using other fuels.

Existing facilities also are required by statute to limit use of natural gas to the proportion of total fuel used during 1974-1976, to refrain from oil-to-gas switches, and to cease use of natural gas entirely by 1990. This latter requirement may be delayed beyond 1990 by filing a "system compliance plan."

Pollution-Control Assistance. The switch to coal involves expanded outlays on pollution-control equipment (for example, scrubbers), and so the act establishes an $800 million loan program to assist utilities that cannot raise the necessary funds for pollution-control equipment.

Industrial Sector

New Boilers. According to PIFUA, new industrial boilers with a fuel-heat input rate of 100 million Btu's (MMBtu) per hour or greater are prohibited from using oil or natural gas unless an exemption is granted by DOE on grounds that the use of coal or an alternate fuel is precluded by environmental regulations, cost, or site limitations, or for other reasons.

Existing Boilers. For existing industrial facilities, DOE may order individual coal-capable units with a fuel-heat input rate of 100 MMBtu/h or greater not to burn oil or gas, with exemptions granted for stipulated reasons. Units that are not coal-capable may be required, where feasible, to burn mixtures of oil and alternate fuels, using only the minimum amount of oil necessary to maintain efficiency.

Public Utility Regulatory Policies Act

The demand for electricity fluctuates by hour of the day, day of the week, and month of the year. This, in connection with the fact that electricity generally cannot be stored, means that utilities must maintain generating capacity that is substantially in excess of average hourly demand. The Public Utilities Regulatory Policies Act (PURPA) of 1978 (Pub. L. 95-617) is directed at fostering retail and wholesale practices that would alleviate the excess-capacity problem.

In the United States, retail transactions (that is, utility sales to ultimate customers) are typically subject to regulation by state commissioners, while wholesale transactions (that is, interutility arrangements) are regulated by the Federal Energy Regulatory Council (FERC). The act seeks to encourage retail and wholesale practices that would promote (1) conservation of energy, (2) efficient use of facilities and resources, and (3) equitable rates to electric customers.

Retail Transactions

Each state ratemaking authority must, within 3 years of enactment, review various innovative rate-design standards to determine if they will result in the optimal use of resources by the utilities and their customers; however, there is no requirement for adoption. The suggested standards include the following:

1. Time-of-day rates—rates that vary according to whether electricity is consumed during peak or off-peak periods of the day.
2. Seasonal rates—rates that vary according to whether electricity is consumed during peak or off-peak periods of the year.
3. Cost-of-service rates—rates that are charged to each class of electric consumers based on the different costs for serving each such class.
4. Interruptible rates—low rates offered to customers who are willing to have their power interrupted at times of highest peak demand.
5. Load-management techniques—physical nonprice techniques designed to reduce the demand on the utility at peak periods.
6. Prohibition of unjustified declining-block rates—discontinuance of rates that incorrectly favor larger users by pricing successive blocks of electricity at lower per-unit prices.

Wholesale Transactions

PURPA contains a number of provisions to increase the power of the FERC to order wholesale transactions having to do with power wheeling and pooling among other things.

With respect to wheeling, FERC can order an electric utility to provide transmission services to allow two noncontiguous utilities to transmit electric power over its system. The FERC must find that a wheeling order will conserve energy, promote efficiency, or increase reliability. No wheeling order may be issued if any other utility is likely to incur an uncompensated loss as a result of the order.

Pooling arrangements are to be reviewed by the Secretary of DOE in consultation with the FERC to identify opportunities for energy conservation and increased efficiency in the use of facilities or resources through pooling arrangements among utilities. In appropriate cases, FERC may exempt utilities from any state law or rule that prohibits voluntary coordination between utilities to obtain more economic use of facilities and resources.

Natural Gas Policy Act

Natural-gas transactions in the interstate market had been controlled, while transactions in the intrastate market had not been controlled. This resulted in the following problems:

1. A slackening of gas exploration and development because the low interstate prices did not provide sufficient incentive to producers.
2. Declining supplies of gas to the interstate market leading to curtailments of industrial service and occasional threats to residential and commercial service.
3. Surplus supplies of gas in the intrastate market.

The Natural Gas Policy Act (NGPA) of 1978 (Pub. L. 95-621) is designed to redress these market distortions. It removes outmoded regulatory burdens on interstate sales and brings the intrastate market under control. It allows high prices to be charged for newly discovered gas to encourage drilling, while restraining price increases on previously discovered gas to prevent significant inflationary impacts. In addition, the bill provides for the protection of residential and small commercial consumers from price increases over current law through incremental pricing of higher-cost gas supplies to industrial consumers.

Wellhead Pricing and Decontrol

Ceiling for Sales of Natural Gas to Interstate Commerce. For natural gas "dedicated to interstate commerce" (that is, gas that must be sold in interstate commerce if sold at all), the maximum lawful price would be either the rate established by the FERC applicable on 20 April 1977, approximately $0.93 per million Btu (MMBtu), plus the inflation adjustment or the rate set by the FERC after 20 April 1977, whichever is higher.

Ceiling Price for Sales under Existing Intrastate Contracts. The prices for intrastate gas are tied to interstate gas. In general, intrastate gas will be sold at a rate equal to the "maximum lawful price" for new gas of $1.75 per MMBtu plus inflation and escalation adjustments. If this "maximum lawful price" is greater than the previous selling price of gas, then the gas must be priced at the lower intrastate contract rate. If the intrastate gas is already selling at a rate in excess of the "maximum lawful price," the price for this gas would be rolled back to the maximum lawful price or would be set at the contract price in effect on the date of enactment of the National Gas Policy Act. If the second procedure is used, the price of the gas may rise each month thereafter only by the annual inflation-adjustment factor applicable for that month.

Ceiling Price for Sales under Rollover Contracts. A dual pricing scheme is established for sales under "rollover contracts" (on the basis of interstate versus intrastate gas). For gas subject to a first sale under a rollover contract that is generally dedicated to interstate commerce, the rate at which the gas may be sold is equal to a base of $0.54 per MMBtu plus the inflation adjustment. For gas subject to a first sale under an intrastate rollover contract, the rate would be calculated on a base of $1 per MMBtu plus the inflation adjustment.

Ceiling Price for New Natural Gas. The ceiling price or "maximum lawful price" for a new natural gas and natural gas produced from the outer continental shelf (OCS) is placed at $1.75 per MMBtu as of April 1977. The maximum lawful price calculated on a monthly basis is scheduled to increase with the GNP deflator plus 3.5 percent through 20 April 1981. From 21 April 1981 through 31 December 1984, the ceiling could increase by the GNP deflator plus 4.0 percent.

Elimination of Price Controls. The following categories of gas are deregulated immediately: geopressurized brine gas, coal-seam gas, Devonian shale gas, and gas from wells below 15,000 feet. After 1 January 1985, four more categories are decontrolled: new OCS gas, new onshore-well gas not committed to interstate commerce on 20 April 1977 and produced from a completion location below 5000 feet, existing intrastate contract gas where contract prices exceed $1 per MMBtu on 31 December 1984 other than by operation of price-escalator clauses, and interstate rollover-contract gas where prices exceed $1 per MMBtu on 31 December 1984 regardless of operation of price-escalator clauses. After 1 January 1987, new onshore-well gas not committed on 20 April 1977 and produced from a location of 5000 feet or less would be decontrolled.

Incremental Pricing

The new ceilings and the decontrol will raise gas prices to the consumer. The intention of NGPA is that the industrial customers absorb a more than proportionate share of this price increase. This is to be effected through the incremental-pricing provision. However, even with incremental pricing, the overall average cost of natural gas to industry should remain below the cost of alternative liquid fuels.

An incremental-pricing threshold is to be computed on a March 1978 base rate of $1.48 per MMBtu plus an inflation adjustment. Amounts paid by the distribution company that exceed the incremental pricing threshold (or some other specified limit) and are associated with expensive imports, costly stripper-well gas, natural gas from Prudhoe Bay, increased state severance taxes, or surcharges paid by one interstate pipeline to another are subject to passthrough provisions. Under the passthrough requirements, amounts paid in excess of $1.45 per MMBtu would have to be placed in a special account. These excess amounts would then be passed through in the form of a surcharge to industrial users until such time as the delivered-gas price to these users equals the cost of alternative fuels.

Allocation and Curtailment

The president may declare an emergency if a gas shortage exists or is imminent that endangers supplies for "high-priority" users. *High-priority use* means the use of gas in a residence or small commercial establishment or any use the curtailment of which would endanger life, health, or maintenance of physical property. During an emergency, the president may authorize certain emergency sales of gas. If these emergency sales are not sufficient to protect high-priority users, he may allocate certain supplies of gas as necessary.

Interstate pipelines are prohibited from curtailing natural gas for essential agricultural purposes for which natural gas is necessary unless the curtailment does not decrease the amount of natural gas needed for essential agricultural purposes or is necessary to meet the requirements of high-priority users. The Secretary of DOE establishes and reviews priorities for curtailment, and FERC implements the priorities.

Notes

Chapter 1
Introduction

1. The statistics presented in this chapter are from Energy Information Administration, *Monthly Energy Review* (Springfield, Va.: National Technical Information Service, August 1980).

2. R. Stobaugh and D. Yergin, *Energy Future* (New York: Random House, 1979).

3. MIT World Coal Study, *Coal: Bridge to the Future* (Cambridge, Mass.: Ballinger, 1980).

Chapter 2
Public-Sector International Energy Modeling

1. Workshop on Alternative Energy Strategies, *Energy: Global Prospects, 1985-2000.* (New York: McGraw-Hill, 1977).

2. A number of MIT Working Papers discuss various parts of the World Oil Project. See, for example, R.S. Pindyck, *International Comparisons of the Residential Demand for Energy* (Cambridge, Mass.: Working Paper MIT-EL 77-027 WP, undated).

3. Pindyck, for example, predicts a 2 percent increase in real world oil price as the most likely case in R.S. Pindyck, *OPEC, Oil Prices, and the Western Economies* (Cambridge, Mass.: Working Paper MIT-EL 78-001 WP, January 1978).

4. Logistics Management Institute, *The International Energy Evaluation System* (report prepared for Energy Information Administration, U.S. Department of Energy, Washington, September 1978); the OMS model is described in Energy Information Administration, *An Evaluation of Future World Oil Prices* (Washington: U.S. Department of Energy, EIA Analysis Memorandum, EIA-0102/4, June 1978).

5. M. Mesarovic and E. Pestel, *Mankind at the Turning Point* (New York: Dutton, 1974); and B. Hughes and M. Mesarovic, "Analysis of Global Energy Developments and a IIASA Scenario: The Use of the World Integrated Model" (paper presented at NATO Science Committee, Brussels, April 1978).

6. Energy Information Administration, *Monthly Energy Review* (Springfield, Va.: National Technical Information Service, various issues).

7. For a summary of MEFS (formerly called PIES), see Federal Energy Administration, *Project Independence Evaluation System (PIES): A User's Guide* (Springfield, Va.: National Technical Information Service, June 1977).

8. Energy Information Administration, *International Energy Assessment* (Washington: U.S. Department of Energy, Analysis Report EIA-0184-1, May 1979).

9. Computer Sciences Corporation, *A Survey of Long-Range Forecasting Models and Data Resources* (prepared for U.S. Department of Defense; approved for unlimited public distribution, April 1978).

Chapter 3
Electricity-Demand Models

1. J. Darmstadter, J. Dunkerley, and J. Alterman, "International Variations in Energy Use: Findings from a Comparative Study," *Annual Review of Energy* 3(1978):201-224.

2. L.D. Taylor, "The Demand for Electricity: A Survey," *Bell Journal of Economics* 6(1975):74-110.

3. For a sophisticated example of an end-use model, see Arthur D. Little, Inc., *Electric Energy Model Structure.* Vol. 2 (report to Illinois Power Company, July 1980).

4. For a discussion of appliance saturation, see Midwest Research Institute, *Patterns of Energy Use by Electrical Appliances* (Palo Alto, Calif.: Electric Power Research Institute, January 1979), pp. 4.2-4.10.

5. W. Lin, E. Hirst, and S. Cohn, *Fuel Choices in the Household Sector* (Oakridge, Tenn.: Oakridge National Laboratory, October 1976), pp. 1-40.

6. Arthur D. Little, Inc., *Classification and Evaluation of Electric Motors and Pumps* (report to U.S. Department of Energy, February 1980).

7. For a discussion of steel industry processes and energy use, see G.R. DeSouza, "A Technoeconomic Policy Model of the Ferrous Scrap Industry," *Business Economics* 3(1980)45-52.

8. Arthur D. Little, Inc., et al., *Industrial Cogeneration Optimization Program* (report to U.S. Department of Energy, 1980).

9. Arthur D. Little, Inc., has in fact used industrial and use-specific modeling techniques in an ongoing conservation study for Pacific Gas and Electric.

10. An example of industrial electricity econometric modeling is provided by Arthur D. Little, Inc., *The Development of an Energy and Peak Demand Forecasting Model* (report to Omaha Public Power District, August 1977).

11. For theoretical background, see E.R. Berndt and D.O. Wood, "Technology, Prices and the Demand for Energy," *Review of Economics and Statistics* 57(1975):259-267.

12. R.F. Wolff, "Peak Growth Down Again, to Only 0.6%," *Electrical World* (November 1, 1979):48-49.

13. The first review of peak-demand modeling is contained in G.R. DeSouza, "On Selecting a Peak Demand Forecast Methodology," *Public Utilities Fortnightly* (June 22, 1978):26-28.

14. H.D. Burbank, "The Connecticut Peak-Load-Pricing Experiment," in *Forecasting and Modeling Time-of-Day and Seasonal Electricity Demands* (Palo Alto, Calif.: Electric Power Research Institute), pp. 1-1 to 1-30.

15. Arthur D. Little, Inc., *Mechanical Controls and Penalty Pricing* (report to Electric Power Research Institute, 1977).

16. For a discussion of time-of-day elasticity, see Research Triangle Institute, *Time-of-Use Electricity Price Effects: Connecticut* (Washington: U.S. Department of Energy, August 1979).

17. For a discussion of techniques for load shifting, see Arthur D. Little, Inc., *The Utilization of Off-Peak Electricity* (report to Electric Power Research Institute, January 1977).

Chapter 4
Coal-Demand Analysis

1. R. Stobaugh and D. Yergin, *Energy Future* (New York: Random House, 1979).

2. World Coal Study, *Coal, Bridge to the Future* (Cambridge, Mass.: Ballinger, 1980).

3. Federal Energy Administration, *Project Independence Evaluation System (PIES): A Users Guide* (Springfield, Va.: National Technical Information Service, June 1977).

4. Stanford Research Institute, *Fuel and Energy Price Forecasts* (Palo Alto, Calif.: Electric Power Research Institute, February 1977).

5. Energy Information Administration, *Annual Report to Congress,* Vol. 3 (Washington: U.S. Government Printing Office, July 1980).

6. A.S. Kydes and J. Rabinowitz, *A Long-Range Assessment of R&D Policy for Gas-Related Conversion Technologies* (Upton, N.Y.: Brookhaven National Laboratory, April 1980).

7. Committee on Nuclear and Alternative Energy Systems, *Alternative Energy Demand Futures to 2010* (Washington: National Academy of Sciences, 1979).

8. Resources for the Future, *Energy: The Next Twenty Years* (Cambridge, Mass.: Ballinger, 1980).

9. The statistics presented in this discussion are from Energy Information Administration, *Monthly Energy Review* (Springfield, Va.: National Technical Information Service, August 1980).

10. "The 31st Annual Electrical Industry Forecast," *Electrical World* (September 15, 1980):55-70; National Electric Reliability Council, *1980 Summary of Projected Peak Load, Generating Capability, and Fossil Fuel Requirements* (Princeton, N.J.: July 1980); National Coal Association, *NCA Economics Committee Long Term Forecast* (1980); and Economic Regulatory Adminis-

tration, *Electric Power Supply and Demand for the Contiguous United States* (Washington, 1980).

11. Electric Power Research Institute, *Coal and Nuclear Generating Costs* (Palo Alto, Calif.: Electric Power Research Institute, April 1977).

12. Pacific Power and Light Company, *Time Differentiated Long-Run Incremental Costs* (submission before Wyoming Public Service Utility Commission, 1979).

13. The statistics presented on metallurgical coal demand are generally from the American Iron and Steel Institute, *Annual Statistical Reports.*

14. American Iron and Steel Institute, *Steel at the Crossroads: The American Steel Industry in the 1980's* (Washington, January 1980).

15. Arthur D. Little, Inc., *Proposed Industrial Recovered Materials Utilization Targets for the Metals and Metal Products Industry* (prepared for U.S. Department of Energy, May 1979).

16. Techniques to optimize energy use in the steel industry are discussed in Arthur D. Little, Inc., *Research, Development and Demonstration of Energy Conservation: Preliminary Identification of Opportunities in Iron and Steelmaking* (prepared for U.S. Department of Energy, January 1978).

17. Resource Planning Associates, *The Potential for Cogeneration Development in Six Major Industries by 1985* (report to U.S. Department of Energy, December 1977); the Resource for the Future Estimate is based on R.H. Williams, "Industrial Cogeneration," *Annual Review of Energy* 3(1978):313–356; and see Energy and Environmental Analysis, Inc., *Technical and Economic Feasibility of Alternative Fuel Use in Process Heaters and Small Boilers* (report to U.S. Department of Energy, February 1980).

18. Bechtel National et al., *Achieving a Production Goal of 1 Million B/D of Coal Liquids by 1990* (prepared for U.S. Department of Energy, March 1980).

19. L. Cleary, *Energy Economic Projections for the 1979 Overview* (Palo Alto, Calif.: Electric Power Research Institute, September 1979).

20. The Engineering Societies' Commission on Energy, Inc., *Synthetic Fuels Summary* (report prepared for the U.S. Department of Energy, August 1980).

21. As reported in Energy Information Administration, *Weekly Coal Report* (Washington: U.S. Department of Energy, March 14, 1980), p. 9.

22. As reported in Energy Information Administration, *Demand for World Coal Through 1995* (Washington: U.S. Department of Energy, May 1979), p. 23.

Chapter 5
Energy-Supply Models

1. The historical statistics presented in this chapter are from Energy Information Administration, *Statistics and Trends of Energy Supply, Demand, and*

Price (Washington: U.S. Government Printing Office, May 1978); and Energy Information Administration, *Monthly Energy Review* (Washington: U.S. Government Printing Office, June 1980).

2. Workshop on Alternative Energy Strategies, *Energy: Global Prospects 1985-2000* (New York: McGraw-Hill, 1977).

3. P.L. Eckbo, H.D. Jacoby, and J.L. Smith, "Oil Supply Forecasting: A Disaggregated Process Approach," *Bell Journal of Economics* 1(1978):218-235.

4. A number of econometric models of oil supply have been developed, see, for example, F.M. Fisher. *Supply and Cost in the U.S. Petroleum Industry: Two Econometric Studies* (Baltimore: Johns Hopkins Press, 1974).

5. R. Turvey and D. Anderson, *Electricity Economics* (Baltimore: Johns Hopkins Press, 1977).

6. California Institute of Technology, *The Cost of Energy: A Required Revenue Methodology for ERDA/EPRI Evaluations* (Pasadena, Calif.: June 1976).

7. See, for example, R.H. Harnett and D.L. Phung, "Three Modes of Energy Cost Analysis," *Energy Systems and Policy* 1(1979):61-72.

Chapter 6
Regulated Energy Pricing

1. *Federal Power Commission et al.* vs. *Hope Natural Gas Company,* 320 U.S. 501 (1949) at 603.

2. H. Markowitz, *Portfolio Selection: Efficient Diversification of Investments* (New York: Wiley, 1959).

3. W. Sharpe, *Portfolio Theory and Capital Markets* (New York: McGraw-Hill, 1970).

4. L. Hyman and J. Egan, "The Utility Stock Market: Regulation, Risk, and Beta," *Public Utilities Fortnightly* (February 14, 1980):21-27.

5. D.R. Harrington, "The Changing Use of the Capital Asset Pricing Model in Utility Regulation," *Public Utilities Fortnightly* (February 14, 1980):28-30.

6. R.L. Hagerman and B.T. Ratchford, "Some Determinants of Allowed Rates of Return to Equity to Electric Utilities," *The Bell Journal of Economics* 1(1978):46-55.

7. ICF Incorporated, *Domestic Rate Survey* (report to U.S. Department of Energy, May 1979).

8. Task Force No. 1, *Analysis of Various Pricing Approaches* (Palo Alto, Calif.: Electric Power Research Institute, February 1977).

9. Task Force No. 4, *Critical Issues in Costing Approaches* (Palo Alto, Calif.: Electric Power Research Institute, January 1978).

10. R.K. Koger, "Is there Economic Justification for a Lifeline Rate," *Public Utilities Fortnightly* (May 10, 1979):11-17.

11. The statistics are from Energy Information Administration, *Monthly Energy Review* (Springfield, Va.: National Technical Information Service, May 1980).

12. Electric Power Research Institute, *Coal and Nuclear Generating Costs* (Palo Alto, Calif.: Electric Power Research Institute, April 1977).

13. Memorandum supplied by Betsy O'Brien of the Energy Information Administration of the Department of Energy to the author and information contained in Energy Information Administration, *Annual Report to Congress,* Vol. 3 (Washington, July 1980).

14. Energy Information Administration, *Cost and Quality of Fuels for Electric Utility Plants* (Washington, 1980).

Chapter 7
Public-Sector Energy Modeling

1. Energy Information Administration, *Annual Report to Congress* (Washington: U.S. Government Printing Office, June 1978).

2. Energy Information Administration, *An Evaluation of Natural Gas Pricing Proposals* (Washington: U.S. Department of Energy, EIA Analysis Memorandum AM/AI-7802, June 1978).

3. Resources for the Future, *Workshop to Review FEA's 1976 National Energy Outlook* (Springfield, Va.: National Technical Information Service, March 1977).

4. W. Hogan and S. Parikh, "Comparison of Models of Energy and the Economy," *Energy and the Economy* (Stanford, Calif.: Stanford University, September 1977), pp. D1–D15.

5. Federal Energy Administration, *Project Independence Evaluation System (PIES): A User's Guide* (Springfield, Va.: National Technical Information Service, June 1977).

6. Federal Energy Administration, *The Integration Model of the Project Independence Evaluation System* (Springfield, Va.: National Technical Information Service, September 1976).

7. Federal Energy Administration, *Coal Supply Analysis* (Springfield, Va.: National Technical Information Service, September 1976).

8. Federal Energy Administration, *FEA Model of Oil and Gas Supply, Data Validation and Update* (Springfield, Va.: National Technical Information Service, September 1976).

9. Resources for the Future, *Workshop to Review FEA's 1976 National Energy Outlook.*

10. E. Hirst and J. Carney, *The ORNL Engineering-Economic Model of Residential Energy Use* (Oakridge, Tenn.: Oakridge National Laboratory Release ORNL/CON-24, July 1978).

11. Federal Energy Administration, *PIES Econometric Demand Model* (Springfield, Va.: National Technical Information Service, September 1976).

12. Energy Information Administration, *An Evaluation of Future World Oil Prices* (Washington: Department of Energy, EIA Analysis Report EIA-0102/4, June 1978).

13. Logistics Management Institute, *The International Energy Evaluation System* (Washington: U.S. Department of Energy, September 1978).

14. Energy Information Administration, *International Energy Assessment* (Washington: U.S. Department of Energy, EIA Analysis Report EIA-0184/1, May 1979).

15. Ibid.

16. Federal Energy Administration, *Project Independence Report* (Washington: U.S. Government Printing Office, November 1974).

17. U.S. Department of Commerce, *Survey of Current Business* (Washington: U.S. Government Printing Office, July 1979).

18. Energy Information Administration, *Energy Supply and Demand in the Midterm: 1985, 1990 and 1995* (Washington: U.S. Department of Energy, EIA Analysis Report EIA-0102/52, April 1979).

19. Resources for the Future, *Workshop to Review FEA's National Energy Outlook*.

20. G. DeSouza, "On Selecting a Peak Demand Forecast Methodology," *Public Utilities Fortnightly* (June 22, 1978):26-28.

Bibliography

Books

Baughman, M.L., P.L. Joskow, and D.P. Kamat. *Electric Power in the United States: Models and Policy Analysis.* Cambridge, Mass.: MIT Press, 1979.

Burby, R.J. *Energy and the Community.* Cambridge, Mass.: Ballinger, 1978.

Conference Board. *Energy Consumption in Manufacturing.* Cambridge, Mass.: Ballinger, 1974.

Connery, R.H., and R.S. Gilmour (eds.). *The National Energy Problem.* Lexington, Mass.: Lexington Books, D.C. Heath and Company, 1974.

Cunningham, W.H., and S.C. Lopreato. *Energy Use and Conservation Incentives.* New York: Praeger, 1977.

Fisher, F.M., and C. Kaysen. *The Demand for Electricity in the United States.* Amsterdam: North-Holland, 1962.

Gordon, R.L. *U.S. Coal and the Electric Power Industry.* Baltimore, Md.: Johns Hopkins Univ. Press, 1975.

Gordon, R.L. *Coal in the U.S. Energy Market.* Lexington, Mass.: Lexington Books, D.C. Heath and Company, 1978.

Inform Inc., *Energy Futures: Industry and the New Technologies.* Cambridge, Mass.: Ballinger, 1977.

Maddala, G.S., W.S. Chern, and G.S. Gill. *Econometric Studies in Energy Demand and Supply.* New York: Praeger, 1978.

Mancke, R.B. *The Failure of U.S. Energy Policy.* New York: Columbia Univ. Press, 1974.

Miernyk, W.H. and Frank Giarrantani. *Regional Impacts of Rising Energy Prices.* Cambridge, Mass.: Ballinger, 1978.

Miller, R.L. *The Economics of Energy.* Glenn Ridge, N.J.: Horton, 1974.

Mitchell, B.M., and Willard G. Manning. *Peak-Load Pricing European Lessons for U.S. Energy Policy.* Cambridge, Mass.: Ballinger, 1978.

Myers, J.G., and L. Nakamura. *Saving Energy in Manufacturing.* Cambridge, Mass.: Ballinger, 1978.

Naill, R.F. *Managing the Energy Transition.* Cambridge, Mass.: Ballinger, 1977.

Oppenheimer, B.I. *Oil and the Congressional Process.* Lexington, Mass.: Lexington Books, D.C. Heath and Company, 1974.

Pachauri, R.K. *The Dynamics of Electrical Energy Supply and Demand.* New York: Praeger, 1977.

Richardson, H.W. *Economic Aspects of the Energy Crisis.* Lexington, Mass.: Lexington Books, D.C. Heath and Company, 1975.

Slesser, M. *Energy in the Economy.* New York: St. Martin's Press, 1978.

Socolow, R.H., (ed.). *Saving Energy in the Home.* Cambridge, Mass: Ballinger, 1978.

Thompson, G. *Building to Save Energy: Legal and Regulatory Approaches.* Cambridge, Mass.: Ballinger, 1980.

Tolley, G.S., C.W. Upton, and V.S. Hastings. *Electric Energy Availability and Regional Growth.* Cambridge, Mass.: Ballinger, 1977.

Turvey, R., and D. Anderson. *Electricity Economics.* Baltimore, Md.: Johns Hopkins Univ. Press, 1977.

Vernon, R., (ed.). *The Oil Crisis.* New York: Norton, 1976.

Vogt, L.J., and D.A. Conner. *Electrical Energy Management.* Lexington, Mass.: Lexington Books, D.C. Heath and Company, 1977.

Warkov, S. *Energy Policy in the United States.* New York: Praeger, 1978.

Articles

Acton P.J., and B.M. Mitchel. "Do Time-of-Use Rates Change Load Curves? And How Would You Know?" *Public Utilities Fortnightly* (May 22, 1980): 15-24.

Ayres, J.M. "Predicting Building Energy Requirements." *Energy and Building* (1977):11-18.

Bagge, C.E. "The Outlook for Better Coal Utilization in Electric Power." *Public Utilities Fortnightly* (April 22, 1976):35-37.

Baughman, M.L. "Energy System Modeling, Regulation, and New Technology." In Michael S. Macrakis (ed.), *Energy Demand, Conservation, and Institutional Problems.* Cambridge, Mass.: MIT Press, 1974.

Baughman, M., and P. Joskow. "The Effects of Fuel Prices on Residential Appliance Choice in the United States." *Land Economics* (1975):41-49.

Benemann, J.R. "Biomass Energy Economics." *The Energy Journal* (1980): 107-131.

Berndt, E.R. "Aggregate Energy Efficiency and Productivity." *Annual Review of Energy* 3(1978):225-273.

Berndt, E.R., and D.O. Wood. "Technology, Prices and the Derived Demand for Energy." *Review of Economics and Statistics* 57(1975):259-267.

Bowden, J.R. "Prospects for Coal as a Direct Fuel and its Potential Through Application of Liquefaction and Gasification Technology." *Energy Sources* 3(1976):1-12.

Breedlove, R.L. "Demand-Triggered Supply Models." In Roland F. Salmonson (ed.), *Public Utility Accounting: Models, Mergers, and Information Systems.* East Lansing, Mich.: Michigan State University, Institute of Public Utilities, 1971.

Bullard, C.W., III, and Herendeen, R.A. "The Energy Costs of Goods and Services." *Energy Policy* 4(1975):268-278.

Bupp, I.C., and F. Schuller. "Natural Gas: How to Slice a Shrinking Pie." In Robert Stobaugh and Daniel Yegrin (eds.), *Energy Future.* New York: Random House, 1979.

Caves, D.W., and L.R. Christensen. "Residential Substitution of Off-Peak for Peak Electricity Usage Under Time-of-Use Pricing." *The Energy Journal* 2(1980):55–84.

Chern, W.S. "Demand and Conservation of End-Use and Primary Energy in the Residential and Commercial Sectors." *Energy Systems and Policy* 3(1978): 267–286.

Consdorf, A., and C.W. Behrens. "Appliance Energy Efficiency." *Appliance Manufacturer* 25 (March 1977):40–59.

Corey, G.R. "A Cost Comparison of Nuclear and Conventional Electric Generation." *Public Utilities Fortnightly* (April 22, 1976):25–28.

Crew, M.A., and P.R. Kleindorfer. "An Introduction to Current Problems in Public Utility Economics and Regulation." In Michael A. Crew (ed.), *Problems in Public Utility Economics and Regulation.* Lexington, Mass.: Lexington Books, D.C. Heath and Company, 1979.

Cyrulewski, J.D., and R.L. McIntyre, "The Practical Benefits of Load Modification for One Electric Utility." *Public Utilities Fortnightly* (December 20, 1979):27–35.

Danielsen, A., and L.C. Few. "A Simultaneous Equations Model of Energy Resources." *Proceedings of the American Statistical Association* (1976): 261–265.

Darmstadter, J., J. Dunkerley, and J. Alterman. "International Variations in Energy Use: Findings from a Comparative Study." *Annual Review of Energy* 3(1978):201–224.

DeSouza, G.R., "Mid-Range Energy Forecasting System: Structure, Forecasts, and Critique." *Energy Systems and Policy* 4(1980):5–24.

DeSouza, G.R. "On Selecting a Peak Demand Forecast Methodology." *Public Utilities Fortnightly* (June 22, 1978):26–28.

Dewees, D.N. "Energy Conservation in Home Furnaces." *Energy Policy* 7(June 1979):149–162.

Dimonte, G. "A Growth Projection for Electricity Demand in San Diego County to the End of the Country." *Energy Sources* 4(1974):383–400.

Dubin, F. "Energy Conservation Studies." *Energy and Buildings* 1(1977):31–42.

Faulhaber, G.R. "Peak-Load Pricing and Regulatory Accountability." In Michael A. Crew (ed.), *Problems in Public Utility Economics and Regulation.* Lexington, Mass.: Lexington Books, D.C. Heath and Company, 1979.

Fowler, R.H. "The Longevity and Searchworthiness of Petroleum Resources." *Energy* 2(June 1977):189–195.

Goldsmith, O.S. "Market Assocation of Exhaustive Resources." *Journal of Political Economy* 82(1974):1035–1040.

Griffin, J.M. "The Effects of Higher Prices on Electricity Consumption." *Bell Journal of Economics and Management Science* 5(1974):515–539.

Halvorsen, R. "Residential Demand for Electric Energy." *Review of Economics and Statistics* 57(1975):12–18.

Harrington, D.R. "The Changing Use of the Capital Asset Pricing Model in

Utility Regulation." *Public Utilities Fortnightly* (February 14, 1980): 28-30.

Hendricks, W., R. Koer, and R. Poslasek. "Consumption Patterns of Electricity." *Journal of Econometrics* 5(1977):135-153.

Hill, G.R. "Coal Liquefaction." *The Energy Journal* 1(January 1980):87-104.

Hirshberg, A.S. "The Challenge and Opportunity for Utilities in Residential Energy Conservation." *Public Utilities Fortnightly* (March 29, 1979):19-23.

Hirst, E. "Effects of Energy Conservation Research, Development, and Demonstration on Residential Energy Use." *Energy Systems and Policy* 1(1979): 37-60.

Hirst E. "Effects of the National Energy Act on Energy Use and Economics in Residential and Commercial Buildings." *Energy Systems and Policy* 2(1979): 171-190.

Horsfield, B., and R.O. Williams. "Energy for Agriculture and the Gasification of Crop Residues." *Energy Sources* 3(1978):277-292.

Horwitch, M., and F. Schuller. "Coal: Constrained Abundance." In Frank Schuller and Daniel Yegrin (eds.), *Energy Future*. New York: Random House, 1979.

Houthakker, H.S. "Residential Electricity Revisited." *The Energy Journal* 1(1980):29-41.

Hudson, E.A., and D.W. Jorgenson. "U.S. Energy Policy and Economic Growth, 1975-2000." *Bell Journal of Economics and Management Science* 5(1974): 461-514.

Hunter, Y.I., E.F.K. Watt, J.E. Flory, P.J. Hunter, and N. Mosman. "The Long-Term Implications and Constraints of Alternate Energy Policies." *Energy* 1(December 1976):375-406.

Hyde, W.H., and F.J. Wells. "The Potential Energy Productivity of U.S. Forests." *Energy Sources* 4(1979):231-258.

Johnson, R.J. "Construction Work in Progress: Planning for the Rate Case." *Public Utilities Fortnightly* (August 2, 1979):15-21.

Just, J. and L. Lave. "Government Analysis of Energy Supply and Demand: A Review." *Energy Systems and Policy* 3(1979):271-307.

Kennedy, M. "An Economic Model of the World Oil Market." *Bell Journal of Economics and Management Science* 5(1974):540-577.

Koger, R.K. "Is There Economic Justification for a So-Called Lifeline Rate?" *Public Utilities Fortnightly* (May 10, 1979):11-17.

Laude, R.H. "A Cost-Benefit Analysis of Electric Peak-Load Pricing." *Public Utilities Fortnightly* (March 29, 1979):9-19.

Limaye, D.R., R. Ciliano, and J.R. Sharko. "Quantitative Energy Studies and Models: A Review of the State of the Art." In Dilip R. Limaye (ed.), *Energy Policy Evaluation*. Lexington, Mass: Lexington Books, D.C. Heath and Company, 1974, pp. 177-214.

Maybee, J.S., and N.D. Uri. "A Methodology for Forecasting Discrete Approximations to the Load Duration Curve." *Energy Sources* 4(1978):125-134.

McDonald S.L. "U.S. Depletion Policy: Likely Effects of Changes." *Energy Policy* 4(March 1976):56-62.

McKenna, J.T., Jr., and U.W. Ruskin. "Gas Supply Planning: Today's Approach." *Public Utilities Fortnightly* (August 30, 1979):32-34.

Mesarovic, M., and B.B. Huges. "Analysis of the WAES Scenarios Using the World Intergrated Model." *Energy Policy* 6(June 1978):129-139.

Mooz, W. "Projecting Electrical Energy Demand for California Manufacturing." In D.R. Limaye (ed.), *Energy Policy Evaluation.* Lexington, Mass.: Lexington Books, D.C. Heath and Company, 1974.

Mork, K.A., and R.E. Hall. "Energy Prices and the U.S. Economy in 1979-1981." *The Energy Journal* 1(April 1980):41-54.

Mount, T.D., L.D. Chapman, and T.J. Tyrell. "Electricity Demand in the United States: An Econometric Analysis." In M.S. Mackrakis (ed.), *Energy: Demand, Conservation, and Institutional Problems.* Cambridge, Mass.: MIT Press, 1974.

Murgatroyd, W., and B.C. Wilkins. "The Efficiency of Electric Motive Power in Industry." *Energy* 4(1976):337-346.

Norgard, J. "Improved Efficiency in Domestic Electricity Use." *Energy Policy* 1(1979):43-56.

Nordhaus, W.D. "The Energy Crisis and Macroeconomic Policy." *The Energy Journal* 1(1980):11-20.

Nordin, J.A. "Residential Electric Load Control Time-of-Use Pricing." *Public Utilities Fortnightly* (July 20, 1978):16-21.

Ogunsola, O.O. "A Corporate Planning Model for an Integrated Oil Company." In T. Naylor (ed.), *Simulation Models in Corporate Planning.* New York: Praeger, 1979.

Olson, M. "Development of Coalbed Methane as an Energy Source." *Energy Sources* 4(1979):353-365.

Pindyck, R.S. "Interfuel Substitution and the Industrial Demand for Energy: An International Comparison." *Review of Economics and Statistics* 57 (1975):259-267.

Reece, D.K. "Competitive Bidding for Offshore Petroleum Leases." *The Bell Journal of Economics* 2(1978):369-389.

Reed, D.J. "Utility Rates Under the National Act, Quo Vadis?" *Public Utilities Fortnightly* (July 20, 1978):11-15.

Renshaw, E.F. "The Decontrol of U.S. Oil Production." *Energy Policy* 8(1980): 38-49.

Renshaw, E.F. "Productivity and the Demand for Electricity." *Public Utilities Fortnightly* (May 6, 1976):17-20.

Rosenberg, N. "Innovative Responses to Materials Shortages." *American Economic Review* 63(1973):111-118.

Saaly, T.L., and R.S. Mariano. "Effects of Energy Conservation Research, Development, and Demonstration on Residential Energy Use." *Energy Systems and Policy* 1(1979):85-111.

Smith, V.L. "Economics of Production from Natural Resources." *American Economic Review* 58(1968):409-431.

Spann R.M., E.W. Erickson, and R. Cibareo. "An Econometric Analysis of Substitution and Usage Effects on Industrial Sector Energy Demands." In Dilip R. Limaye (ed.), *Energy Policy Evaluation.* Lexington, Mass: Lexington Books, D.C. Heath and Company, 1974, pp. 1-12.

Starr, C., and S. Field. "Economic Growth, Employment and Energy." *Energy Policy* 1(1979):2-22.

Schmalensee, R. "Appropriate Government Policy Toward Commercialization of New Energy Supply Technologies." *The Energy Journal* 1(1980):1-40.

Taylor, L.D. "The Demand for Electricity: A Survey." *Bell Journal of Economics* 6(175):74-110.

Tussing, A.R. "The U.S. Outlook for Supplemental Gas." *The Energy Journal* 1(January 1980):63-76.

Uhler, R.G., and B. Zycher. "Energy Forecasting and its Uncertainties." *Public Utilities Fortnightly* (January 17, 1980):27-33.

Uri, N.D. "Price, Quantity and Causality in the Production of Crude Petroleum in the United States." *Energy Sources* 5(1980):31-44.

Uri, N.D. "Price Expectations and the Demand for Electric Energy." *Energy Systems and Policy* 3(1979):73-84.

Uri, N.D. "Short Run Energy Demand and Interfuel Substitution by Electric Utilities." *Energy Sources* 4(1978a):67-76.

Uri, N.D. "The Demand for Electric Energy in the United States." *Energy Systems and Policy* 2(1978b):233-243.

Webb, M.G. "Policy on Energy Pricing." *Energy Policy* 6(1978):53-65.

Wecksler, A.N. "Energy Conservation: Alternative with Flexible Benefits." *Appliance Manufacturer* 10(1979):52-56.

Wenders, J.T., and A. Lyman. "An Analysis of the Benefits and Costs of Seasonal-Time-of-Day Electricity Rates." In Michael A. Crew (ed.), *Problems in Public Utility Economics and Regulation.* Lexington, Mass.: Lexington Books, D.C. Heath and Company, 1979.

Whiting, M. "Industry Saves Energy: Progress Report, 1977." *Annual Review of Energy* 3(1978):181-199.

Wilson, J.W. "Residential Demand for Electricity." *Quarterly Review of Economics and Business* 2(1971):7-22.

Wolff, R.F. "Peak Growth Down Again to Only 0.6%." *Electrical World* (November 1, 1979):48-49.

Yasky, Y., and A.J. Penz. "Uncertainities in Predicting Energy Consumption in Houses." *Energy Systems and Policy* 3(1979):243-270.

Reports

AIA Research Corp. *Phase One/Base Data for the Development of Energy Performance Standards for New Buildings.* Springfield, Va.: National Technical Information Service, 1978.

Amos, J.M. *Energy System Analysis Procedure.* Rolla, Mo.: Business Research Management Center, Department of Air Force, 1977.

Anderson, K.P. *Residential Energy Use: An Econometric Analysis.* Santa Monica, Calif.: Rand Corporation, 1973.

Argonne Nation Laboratory. *Analysis of Coal Development Issues with the Argonne Coal Market Model.* Springfield, Va.: National Technical Information Service, 1979.

Argonne National Laboratory. *Constraints to Increased Coal Use.* Springfield, Va.: National Technical Information Service, 1979.

Argonne National Laboratory. *Environmental Evaluation of the PIES Trendlong Mid-Mid Scenario: Federal Region V.* Springfield, Va.: National Technical Information Service, 1979.

Argonne National Laboratory. *Implications of Seasonal Peak Demand Forecasts for Electric Heating Desirability.* Springfield, Va.: National Technical Information Service, 1979.

Argonne National Laboratory. *Residential Energy Consumption Analysis Utilizing DOE-1 Computer Program.* Springfield, Va.: National Technical Information Service, 1979.

Argonne National Laboratory. *Trends and Issues in Energy Supply and Demand in the Midwest.* Springfield, Va.: National Technical Information Service, 1978.

Arizona State University, Department of Electrical Engineering. *Midterm Simulation of Electrical Power Systems.* Springfield, Va.: National Technical Information Service, 1979.

Arthur Anderson and Co. *Study of the Treatment of Construction Work in Progress and Tax-Timing Differences for Rate-Making Purposes in the Electric Utility Industry.* Springfield, Va.: National Technical Information Service, 1977.

Arthur D. Little, Inc. *An Analysis of Future Electric Power Needs and Sources For The Turlock and Modesto Irrigation Districts Analyses.* Cambridge Mass., 1975.

Arthur D. Little, Inc. *Energy Efficiency and Electric Motors.* Springfield, Va.: National Technical Information Service, 1976.

Arthur D. Little, Inc. *Environmental Considerations of Selected Energy Conserving Manufacturing Process Options,* Vol. 16. Springfield, Va.: National Technical Information Service, 1979.

Arthur D. Little, Inc. *Idaho Power Company's Need For Additional Generating Capacity.* Cambridge, Mass., 1976.

Arthur D. Little, Inc. *Independent Demand Forecast Assessment Forecast Assessment for Capco Power Pool.* Cambridge, Mass., 1976.

Arthur D. Little, Inc., et al. *Industrial Cogeneration Optimization Program.* Washington: U.S. Department of Energy, 1980.

Arthur D. Little, Inc. *Long Term Load Forecast For Potomac Electric Power Company.* Cambridge, Mass., 1973.

Arthur D. Little, Inc. *Topic 9: Mechanical Controls and Penalty Pricing.* Palo Alto, Calif.: Electric Power Research Institute, 1977.

Arthur D. Little, Inc. *Peak Load Forecast for Kansas Power and Light Company.* Cambridge, Mass., 1976.

Arthur D. Little, Inc. *Residential Solar Heating and Cooling Constraints and Incentives.* Cambridge, Mass., 1976.

Arthur D. Little, Inc. *Southeastern Idaho Electric Power Outlook.* Cambridge, Mass., 1979.

Arthur D. Little, Inc. *The Development of an Energy and Demand Forecast and Forecasting Model for Omaha Public Power District.* Cambridge, Mass., 1977.

Arthur D. Little, Inc. *Topic 8: The Utilization of Off-Peak Electricity.* Palo Alto, Calif.: Electric Power Research Institute, 1977.

Ashburn, R.E. *Critical Issues in Costing Approaches for Time Differentiated Rates.* Palo Alto, Calif.: Electric Power Research Institute, 1977.

Battelle Columbus Laboratories. *Development and Establishment of Energy Efficiency Improvement Targets for Primary Metal Industries: SIC 33.* Springfield, Va.: National Technical Information Service, 1977.

Battelle Columbus Laboratories. *Model for Long Range Forecasting of Electric Energy and Demand.* Columbus, Ohio, 1977.

Berndt, E.R., and D.O. Wood. *Consistent Projections of Energy Demand and Aggregate Economic Growth: A Review of Issues and Empriical Studies.* Cambridge, Mass.: MIT Energy Laboratory, 1977.

Brookhaven National Laboratory. *Application of District Heating System to U.S. Urban Areas.* Springfield, Va.: National Technical Information Service, 1978.

Brookhaven National Laboratory. *Applications of Energy Systems Analysis to Policy and Technology Studies.* Springfield, Va.: National Technical Information Service, 1978.

Brookhaven National Laboratory Associated Universities, Inc. *Brookhaven Energy System Optimization Model Methodology and Documentation (Version 2.1).* Springfield, Va.: National Technical Information Service, 1978.

Brookhaven National Laboratory. *Documentation of an Interactive Program for Projecting Space Heating Energy Demand.* Springfield, Va.: National Technical Information Service, 1978.

Brookhaven National Laboratory. *Evaluation of Technological Data in the DFI and PIES Models.* Springfield, Va.: National Technical Information Service, 1979.

Brookhaven National Laboratory. *Energy Optimization of Industrial Energy Use.* Springfield, Va.: National Technical Information Service, 1979.

Brookhaven National Laboratory. *Integrated Methodology for Assessing Energy-Economic Interactions.* Springfield, Va.: National Technical Information Service, 1979.

Brookhaven National Laboratory. *Iron and Steel Industry Process Model.* Springfield, Va.: National Technical Information Service, 1978.

Brookhaven National Laboratory. *MARKAL: A Multiperiod, Linear-Programming Model for Energy Systems Analysis.* Springfield, Va.: National Technical Information Service, 1979.

Brookhaven National Laboratory, Department of Applied Science. *Simulation of Residential Energy Use and Its Dependence on Land Use and Economic Parameters.* Upton, N.Y.: National Science Foundation/Rann Program, 1974.

California Energy Commission. *Natural Gas Demand, 1978–1995: Forecast and Technical Documentation.* Sacramento, Calif., 1978.

California, University of, at Berkeley, Center for Research in Management. *Political Economy of Energy Regulation: A Classification of Policies.* Springfield, Va.: National Technical Information Service, 1978.

Charles River Associates, Inc. *Analysis of Household Appliance Choice.* Palo Alto, Calif.: Electric Power Research Institute, 1979.

Charles River Associates, Inc. *Design for Coal Supply Analysis System.* Palo Alto, Calif.: Electric Power Research Institute, 1979.

Charles River Associates, Inc. *Procedures for Independent Analyses of Electric Energy and Peak Loads by State Agencies.* Springfield, Va.: National Technical Information Service, 1978.

Chern, W.S. *Energy Demand and Interfuel Substitution in the Commercial Sector.* Oakridge, Tenn.: Oakridge National Laboratory, 1976.

Chern, W.S., R.E. Just, and S.B. Caudill. *Energy Demand and Fuel Choices in the Pulp and Paper Industry.* Oakridge, Tenn.: Oakridge National Laboratory, 1978.

Cohn, S., E. Hirst, and J. Jackson. *Econometric Analyses of Household Fuel Demands.* Oakridge, Tenn.: Oakridge National Laboratory, 1977.

Committee for Economic Development, Research and Policy Committee. *International Economic Consequences of High Priced Energy.* New York: Committee for Economic Development, 1975.

Delene, J.G., and J.B. Gaston. *A Regional Comparison of Savings from Various Residential Energy Conservation Strategies.* Oakridge Tenn.: Oakridge National Laboratory, 1976.

Deonigi, D.E., et al. *Investigation of International Energy Economics.* Springfield, Va.: National Technical Information Service, 1977.

Department of Energy. *Assessment of Potential U.S. Petroleum Supply Shortfalls 1978 to 1990.* Springfield, Va.: National Technical Information Service, 1978.

Department of Energy. *Coal Strike Impact Methodologies.* Springfield, Va.: National Technical Information, 1978.

Department of Energy. *Department of Energy Organization and Functions Fact Book.* Springfield, Va.: National Technical Information Service, 1977.

Department of Energy. *EIA Annual Report on Monthly Comparisons of Peak Demands and Energy for Load: 1973 to 1977.* Springfield, Va.: National Technical Information Service, 1978.

Department of Energy. *EIA Input-Output Model Simulation Procedures Technical Memorandum TM/IA/78-03.* Springfield, Va.: National Technical Information Service, 1978.

Department of Energy. *Energy Demand in Devleoping Countries.* Springfield, Va.: National Technical Information Service, 1979.

Department of Energy. *Evaluation of Energy Related Tax and Tax Credit Programs.* Springfield, Va.: National Technical Information Service, 1978.

Department of Energy. *Gasnet: Methodology Description.* Springfield, Va.: National Technical Information Service, 1978.

Department of Energy. *Projected 1985 Automobile Gasoline Savings from the House-Passed Gas Guzzler Tax and Conference Minimum Mileage Standards.* Springfield, Va.: National Technical Information Service, 1978.

Department of Energy. *Sector Employment Implications of Alternate Energy Scenarios.* Springfield, Va.: National Technical Information Service, 1978.

Dole, S.H. *Energy Use and Conservation in the Residential Sector: A Regional Analysis.* Santa Monica, Calif.: Rand Corporation, 1975.

Economics Research Group. *Dynamic Models of the Industrial Demand for Energy.* Palo Alto, Calif.: Electric Power Research Institute, 1977.

Economics, Statistics and Cooperatives Service. *Energy and U.S. Agriculture: Irrigation Pumping, 1974-1977.* Springfield, Va.: National Technical Information Service, 1978.

Edison Electric Institute. *Annual Energy Requirements of Electric Household Appliances.* New York: Edison Electric Institute, Pamphlet EEI-Pub. No. 75-61, 1978.

Electric Power Research Institute. *Demand 77, EPRI Annual Energy Forecasts and Consumption Model Volume 2.* Palo Alto, Calif., 1979.

Electric Power Research Institute. *How Electric Utilities Forecast: EPRI Symposium Proceedings.* Springfield, Va.: National Technical Information Service, 1979.

Energy and Environmental Analysis, Inc. *Data Sources and Methods of Industrial Energy Analysis.* Washington: U.S. Department of Energy, 1979.

Energy Information Administration. *Demand for World Coal Through 1995.* Springfield, Va.: National Technical Information Service, 1979.

Energy Information Administration. *End Use Energy Consumption Data Base.*

Version 110. User's Manual. Washington: U.S. Department of Energy, 1979.

Energy Information Administration. *Energy Supply and Demand in the Short Term: 1979 and 1980.* Springfield, Va.: National Technical Information Service, 1979.

Energy Information Administration. *Review and Application of MULTIREGION as a Regional Economic Impact and Projection Model.* Springfield, Va.: National Technical Information Service, 1979.

Energy Modeling Forum, Stanford University. *Electric Load Forecasting: Probing the Issues with Models.* Palo Alto, Calif.: Electric Power Research Institute, 1979.

Energy System Research Group. *Electricity Requirements in New York State.* Boston, Mass., 1979.

Federal Energy Administration. "Energy Conservation Program for Appliances: Energy Efficiency Improvement Targets." *Federal Register* (July 15, 1977): 36648-35570.

Finger, S. *Electric Power System Production Costing and Reliability Analysis Including Hydroelectric, Storage, and Time Dependent Power Plants.* Cambridge, Mass.: MIT Energy Laboratory, 1979.

Finger, S. *Sysgen Production Costing and Reliability Model User Documentation.* Cambridge, Mass.: MIT Energy Laboratory, 1979.

General Accounting Office. *Hydropower—An Energy Source Whose Time Has Come Again.* Springfield, Va.: National Technical Information Service, 1980.

General Accounting Office. *Analysis of Current Trends in U.S. Petroleum and Natural Gas Production.* Springfield, Va.: National Technical Information Service, 1979.

Gordon, R.L. *Economic Analysis of Coal Supply: An Assessment of Existing Studies.* Springfield, Va.: National Technical Information Service, 1979.

Halvorsen, R. *Industrial Demand for Energy.* Springfield, Va.: National Technical Information Service, 1977.

Hirst, E., and J. Carney. *The ORNL Engineering-Economic Model of Residential Energy Use.* Oakridge, Tenn.: Oakridge National Laboratory, 1978.

Hittman Associates, Inc. *The National Energy Plan: Energy Conservation in Appliances.* Columbia, Md.: Energy Research and Development Administration, 1977.

Hittman Associates, Inc. *The National Energy Plan: Energy Conservation with Insulation.* Columbia, Md.: Energy Research and Development Administration, 1977.

Hittman Associates, Inc. *A Study of the Physical Characteristics, Energy Consumption, and Related Institution Factors in the Commercial Sector.* Springfield, Va.: National Technical Information Service, 1973.

Hoskins, R.A., and E. Hirst. *Energy and Cost Analysis of Residential Water Heaters.* Oakridge, Tenn.: Oakridge National Laboratory, 1977.

Hutchins, P., and E. Hirst. *Engineering-Economic Analysis of Mobile Home*

Thermal Performance. Oakridge, Tenn.: Oakridge National Laboratory, 1978.

Illinois University. *Labor and Energy Impacts of Energy Conservation Measures. First Quarterly Progress Report*. Springfield, Va.: National Technical Information Service, 1979.

Institute for Energy Analysis. *Characterization of Industrial Process Energy Services*. Springfield, Va.: National Technical Information Service, 1979.

Isaac, B.M. *Relationship between Crude Oil Price Controls and Refined Product Prices*. Washington: U.S. Department of Energy, 1978.

Jackson, J.R., et al. *The Commercial Demand for Energy: A Disaggregated Approach*. Springfield, Va.: National Technical Information Service, 1978.

Jaske, M.R., et al., *Technical Documentation of the Residential Sales Forecasting Model: Electricity and Natural Gas*. Sacramento, Calif.: California Energy Commission, 1979.

Jaske, M.R., et al. *The Technical Documentation of the Peak Load Forecasting Model*. Sacramento, Calif.: California Energy Commission, 1979.

Kilgore, W.C., and M. Rodekohr. *Examination of Several World Oil Price Scenarios Given Exogenous Supply and Demand Estimates*. Washington: U.S. Department of Energy, 1978.

Lane, J.H. *Consensus Forecast of U.S. Electricity Supply and Demand to the Year 2000*. Oakridge, Tenn.: Oakridge National Laboratory, 1977.

Lawrence Livermore Laboratory. *Results of the 1978–79 Consensus Forecast Experiment*. Springfield, Va.: National Technical Information Service, 1979.

Lawrence Livermore Laboratory. *New Factors Influencing the Development of Free World Oil Resources*. Springfield, Va.: National Technical Information Service, 1979.

Lawrence Livermore Laboratory. *Lawrence Livermore Laboratory Energy Policy Model: A Brief Overview*. Springfield, Va.: National Technical Information Service, 1979.

Lin, W., E. Hirst, and S. Cohn. *Fuel Choices in the Household Sector*. Oakridge, Tenn.: Oakridge National Laboratory, 1976.

Los Alamos Scientific Laboratory. *Energy Policy and Decision Analysis: New Concepts and Mechanisms*. Springfield, Va.: National Technical Information Service, 1979.

Macal, C.M. *Analysis of Coal Development Issues with the Argonne Coal Market Model*. Illinois: Argonne National Laboratory, 1979.

Metrostudy Corporation. *Commercial Sector Energy Consumption: Analysis and Recommendations for Data Collection*. Springfield, Va.: National Technical Information Service, 1977.

Midwest Research Institute. *Patterns of Energy Use by Electrical Appliances*. Palo Alto, Calif.: Electric Power Research Institute, 1979.

Mitre Corporation. *Energy Resources for the Year 2000 and Beyond.* Springfield, Va.: National Technical Information Service, 1975.

National Association of Counties. *Impact of State Mandated Thermal Efficiency Standards on Counties.* Springfield, Va.: National Technical Information Service, 1977.

National Bureau of Standards. *Cost Effectiveness of Energy Conservation Investments in New United States Residences.* Springfield, Va.: National Technical Information Service, 1979.

National Bureau of Standards. *Economics and the Selection and Development of Energy Standards for Buildings.* Springfield, Va.: National Technical Information Service, 1979.

National Bureau of Standards. *Life-Cycle Costing Guide for Energy Conservation in Buildings.* Springfield, Va.: National Technical Information Service, 1979.

National Center for Analysis of Energy Systems. *Modeling Market Penetration with Emphasis on the DFI Energy Economy System.* Springfield, Va.: National Technical Information Service, 1979.

National Center for Atmospheric Research. *Residential Electricity Demand in Colorado Municipalities: A Time-Series Cross-Section Study.* Springfield, Va.: National Technical Information Service, 1979.

Spann, R.M., and Beauvais, E.C. "Econometric Estimation of Peak Electricity Demands." In *Forecasting and Modeling Time-of-Day and Seasonal Electricity Demands.* Palo Alto, Calif.: Electric Power Research Institute, 1977, pp. 2-11- 2-22.

Wen, C.F., and R.T. Newcomb. *The Potential of Coal Based Fuel and Energy Complexes: A Regional Appraisal.* National Science Foundation—RANN Report, January 1974.

Wenders, J.T. "Theoretical Determinants of the Industrial Demand for Electricity by Time of Day." In *Forecasting and Modeling Time-of-Day and Seasonal Electricity Demands.* Palo Alto, Calif.: Electric Power Research Institute, 1977, pp. 3-90–3-92.

Index

Accelerated depreciation, 97, 136, 142, 183

Accounting, flowthrough/normalized, 142

Adelman, Morris, 7, 8

Administrative expenses, 163

Air conditioners: central, 47; customer disaggregation, 67; efficiency, 32; load controls, 64, 65, 151; room, 32, 46

Air-pollution requirements, 80, 97

Air-quality control regions, 82

Alcoa, 54

Algeria, 1

Aluminum industry, 53, 54

American Iron and Steel Institute, 91, 92

American Society of Heating, Refrigerating, and Air Conditioning Engineers: Standard 90-75, 33, 47-48

Ammonia production, 94

Anderson, D., and R. Turvey, 129

Annualized capital charge, 161

Annualized capital costs, 162

Annualized fixed-charge rate, 132-133

Appliance-efficiency standards, 32-33, 44-47, 67, 68, 79, 179-180

Appliance-saturation ratio, 31

Appliance-saturation submodels, 42-44

Appliance units, number of, 30-32

Arthur D. Little, Inc., 33, 45, 53, 54, 55, 60, 70, 75, 80, 88, 90, 91

ASHRAE. *See* American Society of Heating, Refrigerating, and Air Conditioning Engineers

Atmospheric fluidized-bed boilers, 87

Attainment regions, 82

Australia, 107

Automobiles, 79, 173, 182, 183

Average system price projection, 155-157

Base-load units, 125, 171-172, 184; costs, 144, 145, 158-164; generating capacity, 84-85; heat rates, 86-88

Basic-oxygen furnaces, 89, 90, 91, 92

BEPS. *See* Building Energy Performance Standards

Bergius-Pier technology, 103

Beta coefficient, 139, 140, 141

Blackouts and brownouts, 127, 128

Boilers, 98-100, 184

Bonner and Moore, 170

Boston Edison, 146, 148-149

Brazil, 106

British thermal unit (Btu), defined, 20

Brookhaven National Laboratory, 74, 77-78, 88, 102

Building efficiency improvements, 33, 47-49

Bull Run Plant (TVA), 86

Building Energy Performance Standards (DOE), 33, 47-49, 79-80

Canada, 1, 20, 105, 106, 108

Capacity costs, 145

Capital-asset pricing model, 138-141

Capital costs, 105, 144, 160-161

Capital-recovery factor, 130-131, 161

Capitalization ratio, 161

Carter administration, 81

Case Western Reserve University, 15

Cement production, 101

Central-equivalent concept, 67

Char, 103

China, 108

Chlorine production, 70

Class peak, defined, 145

Class-price differentials, 155, 185

Clean Air Acts (1970, 1977), 82

Clothes dryers, 46

Club of Rome, 15

Coal: Btu's, 169; byproducts, 94; -coke ratio, 94; conversion program,

81–82, 125, 184; demand analysis, 73–115; demand studies, 73–75; demand-total primary energy demand, 75–78; depletion effect, 112; exports, 106–109; -fired base-load units; forecasts, 175; -gas, 103, 105; gasification, 103; generating capacity, 84–85; liquefaction, 103, mine costs/categories, 169; -oil, 94, 105, 106; preheating system, 95; price, 169; producing regions, 87, 111–115, 177; production U.S., 109–115; production costs, 113, 114; share, 80–86 (electricity generation), 99–100 (boiler fuel), 101–102 (nonboiler-process heaters); sulfur, 113, 169; supply model, 168–169; -tar, 94; transport costs, 84, 114. *See also* Base-load units
Coke, 89, 90, 92–95, 96
Coincidence factor, 71
Coincident demand, 71
Cold reserves, 124
Commercial sector: electricity demand, 49–52, energy policies, 180–181, 182–183
Committee on Nuclear and Alternative Energy Systems, 74
Computer Sciences Corporation, 16
Con Edison, 155
Conservation financing program, 180
Conservation grants, 180–181
Conservation programs, 33–34, 51–52, 53–54, 179–188
Conservation tax credit, 182–183
Consol-BNR process, 95
Constant-dollar estimates, 158–159
Construction costs, 158–159
Construction labor pool, 104–105
Construction work in progress, 142, 159, 160
Consumer-loss cost, 128
Consumer surplus, 127
Cost minimization, 57, 142
Customer charges, 145, 146
Customer costs, 144, 163

Customer-population growth rate, 30–31

Darmstadter, J.; J. Dunkerly; and J. Alterman, 20
Debt-equity ratio, 141
Declining-block structure, 146, 152, 185
Deferred tax account, 142
Demand charges, 69–70, 145, 146, 151
Demand-controller concept, 70
Demand costs, defined, 144
Demand curves versus point estimates, 172
Demand inelasticity, 149
Demand models: IEES, 12; MEFS, 172–173, 177–178
Demand probability distribution, 126
Demonstrated-reserve base, defined, 112
Department of Energy Organization Act (1977), 8, 74
Design energy budget, 48, 49, 79–80
DeSouza, G.R., 178
Detroit Edison, 150
DOE. *See* U.S. Department of Energy
Domestic oil, defined, 76
DRI Macroeconomic Model, 176–177
Dry-well ratio, 118
Duke Power, 153

EIA. *See* Energy Information Administration
EPRI. *See* Electric Power Research Institute
Eckbo, Jacoby, and Smith, 121
Econometric models, 26, 27–28, 57, 60, 122–123
Economic factors in investment return, 141
Economic optimum versus thermodynamic optimum, 57
Effective tax rate, 161
Electric and Hybrid Vehicle Program (DOE), 79
Electric cars, 79

Electric furnaces, 89, 90, 91, 95
Electric heat pump, 31, 32
Electric motors and pumps, 53–54, 57, 181
Electric-output ratio, 56
Electric Power Research Institute, 70, 83, 105, 149, 159, 165, 172
Electric ranges and ovens, 46
Electric-resistance heating, 31, 32
Electric Space heating, 31, 51, 151
Electric utilities, 78–89; coal consumption, 78, 80, 85–86, 88–89, 123; cogenerators, 55–56; conservation programs, 79, 179, 184; generation costs, 160, 162, 163; models, 13 (IEES), 171–172 (MEFS); oil and gas consumption, 80, 85–86, 123; power wheeling and pooling, 186; public/private, 161; regulated rate structures, 137–158; size and investment return, 141; supply models, 4, 123–130; wholesale/ retail transactions, 185–186. *See also* Base-load units; Peak-load facilities
Electrical World, 60
Electricity: conservation, 33–34, 53–54; demand models, 4, 19–72; generation patterns and forecasts, 79–80; outages, scheduled/forced, 125, 127, 128; peak demand, 30, 60–72, 147; price, 56, 154–158; sales modeling, 22–30; use profiles, 34–35. *See also* Electric utilities
Electricity-penetration rates, 52
Electricity-utilization rates, 52
Electrification, defined, 79
Electrolytic processes, 52, 53, 54
End-use models, 26, 27, 28, 52, 57
Energy: audits, 34, 180, 181; budgets, 48–49; charge versus demand charge, 69, 145–146, 151; consumption by fuel shares/sector, 21–22, 117; conversion factors, 20; cost allocation, 144, 147; demand patterns, 20–22; efficiency ratio, 32; management devices,

70; -GNP ratio, 20–21, 75; modeling, 3–4; price-GNP forecast, 176–177; price regulation, 137–164; supply models, 117–136; units, 20. *See also* Models
Energy and Environmental Analysis, 98, 101
Energy and Environmental Associates, 147
Energy Conservation and Production Act (1976), 32, 33
Energy Conservation Standards for New Buildings Act (1976), 47
Energy Futures Report (Harvard Business School), 3, 73, 75
Energy Information Administration (DOE), 8–15, 74, 77, 85, 86, 88, 98, 99, 100, 102, 106, 115, 158, 165, 166, 173
Energy Modeling Forum, 165
Energy policy. *See* U.S., energy policies
Energy Policy and Conservation Act (1975), 32, 33
Energy Research and Development Administration, 130
Energy Security Act (1980), 103–104
Energy Supply and Environmental Coordination Act (1974), 80, 81
Energy Tax Act (1978), 34, 79, 97, 136, 182–183
Engineering labor pool, 104
Engineering Societies' Commission on Energy, Inc., 105
Environmental Protection Agency, 87, 169
Europe, 106, 107, 108
Expected value, 138

FUA. *See* Powerplant and Industrial Fuel Use Act
Fall River Electric Light Company, 146
Farmers Home Administration, 180
Federal building, conservation of energy in, 181
Federal Energy Administration, 8, 74, 165, 166, 176

Federal Energy Regulatory Council, 154, 158, 185, 186
Federal Trade Commission, 44
Financing programs, 180
Fischer-Tropsch synthesis, 103
Fixed-charge factor, 161, 162
Flowthrough accounting, 142
FMC process, 95
Food industry, 55
Forced outage, 125
Ford Foundation, 75
Forecasting energy-management devices, 70
Forecasting methodologies, 26–28, 62–63, 98
Fossil fuels, 55, 79
France, 106, 107
Freezers, 45
Fuel-adjustment clause, 142–143, 146
Fuel costs, 162–163
Fuel-heat input rate, 184
Fuel shares of energy consumption, by sector, 21–22, 117

Gas, categories of, 187
Gas-guzzler tax, 183
Gas heating, 31
Gas Research Institute, 74
Gas reserve-production ratio, 117, 118
Gas-turbine and diesel systems, 55
Gas wells/oil wells ratio, 118
Gasification processes, 103
Gasohol tax exemption, 183
General Electric, 80
Generation probability distribution, 126
Geothermal power, 84
Germany, 103
Gibbs & Hill, 55, 60
GNP deflator, 187
GNP-energy price forecast, 176–177
GNP-energy ratio, 20–21, 75
Government National Mortgage Association, 180
Greene County Project (N.Y.), 82
Gross reserve margin, 124
Gross reserve, defined, 120

HUD. See U.S. Department of Housing and Urban Development
Hagerman, R.L., and B.T. Ratcherford, 141
Harrington, D.R., 140
Harvard Business School: Energy Project, 3, 73, 75
Heat pump, 31, 32
Heat rate, defined, 124
Heat rates, coal-fired, 86–88
High-priority use, defined, 188
Hirst model, 172
Hogan, W., and S. Parikh, 165
Hooker Chemical Company, 70
Hope Natural Gas case (1944), 137, 149
Hot-metal charge rate, defined, 92
Household size, decline in, 30–31
Housing units, multifamily versus single family, 33, 34–35
Hydrogenation, 103
Hydropower and renewable resources, 84
Hyman, L., and J. Egan, 140

IEES. See International Energy Evaluation System
Idaho Power, 155
Ideal-rate demand-control devices, 70
Illinois, 141
Incremental pricing, 97, 158, 164, 186, 188
Indirect conversion, 103
Industrial sector: cogeneration, 55–56, 79, 107, 153–154; electricity pricing, 155, 157; energy policies, 56–57, 181, 182–183, 184; fuel coal demand, 96–102; peak-demand model, 69–71; sales model, 52–60
Inflation-adjustment factor, 187
Instantaneous demand-control devices, 70
Insulation-investment credits, 182
Insulation standards, 33
Integration models: 13–14 (IEES), 168 (MEFS)
Interest during construction, 159–160

Interfuel substitution, 55, 79, 107
International Energy Evaluation
    System, 11–15, 173
International energy models, 7–17
Interruptible tariff, 70–71, 150, 185
Inverse-elasticity rule, 149
Investment risk, 138–141
Investment tax credits, 34, 53, 79, 97,
    136, 142, 161, 182–182
Italy, 106, 107

Jackson, Henry M., 165
Jacoby, Henry, 7
Japan, 1, 106, 107, 108

Koger, R.K., 153

Labeling requirements, 44–45, 181
Level of detail, 26
Levelized costing, 130–136
Libya, 1
Life-cycle costs, 31–32, 181
Lifeline rates, 152–153
Lighting efficiency, 32, 54
Linear program, 128–129
Load controls, 64–65
Load-duration curve, 171, 178
Load-management rates, 150–151,
    185
Load-shift factor, defined, 68
Loans and grants, 180–181
Long Island Lighting Company, 155
Long-run Energy Analysis Program, 74
Loss of largest generator method, 126
Loss-of-load probability, 126–127
Low-income conservation grants, 180
Low-income families, defined, 180
Lurgi process, 103

MEFS. See Mid-Range Energy Fore-
    casting System
Magnetohydrodynamics, 87
Maine, 141
Marginal-analysis rule, 128
Marginal-cost pricing, 149
Market return and risk-free return,
    139–140

Markowitz, H., 138
Maximum lawful price, 187
Merit-order dispatch, 128
Mesarovic, M., and E. Pestel, 15
Metallurgical-coal demand, 89–96
Metallurgical-coal exports, 106–109
Methanation, 103
Metropolitan Edison, 150, 152
Mexico, 1, 55
Mid-Range Energy Forecasting System,
    10, 12, 74, 165–178
Middle East, 119–120
Minimum-efficiency standard, defined,
    45
Minimum Property Standards (HUD),
    33, 47
Minnesota, 141
Missouri, 141
MIT: Energy Laboratory model, 8,
    120–122. See also Workshop on
    Alternative Energy Strategies;
    World Coal Study; World Oil Project
Models: demand, 4, 12, 19–72, 172–
    173, 177–178; electric utility, 13,
    171–172; end-use, 26, 27, 28, 52,
    57; evaluation criteria, 25–26;
    forecasting, 26–28; industrial
    electricity sales, 57–60; integration,
    13–14, 168; international, 7–17;
    logic, 35–42, 52, 71, 166; national,
    3; public-sector, 7–17, 165–178;
    sectoral, 3–4; supply, 4, 117–136,
    time-series, 26, 27
Moderate income, defined, 180
Modular structure, 28–30
Monopolies, natural, 137
Motive-power function, 52–53
Motor vehicles, recreational, 182
Motors and pumps, 53–54, 57, 181

Naphthalene, 94
NASA, 54
National Association of the Regula-
    tory Utility Commissioners, 149,
    150
National Energy Act (1978), 57, 179.
    See also Energy Tax Act; National

Energy Conservation Policy Act;
Natural Gas Policy Act (1978);
Powerplant and Industrial Fuel Use
Act, Public Utility Regulatory Poli-
cies Act
National Energy Conservation Policy
Act (1978), 33, 34, 45, 53, 67, 68,
79, 96, 179–182
National energy models, 3
National Research Council, 74
Natural gas, 55, 79, 89, 97, 105, 186–
188
Natural Gas Policy Act (1978), 97,
186–188
NERCO, 84
Nigeria, 1
Nixon, Richard M., 8, 74, 165
Nominal dollar estimate, 159
Nonboiler fuel use, 100–101
Noncoincident demand, 71
Normalized accounting, 142
North Sea Region, 121
Northeast Utilities, 64
Norway, 55
Nuclear power, 80, 82–84, 88–89,
107, 124
Nuclear Regulatory Commission, 83

Oakridge National Laboratory, 43,
130, 172
Off-road vehicle study, 182
Office of Technology Assessment, 115
Oil, crude, types of, 171
Oil-and-gas curtailment policies, 80–
82, 97–98, 183
Oil and Gas Journal, 119
Oil-and-gas-supply models, 117–123,
169–170, 175
Oil import quotas, 80
Oil Market Simulation Model, 8–11,
173
Oil prices and decontrol, 123, 170
Oil recovery methods, 118–119
Oil reserve-production ratios, 117,
118, 120, 170
Oil wells, 118, 122, 123

OMS. See Oil Market Simulation
Model
OPEC, 8, 175
Open-hearth process, 89, 90, 91, 92
Optimized generation-planning model,
128–130
Oregon, 141
Outer continental shelf, 187

PURPA. See Public Utility Regulatory
Policies Act
Pacific Power and Light, 84
Passthrough requirements, 97, 188
Payback ratio, defined, 34
Peak-demand models. See Electricity
Peak-load facilities, 125, 144–145, 172,
184
Peak-load multipliers, defined, 66
Peak-load pricing. See Time-of-day
pricing
Pennsylvania, 141
Pennsylvania Power Company, 152
Phosphorus production, 94
Photovoltaic-energy devices, 181
Pig iron, 89, 90, 91–92, 93, 95
Pindyck, Robert, 7, 8
Point-of-use load controls, 65
Poland, 107, 108
Political factors and investment
return, 141
Pollution-control assistance, 184
Pollution-control equipment, 87, 125,
184
Portfolio theory, 138–139
Power pooling and wheeling, 186
Power-to-steam ratios, 55
Powerplant and Industrial Fuel Use
Act (1978), 80–81, 82, 97, 100,
125, 183–184
Present value of capital investment,
131–132
Present value of variable costs, 133–
134
Pretax cost of capital, 161
Price elasticity, 123
Price-escalator clauses, 187

Primary energy demand/forecasts, 75–78
Probabilistic methods, 126
Process heaters, 100–102
Process steam, 99, 153–154
Profit, fair/excessive, 149
Profit maximization, 57
Project Independence Evaluation System, 12, 74, 165
Public buildings, schools, and hospitals, conservation in, 180–181
Public-sector energy modeling, 7–17, 165–178
Public Service Company of Colorado, 151
Public Utility Regulatory Policies Act (1978), 63, 79, 143, 147, 152, 154, 158, 185–186
Pulp and paper industry, 99
Pyrolysis, 103

Ratchet clauses, 146, 152
Raw steel, 90–91, 95
Real dollar estimate, 158–159
Recycling targets, 96, 181
Refineries Petrochemical Modeling System, 170
Refinery models: IEES, 13; MEFS, 170–171
Refrigerators, 45
Regional submodel, 28–29
Regulatory commissioners' term of office, and investment return, 141
Regulatory lag, 142–143
Remote-control devices, 65
Reserve-requirement models, 125–128
Residential-demand charges, 151–152
Residential financing programs, 180
Residential peak-demand model, 63–69
Residential sales model, 30–49
Residential sector: energy policies, 179–180, 182
Resource Planning Associates, 98
Resources, renewable, 84
Resources for the Future, 75, 98, 165

Retail transactions, 185
Retrofit programs, 34, 52, 181
Revenue requirement, 137, 156, 164
Revenues, timing of, 141–142
Revised New Source Performance Standards, 87
Risk minimization, 138–141
Rollover contracts, 187

Sales submodels, 30
Sasol plant, 103
Saudi Arabia, 1
Scheduled outage, 125
Scrap iron, 89, 96
Scrubbers, 87, 125, 184
Sectoral energy models, 3–4
Shale oil, 105
Sharpe, W., 138
Shed loads, 70
Simplicity criterion, 25
Siting requirements, 82
Social welfare, 152–153
Societal-cost equation, 127, 128
Socioinstitutional constraints, 177
Solar-energy programs, 180, 181, 182, 183
Solvent-refined coal, 103
South Africa, 107, 108
Space heating, 31, 35, 51, 151
Spinning reserves, 124
Stagflation, 140
Standard percent-reserve method, 125–126
Stanford Research Institute–Gulf model, 74
Stanford University, 165
State, the: coal reserves and reserve-production ratios, 112; utility regulation, 105, 141, 185
Statistical-validity measures, 25–26
Steam coal exports, 106–109
Steam generation, 55
Steel industry, 53, 55, 89–96
Straight-line depreciation, 97, 136, 183
Submodels, 28–30

Sulfur, 113, 169; desulfurization, 87, 125, 184
Supplemental Social Security Income, 153
Supply models, 4, 117–136
Synfuels, 102–106
Synthetic Fuels Corporation, 104

Tax preferences, 136. *See also* Accelerated depreciation; Investment tax credits
Technical University (Germany), 15
Technologies, evaluating new and existing, 130–136
Test year, future/historical, 142
Thermal efficiency, 86, 124
Thermal-integrity factor, defined, 68
Thermodynamic optimum, 57
Three Mile Island incident, 82, 83
Time-of-day pricing, 143, 147–148, 185; industrial, 69–70; residential, 63–64
Time-series models, 26, 27
Time-Stepped Energy System Optimization Model, 74
TOD. *See* Time-of-day pricing
Transmission-capital costs, 160–161, 162, 163
Transport costs, 84, 114
Transportation models: IEES, 13; MEFS, 173
Transportation sector: energy policies, 182, 183

Unit-electricity intensity index, 51
U.S.: coal exports, 106–109; coal production, 109–115; coke production, 93; electric-utilities production and fuel consumption, 78, 123; electricity-use patterns, 23–25; energy demands, 21–22, 75–76, 117; energy-GNP ratio, 20–21; energy policies, 1–3, 96, 97–98, 179–188; oil reserve-production

ratio, 117, 118, 120; raw-steel production and trade policy, 90–91
U.S. Department of Energy, 79, 130; BEPS, 33, 47–49, 79–80; efficiency standards, 32–33, 44–45, 53–54
U.S. Department of Housing and Urban Development, 33, 47, 180
U.S. Department of Transportation, 182
U.S. Steel, 90
U.S. Supreme Court, 137–138

Vanpooling exemption, 183
Variable costs, 127, 162–163
Variance (portfolio), 138
Vehicle miles traveled, 173
Venezuela, 1
Vintaging, 52, 173

WAES. *See* Workshop on Alternative Energy Strategies
WOCOL. *See* World Coal Study
Washington Water Power, 155
Water heaters, 45–46; load controls, 64, 65, 151
Weatherization grants and loans, 79, 180
Weighting-factor approach, 49
Wellhead pricing, 186–187
Westinghouse, 55, 60
Wholesale transactions, 185–186
Wilson, Carroll, 7, 73
Wisconsin Public Services Corporation, 152
Workshop on Alternative Energy Strategies (MIT), 7, 119–120
World Coal Study (MIT), 3, 7–8, 73–74, 77, 88, 106, 107–108, 115
World Integrated Model, 15–17
World Oil Project (MIT), 7–8, 121
"World Outside Communist Areas," 119

About the Author

Glenn R. DeSouza received the B.Com. in accounting from the University of Madras (Loyola College Division). He received the Ph.D. in economics from Fordham University, where he specialized in the international and monetary areas. At Fordham he held a fellowship and subsequently a full-time faculty appointment as an instructor in statistics and economic theory.

Since June of 1976 he has been employed by Arthur D. Little, Inc., where he has worked on projects for the Department of Energy, the National Energy Laboratories, the National Science Foundation, the Environmental Protection Agency, the State Department, General Electric, Burlington Northern, U.S. Steel, and various electric and gas utilities. These projects have involved energy-demand modeling, electricity-rate analysis, coal-sector modeling, the economics of research and development, technology-diffusion assessment, environmental-policy analysis, metal-industry economics, socioeconomic-impact analysis, and regional economics.

Dr. DeSouza's publications include *System Methods for Socioeconomic and Environmental Impact Analysis* (Lexington Books, 1979) and articles in *Materials and Society, Journal of Energy and Development, Energy Systems and Policy, Business Economics,* and *Public Utilities Fortnightly.* He has also presented papers at various professional society meetings.